# Rendezvous with Reality

# RENDEZVOUS WITH REALITY

## The American Economy After Reagan

## MURRAY WEIDENBAUM

Basic Books, Inc., Publishers

NEW YORK

Library of Congress Cataloging-in-Publication Data

Weidenbaum, Murray L.
  Rendezvous with reality.

  Includes index.
  1. United States—Economic conditions—1981–
2. United States—Economic policy—1981–
3. Fiscal policy—United States.   I. Title.
HC106.8.W43  1988        338.973        88–47671
ISBN   0–465–06914–2

To Arthur F. Burns and Walter W. Heller

Their wise counsel, continued encouragement, and friendship meant so much to me over the years. In their very different ways, each was a role model for economists who have the opportunity to participate in making public policy.

# CONTENTS

# PART D

## Facing Social Concerns—Economically

# PART E

## An Agenda for Post-Reagan America

# PREFACE

# *What Is Past Is Prologue*

It has become fashionable in recent years for former members of a presidential administration to rush into print with their versions of how the momentous events in which they participated really occurred. Kiss-and-tell, and occasionally kick-and-tell, reports can titillate the reader. Spilling the beans is a literary form that seems to meet the test of the marketplace. Such works may even be useful for the professional historian, but they contribute little if anything to solving the problems that currently face the United States.

Alas (or perhaps fortunately), I kept no diary during my service in the Reagan administration, nor did I write contemporaneous memoirs. Thus, of necessity, the focus in this book is forward- rather than backward-looking. To provide some special illumination, I from time to time draw upon my service in 1981–82 as chairman of the President's Council of Economic Advisers and my far more modest membership since then on the President's Economic Policy Advisory Board.

This book is not intended to demonstrate that I was generally more correct than other members of the Reagan administration—although, with a little coaxing, I could defend that position quite tenaciously. The reader will be spared yet another tedious and biased account of the infighting among Washington insiders. In any event, I have been back at the university far longer than I was away, so I believe a position of informed detachment is the proper one to take.

This book is addressed to interested citizens rather than only to my fellow economists. It is not a treatise in economics or even an attempt to insinuate economic analysis into the public policy debate. Rather, it is an attempt by the author, who happens to be an economist, to draw on his firsthand knowledge of both governmental and business affairs to deal with some of the key issues that will face the American people in the years ahead. The challenge of this book is to draw on a combination of professional analysis and personal experience to develop ways of dealing with the many difficult and interrelated issues of public policy.

When I worked for him in 1981–82, Ronald Reagan used to tease me about my being a practitioner of "the dismal science," drawing on Carlyle's classic description of economics. I will not disappoint my former boss. However, this book does end on a strong upbeat, but that comes much later.

If there is any significant formal economic content in the pages that follow, that may be primarily in the eyes of the beholder. I very much hope that the thoughts expressed here will be useful to those who like to make up their own minds on important questions. If some readers find a few portions heavy going, I can respond only that I have tried to avoid what the columnist Mary McGrory has called the Cuisinart approach to public policy—where issues are "chopped, pureed, sliced and minced," to the point where the substance becomes unrecognizable. On the other hand, if some readers are put off by my attempts at humor, I can respond only that I have tried to take the subject rather than myself quite seriously. The examination of issues of public policy provides many examples where laughter can replace tears.

A few special words of appreciation are in order. I am indebted to Melinda Warren for her conscientious and occasionally heroic efforts in converting my hieroglyphics into readable form and to Stephen Vogt for serving as my research assistant on this book and as colleague on some of the underlying research. The Center for the Study of American Business, and especially Associate Director Kenneth Chilton, created an atmosphere in which we could work productively and had the resources to do so. James Davis demonstrated his friendship by reading the entire manuscript and offering numerous helpful suggestions.

My editor, Martin Kessler of Basic Books, goaded me into writing what undoubtedly is a much better book than I originally envisioned. My wife, Phyllis, gave me the special support without which this undertaking, as well as many others, could not have been completed.

# PART A

## Introduction

# 1

# The Reagan Legacy
# and the Task Ahead

## Setting the Stage

The party will soon be over. Since 1981, the United States has enjoyed an unusual era of good feeling. Americans are getting along with one another with less open hostility than in the 1970s. Riots in urban ghettos have faded into distant memory. Strikes have become an infrequent phenomenon. Campus disruptions petered out with the end of the Vietnam War and the elimination of the draft.

On the economic front, taxes have been cut. Inflation has been brought down. Interest rates have returned to normal size. New jobs have been created at a rate unparalleled among Western nations. Aside from rumbles of warning from financial markets, we are experiencing the longest period of national calm simultaneously with the most durable economic expansion in more than half a century.

Nevertheless, chips are being called in; the bills are coming due. Citizens concerned with the future of America must take on a role akin to that of the cleanup crew the morning after the big blast.[1] There is no substitute for tackling those lingering problems that have been swept under the national rug—the unparalleled string of huge budget deficits that would have threatened any less popular President, the large pockets of genuine distress in many urban and rural areas, and the tremendous weakening of this nation's position in world trade as symbolized by its becoming the world's largest debtor nation.

The national meter is running. The public debt and interest on it are rising at rates unprecedented prior to the 1980s. The longer we delay, the more intractable these problems will become; the principle of compound interest assures us that any solutions will be increasingly costly.

We can derive scant comfort from the knowledge that, in the past, when a situation became critical enough, Americans acted decisively. The hallmark of intelligent public policy is not to let problems fester but to make tough decisions promptly. The United States is approaching a crucial fork in the road. The decisions we make at the present time will not only influence events far in the future; they will be hard to reverse.

Wherever one looks—whether it is a matter of setting new priorities for the public sector or of responding to the inroads of foreign competition on the private sector—tough realities need to be faced. Each recent presidential administration—be it that of Nixon, Ford, Carter, or Reagan—has enjoyed the benefits of actions whose costs will be borne by future generations.

The 1970s and 1980s have been a period in which we Americans postponed making hard choices. We have advocated a balanced budget in the abstract. But we have voted rapid expansions in expensive government activities—ranging from national defense to farm subsidies and pensions for the aged—without the taxes to pay for them. We have legislated increasingly ambitious environmental cleanup goals while doing little to slow the growth of the mountain of pollution. We have added to the tax and regulatory burdens of old-line industries and then were taken by surprise when those same companies asked to be rescued by means of trade restrictions and, occasionally, direct bailouts.

As citizens of the United States, we are consuming more than we are producing, borrowing more than we are saving, and spending more than we are earning. We are rapidly approaching the time when we have to pay the piper. Neither Republicans nor Democrats in the Congress have shown much interest in voting for the taxes to pay for those rapidly rising costs. A search for scapegoats is both fruitless and counterproductive. As Pogo said, "We have met the enemy and they is us."

Americans can confront the tough issues facing this country and make those difficult choices that will lead to a stronger nation in the 1990s. Realistically, and with a reasonable degree of objectivity, we can correct the weaknesses of Ronald Reagan's policies. We should simultaneously build on the strengths of the Reagan years—and fairness requires that we should not overlook those positive factors either. If patient readers bear with me, they will find that this book comes up with the specifics of what can be done.

The events since 1980, as well as earlier ones, will continue to cast a long shadow on the outlook for the rest of this decade—and beyond. The economic/political/social problems facing the United States are far too urgent for their consideration to be dominated by any "apologia," personal or institutional. Thus, this is a book about the future, not the past. In retrospect, 1981 was a watershed year, a period of important change. In a different way, 1989 promises to provide another watershed. As someone who was present at, and played a part in creating, the earlier set of changes, I believe I have something to contribute to the impending public policy debate. After all, the nation should expect that we have learned some lessons from the successes—and the failures—of the past eight years.

This book is designed to provide interested citizens with a guide to the problems that lie ahead for the next presidential administration. The array of likely choices is accompanied by suggestions on the selection of specific public policy options. In writing this book, I have drawn on my business background as well as my public service. Because so many of our national problems arise at the intersection of the public and private sectors, it is particularly helpful to have experienced the difficulties that decision makers in both business and government have faced—and subsequently to have enjoyed a substantial period of reflection. But history does not repeat itself precisely. Answers to previous problems may not be appropriate for future questions. Thus, dealing with the national issues of the coming decade is both an exciting and an innovative prospect.

## What Reagan Hath Wrought

As we approach another round of impending change, let us begin by examining the problems and the opportunities that President Ronald Reagan will bequeath to his successor. This will set the stage for the specific chapters that follow. Inevitably, we will defer most of the detailed analysis to those later chapters. As a prelude, it is helpful to understand that David Stockman was wrong. The Reagan program is not, as he described it in the subtitle of his semiautobiographical book, a "revolution" that "failed."[2] Neither is the "Reagan revolution" (some have called it a counterrevolution) the unalloyed blessing that the Republican National Committee would have everyone believe. As is customary in any new presidential administration, the comprehensive program of change announced in early 1981 was described in very enthusiastic language (which, fortunately, stopped short of claiming a cure for baldness):

> The program we have developed . . . will revitalize economic growth, renew optimism and confidence, and rekindle the Nation's entrepreneurial instincts and creativity. . . . These positive results will be accomplished simultaneously with reducing tax burdens, increasing private saving, and raising the living standard of the American family.[3]

The overpromising by President Reagan in 1981 is not unprecedented. It pales before the bombast contained in some earlier presidential statements. For example, in his inaugural address, President John Kennedy stated that "we will pay any price and share any burden" to maintain freedom anywhere in the world. That piece of eloquence did not hold up as an accurate declaration of national intentions.

In contrast to the ringing rhetoric, the results of Reaganomics constitute a mixed bag. If it was revolutionary in purpose, it has been evolutionary in practice. A carefully balanced study by the Urban Institute concluded that the Reagan administration, more than most others, had a clear vision of what it was trying to accomplish—"to reduce the size and influence of government, to restore economic prosperity, and to improve national security."[4] Viewed in that light, both its accomplishments and its shortcomings are substantial.[5] In any event, they set the stage for many important decisions that will affect the course of the nation in the years ahead.

## THE SUCCESSES OF REAGANOMICS

The most fundamental change on the American economic scene since January 21, 1981, is the new sense of realism in business and personal decision making. Management and labor alike have become more cost conscious. They have learned—many of them the hard way—the advantages of being competitive in a society in which the federal government does not readily come to rescue the losers in the marketplace.

*Living in a Low-Inflation Environment.* Businesses making ill-conceived outlays—be they on personnel or on equipment—are no longer automatically bailed out by inflation. Consumers once again are looking on purchases of cars, homes, and furnishings as primarily a form of consumption—and not as a sage investment in a continuously rising price level.

Employees have learned that their wages, salaries, and fringe benefits are vitally dependent on the future success of their employer. Workers are increasingly willing to accept changes in work rules and job practices necessary to ensure the future of their company—and their jobs. This new sense of realism did not come easily, and it contains no guarantee of permanency.

Although few people realized it at the time, one of the most important labor events in the past decade was the President's tough response to the illegal strike by the Professional Air Traffic Controllers (PATCO) in 1981. Firing the air traffic controllers was a difficult but decisive move that signaled a fundamental turn in American labor-management relations. This shift was the main reason that several years later the pace-setting postal unions talked—or, rather, whispered—about going on strike and promptly settled.

But the repercussions of the President's action extended to the private sector as well. The signal was strong and clear: this White House will not get involved in disputes between companies and unions. In most past administrations, the federal government put pressure on management to settle promptly with their unions, and the result was escalating wage settlements. Our high-cost steel industry, so beset by foreign competition, is a cogent example of the dangers and results of such government intervention.

In contrast, a remarkable slowdown in labor demands has occurred since 1981. This has aided in reducing inflationary pressures. But what is most fascinating is that it has helped the average worker. Contrary to the prevailing notion, the typical working family is now experiencing a stability in living standards; median family income (in 1985 dollars) actually rose slightly, from $26,481 in 1981 to $27,735 in 1985. This modest trend compares favorably with the declines in real earnings during years when wage rates were rising far more rapidly; median family income (in 1985 dollars) declined from $29,087 in 1978 to $26,481 in 1981.[6] The American people are finally off the inflationary treadmill. Whether we can stay off it is another matter; it depends on how we respond to the many difficult choices presented in the forthcoming chapters.

The labor environment for production has improved very substantially. The portion of working time lost to strikes is the lowest since the Department of Labor started to gather the data. Likewise, the number of people out on strike since 1981 has been at a modern low. Fewer than 70 major work stoppages occurred in 1986 ("major" is defined as those involving 1,000 or more workers). This compares with a peak of 424 in 1974, when the economy and the work force were much smaller.[7] Such a sustained period of labor peace invariably contributes to stability in planning work routines and thus to raising productivity, a key to enhancing international competitiveness.

*Wrestling with the Budget.* Turning to the public sector itself, we find that the federal budget has moved out of its traditional category of technical obscurity to rival the weather as a topic for everyday discussion. It is tempting to paraphrase the trite old saying to the effect that, as with the weather, everybody now talks about the budget and the deficit without doing anything about them. Dealing with the escalating expenditures of the federal government is a topic that will be covered in detail later on. But, despite the rise of triple-digit budget deficits, important changes have occurred during the Reagan years in the composition of federal spending programs.[8]

For example, as a result of the budgetary pressures, the era of big dams and water power projects appears to be drawing to a close. The 1988 budget virtually eliminated funds for planning new large water resource undertakings, although some congressional backsliding may occur.[9] This is one area of government policy where conservative economists and liberal conservationists come close to seeing eye to eye. Often characterized by cost overruns and disregard for environmental impacts, these huge construction projects have proliferated solely because of political support from the specific interest groups that benefit from them. Prior to the concern over "those $200 billion deficits," there was no way effectively to turn down these outlays that, for the nation as a whole, have generated far more costs than benefits.

In an equally significant but less dramatic way, coping with the budget deficits has forced an important reallocation of functions between the federal government and state and local agencies. State, county, and city governments are increasing taxes—and/or reducing services—to cope with the reduced flows of revenue sharing and grants-in-aid from the federal government. The locus of governmental initiative has shifted markedly. Many towns receive no direct aid from Washington for the first time since the enactment of the Great Society programs more than two decades ago, in the administration of President Lyndon Johnson.[10]

## The Reagan Legacy and the Task Ahead

In the words of the executive director of the Advisory Commission on Intergovernmental Relations, "A sea change has occurred in the expectations of state and local officials—when forced to search for 'new money,' they once again look to their own resources."[11] The Reagan administration has created an environment that forces states and localities to be more self-reliant.

On the revenue side of the budget, a series of reductions in federal income tax rates and changes in other provisions of the Internal Revenue Code have succeeded in reducing the Treasury's share of the national income—from 20 percent in 1981 to 18 percent in 1986. A 2 percent drop in the federal share of the national income may not sound like much, but 2 percent of a $4 trillion economy is $80 billion a year. The successive reductions in income tax rates signaled the direction in which the administration desired to move—shifting money and power from the public sector to individuals and private institutions.

*Reforming Regulation.* Unlike the tax or budget bills, no single piece of legislation embodying the administration's regulatory program has commanded public attention. The struggle to reduce the burden imposed by federal rule making had to be waged on many fronts. Nor have all changes necessarily been victories, even minor ones. As will be shown in chapter 6, the regulation of foreign trade (both imports and exports) has intensified in recent years.

Yet, dozens of specific actions have been taken that curtailed the burden of complying with the multitude of federal directives and prohibitions. Examples range from reducing record-keeping requirements for credit unions (generating an annual saving of $670 million) to permitting mechanical deboning of meat in processing foods (a cost reduction of $500 million a year) and to liberalizing the rules on patient package inserts on medicine (a $20 million annual economy).[12]

The most significant development on the regulatory front is along the lines of that Sherlock Holmes story in which the decisive point was the fact that the dog did not bark. During the past eight years, not a single major new regulatory law has been enacted (although several have been toughened). Nor has a new regulatory agency been established. This has been the first such extended period in the past half century when the federal rule-making dog did not bark. The state is not withering away, but some high-cost resources are being reoriented to more productive pursuits.

*Controlling Inflation.* The most obvious economic achievement of Ronald Reagan's administration has been to tame the inflationary beast.

After an escalating, double-digit rate in early 1981—the consumer price index rose by 12.0 percent in 1980—price increases in 1986 averaged a modest 2.5 percent. The acid test is the one in the beginning of this decade. Virtually every public opinion poll of the American people reported that inflation was the number one problem facing the United States. By 1987, those taking that position were down from 70 percent to 2 percent of the population.[13]

The progress toward deregulation—plus the tide of imports—helped reduce costs and increase productivity. But it was the tight money policy of the Federal Reserve System that directly squeezed the bulk of the inflation out of the American economic system during 1981 and 1982. However, that policy was extremely unpopular at the time, and the Reagan administration deserves credit for its support of the Fed. Aside from a bit of public needling by the Treasury, the Reagan administration deflected many of the political pressures that were generated by the high interest rates that accompanied the low growth of the money supply. As the reader might suspect, that supportive position was taken only after considerable internal debate.

Probably the single most significant feature of the 1980s to date has been the renewal of confidence in market forces, with some of the strongest support coming from the younger generation.[14]

### THE FAILURES OF REAGANOMICS

If there has been any single fundamental theme in Reaganomics from the outset, it has been the emphasis on reducing the size and power of government, especially at the national level. Yet, in terms of objective measurements, the federal government looms larger in the American economy today than it did at the beginning of 1981. The San Andreas fault of the Reagan administration's domestic program has been the failure to curb federal spending and thus to control the size of government, including its voracious appetite for deficit financing.

*The Inability to Curb Government Spending.* The prevailing notion is that the Reagan administration used the proverbial meat ax on all social programs. The record shows that the deepest cuts were proposed (and not always enacted) for the relatively small programs serving the poor, notably school lunch subsidies and food stamps. These programs were viewed with hostility because they were deemed ineffective. Very little has been done since 1980 to reduce the increasingly expensive body of statutory "entitlements" for predominantly middle-class voters, such as Social Security, Medicare, and veterans benefits.

## The Reagan Legacy and the Task Ahead

The divergence between image and reality was underscored by the results of a survey taken in late 1982. A sample of Connecticut residents was asked to designate the specific areas where a real loss of government services had occurred. More than 28 percent cited Social Security and aid to the elderly; 15 percent mentioned education and 14 percent welfare. However, when the same group was asked if any member of their own family had suffered a loss of government aid, only 4 percent mentioned Social Security, 1 percent welfare, and less than 1 percent education.[15]

The most damning fact in terms of both public perception and budget reality was that the Department of Defense got what amounted to a blank check in those crucial early years of the Reagan administration when enthusiasm for the general notion of budget cutting was running high. As a practical matter, it was very difficult for the heads of the civilian departments to accept large cuts in the "controllable" programs supported by their traditional constituencies at a time when the two largest categories of federal expenditure—defense spending as well as entitlements—were virtually getting a free ride.

The inconsistent treatment of the different items in the budget was especially galling to those of us in the administration who took seriously the rhetoric about getting big government off the back of the average citizen. To compound the problem, the Congress gave the President only about one-half of the cuts in civilian spending that he requested. In his first term, both houses tended to vote almost all of the proposed increases in the military budget—of course, only after a dazzling display of rhetoric questioning the desirability of such a rapid buildup.

Total federal spending is much higher today than it was at the start of the 1980s, even after the effects of inflation have been boiled out. But that is not surprising in a society whose population and economy are expanding. The truly relevant point is that federal expenditures have been growing more rapidly than the rest of the economy. In the fiscal year 1981, federal spending equaled 23 percent of the gross national product (GNP). In 1986, the ratio stood at 24 percent.

As my colleague Richard McKenzie is fond of saying, the administration and Congress have done a better job of getting the IRS's hands out of our wallets than in getting government off our backs. Because the revenue-to-GNP ratio was moving in the opposite direction at the very time when federal spending accelerated, the result was unprecedented triple-digit budget deficits for six years in a row—and no end is yet in sight.

Other measures of the size of the federal government are equally discouraging. Total federal debt was nearing $1 trillion when Ronald Reagan took office. It has since more than doubled, surpassing $2 trillion during 1986. In 1981, the head count of federal civilian employees was 2.8 million. In 1986, the total exceeded 3.0 million. Nobody—Democrat or Republican—had forecast such results.

The repercussions of this unplanned expansion in the public sector have been numerous and powerful. Initially, the economic stimulus provided by rising federal outlays was seen as a positive factor, helping to get the United States out of the deep recession of 1981–82. But that is too sanguine a view. The expectation of future deficits drove up interest rates and contributed to the length and severity of that recession.

In the 1980s to date, the federal budget deficit has absorbed roughly two-thirds of the saving by business and consumers—funds that normally would be invested in productive enterprises. Albeit painful to capital-intensive sectors of the domestic economy, rising real interest rates in the United States were helpful in attracting the foreign capital needed to fill the gap.

The failure to match the 1981 tax cuts with spending cuts put the main burden of fighting inflation on the Federal Reserve System. The specter of the rising tide of red ink—and its potential for generating inflationary pressure—scared the Fed chairman at the time, Paul Volcker, and his colleagues at the Federal Reserve System into maintaining an extremely tight monetary policy in 1981 and most of 1982. I recall from my own regular breakfast meetings with the Fed chairman that the expectation of large and rising budget deficits was a major concern to the nation's number one central banker.

Not too surprisingly, in 1981 the money supply grew at a rate below the bottom end of the Fed's own target for monetary expansion, which provides a good working definition of tight money. This policy development, coupled with the tendency of financial markets to react adversely to the impending budget deficits, resulted in depressed investment and thus a weaker economy.[16]

*Long and Deep Recession.*  The large deficit financing collided with the reduced supply of credit. The result was the highest interest rates "since Jesus Christ," in the words of Helmut Schmidt, at the time West Germany's chancellor. The combination of high interest rates and monetary stringency was a major contributor to the unusual depth and duration of the resulting recession. But, like a higher power, the Fed giveth and the Fed taketh away. The recession accounted in large part for the swift drop in the inflation rate as well as for much of the rise in the budget deficit.

The long string of budget deficits had many negative effects on the economy. The relation with the triple-digit trade deficit is intricate. Most analysts believe that the combination of huge Treasury borrowings and the closely related high domestic interest rates attracted large amounts of foreign capital into the United States. But that inflow of foreign money required a conversion of foreign currency into dollars.

Aye, there was the rub. The rapid increase in the worldwide demand for American money bid up the price of dollars in global currency markets. That high-priced dollar in turn made U.S.-produced products more expensive to foreign customers. A double whammy resulted. The other side of the international-trade equation was the newly low-priced foreign currencies (in terms of dollars), which meant that imported goods were suddenly much cheaper to American consumers.

All that helped dampen any inflationary trends in the United States and was an important factor in controlling labor and other costs. Yet, the promoting of imports and discouraging of exports inevitably led to painfully high trade deficits. The resultant hard times in agriculture, steel, automobile manufacturing, and other parts of the economy especially vulnerable to foreign competition have generated the greatest surge of protectionist pressures since the depression of the 1930s.

The 1981–82 recession, long and painful as it was, eventually came to an end. In late 1982, sensing that the main economic villain had become unemployment rather than inflation, the Federal Reserve shifted to a policy of monetary ease. The credit crisis in Mexico and the plight of other overextended Latin-American borrowers were the precipitating elements in the policy shift. By the end of 1982, the American economy began a strong and sustained upturn—which has lasted longer than any other peacetime recovery.

In 1983 and 1984, consumers began to enjoy relatively stable prices and generated rising real levels of purchases, of both domestic and foreign products. Consumer credit financed the gap between the income Americans earned and the money they spent. Moreover, business investment expanded substantially, bolstered by the new incentives contained in the 1981 tax law. Business capital outlays rose 11 percent a year, almost double the rate experienced in the average expansion since World War II.

But credit expansion has its limitations. Fundamentally, income from domestic production provides the ability to buy those goods and services. As a result of the sustained triple-digit trade deficits, economic growth in the United States slowed down very substantially in 1985, to a lackluster rate of approximately 3 percent, and stayed at that growth plateau for several years.

Simultaneously, unemployment declined from a high of 9.5 percent in 1982 to less than 7.0 percent in 1986. That was still a substantial amount of unutilized human resources, and severe hardships occurred in individual families and in specific regions. Nevertheless, in recent years, unemployment has not generated the urgent national concern that inflation did a decade earlier.

Several explanations come to mind. With the higher incidence of two or more breadwinners in the same family, the loss of a job by one member is no longer as catastrophic as in the past. Moreover, despite the talk about their decimation under the Republicans, unemployment compensation, welfare, food stamps, and other assistance continued to be available in large quantities.

A SUMMING UP

Reaganomics was the most ambitious reform effort in the United States since the New Deal. Table 1-1 is a statistical attempt to answer, for the current presidential administration, the type of question that Ronald Reagan posed to Jimmy Carter in 1980—are the American people better off today than they were at the beginning of your term of office? The data reinforce the point made at the outset of this chapter: the performance of Reaganomics is mixed.

In important ways, the average American was better off in 1986 (the latest year for which annual data were available when this book was being written) than at the end of the Carter administration. Inflation is much lower (2 percent versus 14 percent), unemployment is a bit less (7.0 percent versus 7.2 percent), real take-home pay is up ($10,780 versus $9,722), and real growth has moved from a negative position ($-0.2$ percent) to a positive stance ($+2.5$ percent). On the other hand, the budget deficit has grown rapidly (from 2 percent of the GNP to 5 percent), the national debt has more than doubled ($906 billion versus $2.1 trillion), U.S. foreign trade has moved from a slight surplus ($2 billion) to an unprecedented deficit ($141 billion), and the United States has shifted from being a net creditor in the world economy ($106 billion) to being a large debtor ($-$117 billion).

The most fundamental changes since 1980 have been below the sur-

TABLE 1-1

*Are Americans Better Off Than in 1980?*

| U.S. Economic Indicators | 1980 | 1986 |
|---|---|---|
| *Successes* | | |
| Economic growth (real GNP) | −0.2% | +2.5% |
| Inflation (increase in consumer prices) | +14% | +2% |
| Unemployment rate | 7.2% | 7.0% |
| Real take-home pay (per capita disposable income in 1982 dollars) | $9,722 | $10,780 |
| Saving by individuals (billions of 1982 dollars) | $219 | $335 |
| Industrial production (1977=100) | 109 | 125 |
| Interest rates (prime rate) | 15% | 8% |
| *Failures* | | |
| Federal government deficit (percentage of GNP) | 2% | 5% |
| Foreign trade (current account in billions) | +$2 | −$141 |

SOURCE: Computed from data in *Economic Report of the President, January 1987.*

face and more subjective. They flowed from President Reagan's belief that government itself was the main source of the problems facing the United States. Unlike other recent Presidents, both Democratic and Republican, he did not assume that, if something was wrong, it automatically was the government's responsibility to fix it.

As a result, the domestic agenda is now substantially leaner than when President Reagan took office. In effect, he established tougher standards against which to measure new domestic initiatives. The burden of proof shifted subtly but perceptibly from those who would have the government do less to those who advocate its doing more.

Perhaps the most basic way of judging the impact of the Reagan administration is to get the reaction of the American people. A sample of U.S. residents were asked in January 1981 if they were "satisfied or dissatisfied with the way things are going in the United States at this time." Only 17 percent said they were satisfied. By June 1986, the proportion giving a positive answer had risen to 69 percent.[17]

Reaganomics was an ambitious effort. To succeed fully, it required delicate balancing. Monetary policy had to be tightened enough to bring down the inflation, but not so much as to create severe recession. Taxes had to be cut, but without raising the specter of vast deficits that would scare the Fed into a restrictive credit policy. National defense had to be expanded, but not so rapidly as to offset reductions in civilian spending. Regulation had to be cut enough to provide a significant boost to productivity and hence to growth, but without eliminating public support for the needed reforms.

In any event, taxes were cut too much and spending not nearly enough. Visions of soaring deficits proved all too accurate, the Fed was supertight, the economy nose-dived, and regulatory reform took a backseat. With monetarists, supply-siders, and politicians each going off in separate directions, as chairman of the Council of Economic Advisers, I often felt like a one-armed trainer in an unruly circus.

With the wisdom of hindsight, I believe that the costs of the 1981–82 recession would have been lowered if government decision makers had followed more closely the original design of the Reagan economic program, as presented in February 18, 1981.[18] For example, tighter fiscal policy—smaller tax cuts and bigger reductions in spending—coupled with a somewhat looser monetary policy (faster growth in the money supply) would also have succeeded in reducing inflation, and perhaps with fewer adverse effects on the national economy. Federal policymakers now face the dilemma of canceling low-priority projects after considerable money has been spent on them—and of answering the inevitable question "What is the value of half a dam, or two-thirds of a nuclear carrier?" Hindsight tells us that it would have been much easier to stop such projects at the outset.

The original approach would not have required wrenching changes to bring the deficits under control. It also might have avoided the high interest rates and the superstrong dollar that made it so difficult for American industry and agriculture to compete in world markets, and it would probably have put the economy on a path toward higher long-term growth. But exercises in what might have been accomplish little. Our task in this book is to tackle the serious problems and challenges that remain.

The response of public policy to the sharp decline in the stock market on October 19, 1987, is setting the tone for the post-Reagan economy. For the remainder of its time in office, the Reagan administration will be fighting a rearguard action on domestic economic and financial matters.

The main possibility for an important new initiative is in the field of foreign policy, particularly in the form of one or more arms control agreements with the Soviets.

For practical purposes, the chapter of American economic history entitled "Reaganomics" is closing. Any doubt on that score can be quickly resolved by comparing the major thrusts of President Reagan's economic policy during the years 1981–86 and the current debate in Washington. Those features that constituted the heart of the Reagan policies are a thing of the past. On the tax front, the issue is no longer tax reduction, but whether—and how much—taxes should be raised. On the budget front, the effort to increase defense spending is behind us, at least for the next few years (providing, as always, that no major foreign crises erupt).

Rather than slowing down the money supply to fight inflation, the thrust of monetary policy now is to provide sufficient liquidity to stave off recession and to prevent a financial panic. In the regulatory area, the staff and budgets of regulatory agencies—especially of the Environmental Protection Agency (EPA)—are already turning up; "regulatory relief" is no longer an active term in the policymakers' vocabulary. None of this diminishes the long-term impact of the past accomplishments of Reaganomics, as discussed earlier in this chapter. Rather, the point is that the United States is currently in the midst of a transition to another era of public policy-making. While the memories are fresh, let us see what lessons can be learned from recent experience.


## Lessons from the Reagan Era


Even though dramatic contrasts are more striking, Ronald Reagan has not altered the American environment as much as liberals had feared or conservatives had hoped. Moreover, the lessons of the Reagan years are reinforced by the nation's experiences in Lyndon Johnson's administration, as well as in each of the presidencies since then.

1. *Spending more money for a high-priority national purpose does not guarantee success; it is just the beginning.* This was a lesson partially learned during the Great Society experiments of the Johnson administration. But, the outpouring of money for national defense since 1981—unparalleled in peacetime—reveals similar shortcomings. In ret-

rospect, we can now see that indiscriminately buying virtually every weapon in sight was a costly mistake. If that sounds like an exaggeration, consider the fact that virtually no new weapon system approved by the Carter administration was rejected by President Reagan. Rather than changing military priorities, the Reagan administration hastily added new requirements on top of the old.

I still recall the justification given by former Secretary of Defense Caspar Weinberger in 1981 during the vigorous internal debates on the size of the military budget: because Jimmy Carter wound up proposing in his last budget message the same 5 percent yearly real growth in military spending that Ronald Reagan had campaigned for in 1980, the Reagan administration would have to go higher. As a result, the 5 percent ceiling of the military budget was quickly transformed into a floor. As we will see, despite the liberal funding, the U.S. defense establishment still falls short of meeting basic readiness needs.

2. *There are compelling limits to what government can do to redistribute income and wealth.* The notion that officials on the banks of the Potomac can merely twist the appropriate policy dials and readily achieve the desired distribution of income and wealth in the United States has surely been discredited. Yet, our cynicism is aroused when the same interests that oppose programs for the poor support increased spending on programs benefiting upper-income groups that happen to be politically powerful.

We have found that arbitrary attempts to redistribute income to the poor are often counterproductive because they reduce the work incentives of the recipients. We still have to learn that arbitrarily redistributing income to the top of the income pyramid is even more counterproductive—because of adverse effects on the economic and political incentives of the rest of society.

3. *Neither compassion nor frugality provides sufficient guidelines.* Indiscriminate use of scarce resources in response to heart-rending appeals results in two kinds of backlashes—from taxpayers who see their money wasted and from recipients whose heightened expectations remain unfulfilled. Nevertheless, frugality is not a sufficient motivation for public policy. In the decade ahead, considerations of efficiency will be a necessary but not a sufficient element in the allocating of government funds. The dominating concern very likely will once again be the achievement of one of the basic purposes of government—in the words of the Constitution, "to promote the general welfare." Cutting the welfare rolls means more than just reducing federal social spending. It

requires expanding the nation's work force during a time when the number of people of working age is ceasing to grow.

4. *It is wishful thinking to believe that the way to reduce government spending is to cut taxes.*[19] In its extreme form, this idea has been expressed as follows: "The only way to reduce spending is to reduce revenues." As many suspected from the beginning, and as recent experience has confirmed, the truly effective way to cut government spending is for Congress to appropriate less. Of course, that is easier said than done. That every interest group wants its share of the goodies and will attempt to sandbag any effort at economy in government is hardly a novel observation. After all, Victor Hugo said as much: "The budget, strange fish and monster vast, to which from all sides the hook is cast."

5. *Supply-side rhetoric must be separated from supply-side economics.* Supply-side economics has made a useful positive contribution in moving the issue of incentives to production and entrepreneurial activity from the learned journals to the front pages of our newspapers. Unfortunately, a great deal of suspicion has been engendered by the extravagant claim that cutting tax rates would quickly unleash the latent strength of a dynamic economy. The sudden onrush of work, saving, and investment would supposedly generate such new heights of production and income that the citizenry would no longer have to worry about budget deficits.[20] In fact, at least one of the "high priests" contended that deficits would be declining so rapidly that it would be feasible to expand government spending simultaneously with the reductions in tax rates. The main budgetary problem would quickly become how to dispose of an embarrassingly large surplus.[21]

That was nonsense from the start. However, many noneconomists were attracted by the optimism and easy answers. To a member of the Senate or the House struggling with the annual appropriations bills, it was comforting to be told that there was no need to curtail government spending, that just cutting taxes was enough.

Thus, the battle of the budget at the critical junction in 1981 quickly turned into a two-front war. On the conventional front, budget cutters encountered, as would be expected, the vehement opposition of each of the interest groups whose program might be reduced. The unanticipated, second front consisted of those who saw no need for the effort at expenditure restraint, because they had fallen for the oversimplified version of the supply-side line. It led them to support even larger and longer-term reductions in taxes, notably indexing of the personal tax system. The result was the unprecedented array of triple-digit budget deficits that became the Achilles' heel of Reaganomics.

Martin Feldstein has written, "I have no doubt that the loose talk of the supply-side extremists gave fundamentally good policies a bad name. . . ."[22] In that spirit, we should not overreact and discard the well-developed supply-side notions that taxes affect the incentives of workers and savers and that investment is basic to economic growth.

6. *Business ethics should no longer be considered an oxymoron.* Those who equate the emphasis on competition in the marketplace with fraud, dishonesty, and lawbreaking are generally mistaken. Even in the most stripped-down version of the conservative state, there is a vital role for government in establishing what are called "the rules of the game." Business executives who achieve positions of wealth and power through unscrupulous and illegal practices are no credit to the private-enterprise system.

It is not evidence of disloyalty to the notion of private capitalism to urge throwing the book at the Ivan Boeskys and the other Wall Street insiders whose illegal and immoral actions gave the financial community a black eye. Quite to the contrary, continued public support for the market system requires a high level of enforcement of the society's legal and moral codes. The alternative is another wave of government intervention in internal business decision making.

It would be ironic if Americans lost their faith in a free-market economy just at the time when so many other parts of the world are becoming aware of the benefits of competition, incentives, and entrepreneurship. The ten million new jobs created in the private sector of the United States since 1982 may have escaped the attention of many of our fellow citizens. But that growth is surely envied by Western Europeans, who have seen virtually no increase in their own employment level during the same period.

Despite the great confidence that the business system has earned for its economic capability, we should continue to be suspicious of the political motives of individual companies. Too many business executives do not practice what they preach. They have yet to learn that the most high-powered public relations effort cannot convert self-serving actions into visions of statesmanship.

7. *A global economy is a two-way street.* For the quarter of a century following the end of World War II, Americans were told of the great opportunities being generated by a global economy increasingly accessible to business firms and investors as a result of remarkable advances in transportation and communication. During that period, U.S.

firms invested in many overseas ventures, locating factories and offices throughout the world. In the process, American people and American goods and services were distributed in foreign markets of every size and description.

Occasionally, there were voices of protest. Some objected to the "Coca Colanization" of Western Europe, concerned that American investments were pushing out local companies.[23] In response, Americans explained that U.S. investment was good for France, England, Germany, and other countries because it created jobs and income for their citizens and tax collections for their governments. Moreover, the competition of American goods and services helped to keep their producers on their toes and surely benefited their consumers.

Nobody has ever accused American leaders—in government, business, or labor—of excessive consistency. What we have been witnessing in the past decade is the simple application of the age-old notion that "what is sauce for the goose is sauce for the gander." Let us recall the obvious, which is too often overlooked. There were no objections on this side of the Atlantic to our large trade surpluses with Western Europe in the 1950s, 1960s, and 1970s. Back then, nobody in the White House or the Congress—or in Western Europe—suggested that we restrict our exports, much less enact legislation to require the careful balance of exports and imports that flow between the United States and each nation that we do business with.

But now that the shoe is on the other foot, we learn that it pinches. As the world's largest exporter, America cannot pick up its economic marbles and go home. White House and congressional grandstanding on trade issues is no solution. It is fascinating to note that, at a time when competitiveness has become a national buzzword, few people really support competition when it squeezes their company or their job prospects. Our companies—their management and labor alike—must learn to produce more efficiently and to compete in the marketplace and not in the arena for government handouts. That, of course, gets back to point 2; it is hypocritical to oppose welfare for poor people and propose the equivalent for those better off.

8. *Most swings of the pendulum are ultimately reversed.* The emphasis during the Reagan years has been on the reduction of the size, scope, and burden of government, especially at the federal level. Many of us strongly shared that view—and continue to believe that some public-sector activities are misguided, wasteful, or merely unnecessary and surely not worth the taxes that the public pays for them. But, on reflection, we may have conveyed an unintentional message—to

the effect that the typical government worker is dumb, lazy, and incompetent.

Whatever the desired size of the public sector, it is vital that government perform well the tasks that society assigns it. One reason for advocating a crash diet for federal agencies is the belief that more responsibilities have been given to them than they can possibly perform to any degree of satisfaction.

But public policy will not benefit from continued attacks on the integrity and industriousness of government employees. From my own personal experience—extending back to Governor Thomas Dewey's administration in New York State four decades ago—I must report that most civil servants are as honest and dedicated and competent as their private-sector counterparts. Moreover, taxpayers should want it that way.

We can, and should, debate what the desirable level and scope of government services are. But whether government employees are soldiers or teachers or foresters or tax collectors, they should be expected to meet society's prevailing standards of performance. The stereotype of the lazy bureaucrat should be eliminated from public discourse, along with the equally inaccurate stereotype of the crooked businessman.

What is really required—and a task to which this book is dedicated—is to reconcile the national desire for continued high levels of benefits from government with the limited resources that taxpayers are willing to make available to the public sector. Solving that fiscal problem will be neither quick nor easy. It will mean making many hard choices.

Deep down, the American people have begun to sense that easy answers and popular panaceas will only delay and make even more difficult the accomplishment of the serious governing responsibilities that face the citizens of a free society. The American people will be disappointed once again if they expect government to cure all their ills. But they will be needlessly discouraged if they despair of future progress—in both the public and the private sectors.

## A Needed Framework for Decision Making

In developing a framework for decision making on public policy, this book avoids any grand design for the future of the United States. That is partly the result of past experience. Whether it is Keynesian economics, monetarism, or supply-side economics—or even a newer and yet more sophisticated approach—I am not inclined to accept any one school of thought as the overriding basis for making national policy.

The reason is basic. An advanced society has a multiplicity of goals and problems, and many of them are not economic. Each individual has an almost infinite variety of needs and desires, and the priorities of those individuals are constantly changing. Thus, it is futile to make any once-and-for-all-time choice of a way of looking at economic endeavors.

Each of the major schools of economic thought can be useful on occasion. The insights of Keynesian economics proved appropriate for Western societies attempting to get out of deep depression in the 1930s. The tools of monetarism were powerfully effective in squeezing out the inflationary force of the 1970s. Supply-side economics played an important role in getting the public to understand the high costs of taxation and thus to support tax reform in the 1980s. But sensible public policy cannot long focus on any one objective or be limited to one policy approach.

It is useful to consider the kind of society that most Americans desire and then to examine the mechanisms available to advance that vision. Fundamentally, the citizens of the United States want to live in a country where each individual has a reasonable chance of achieving a good living standard, what is "good" being based on both experience and comparisons with other members of the community. For a nation with a growing population, this means an economy with rising levels of production, employment, and income. It is an economic system where the bulk of the employment occurs in the business sector, which, in turn, requires substantial levels of saving and investment.

The appropriate government policy is one that provides a stable environment in which private citizens can confidently plan and make their commitments and choices. This view of the principles of limited government consistent with a market system is hardly new. Adam Smith came to the same conclusion over two centuries ago when he conducted his inquiry into the nature and the causes of the wealth of nations. The society he envisioned surely was not anarchic. Rather, it was characterized by limited government, with the expectation that government would perform well the important tasks that only it could carry out, notably defense, justice, and those major public works we now call infrastructure.[24]

The tools of government policy are too limited in their reach to permit the discarding of those that work with reasonable effectiveness. It is sensible to focus initially on the "macroeconomic" mechanisms of monetary and fiscal policy. Different combinations of tax changes, shifts in government expenditures, and alterations in the rapidity of monetary expansions can help set the appropriate economic environment.

There are other policy instruments that, if properly employed, can help macroeconomic policies work better. This second category, consisting of "microeconomic" mechanisms, deals with individual enterprises and specific markets. There is near-universal agreement in the economics profession on microeconomic matters that is not appreciated by the public generally.[25] For example, when government clamps a ceiling on rents (albeit from the most altruistic motive), economists know, it produces a shortage of housing. New York City provides a dramatic example of the results. The oil "shortages" of the 1970s were a variation on the same theme. Indeed, as a general proposition, the artificial depressing of the price of any product or service will generate a situation where more people will want to buy and consume the item than are willing to produce and sell it at that price.

The converse is equally true. Artificially prop up the price of a given product, and surpluses quickly occur. The farm subsidy program is an ever-present example of the results. That elementary bit of economic understanding continues to have powerful applications in policy-making.

In that spirit, the individual chapters that follow deal with ten key and closely interrelated segments of national policy-making, some macroeconomic and others more microeconomic in orientation:

- Reducing what seems to be an endless array of triple-digit budget deficits
- Controlling the costs of our vast military establishment while adequately protecting the national security
- Reconciling such tax reform objectives as fairness and simplicity with the overall well-being of the American economy
- Reversing the tide of imports—and doing that in a constructive way
- Dealing with the concern that the United States is becoming a service economy
- Responding to the unprecedented wave of hostile takeovers of U.S. business firms
- Coping with continued pressures for the federal government to bail out individual business enterprises
- Facing up to the fact that many of our fellow citizens do not participate in the expanding income and wealth generated by a growing economy
- Protecting the American environment in an effective manner in order to enhance the nation's productivity and competitiveness
- Reforming a regulatory structure whose reach far exceeds its grasp

## The Reagan Legacy and the Task Ahead

A new set of policy initiatives is in the offing. Given the success in fighting inflation, the 1990s may well be a time when growth and the combating of unemployment once again become the dominant objectives, and when questions of fairness and adequacy of the distribution of income and wealth are raised with renewed vehemence. Accompanying the likely stability—or even decline—in defense outlays over the next several years will be rising budgets for such civilian areas as education, training, research and development, and governmental capital investments, notably airports. A larger role for government may well accompany the next swing of the public policy pendulum.

Much will depend on the outcome of the 1988 presidential and congressional elections. The policy shifts under a conservative Republican President would be quite different and probably less radical than under a liberal Democratic occupant of the Oval Office. Whether the nation elects a supporting or an antagonistic Congress will also be a key factor. As in the past, unexpected developments overseas may overshadow considerations of domestic policy. Examples range from a renewed crisis in the Mideast to the outbreak of war in Latin America and to an eventuality that does not now even come to mind.

In any event, public policy for the next several years is not likely to take the form of a cold shower for an overheated economy. If the related but growing concern over federal deficits results in substantially reducing the tide of federal red ink—and thus the flow of governmental purchasing power—perhaps artificial respiration for a soft economy may be a more apt description of the future direction of American economic policy in the post-Reagan era.

As we approach the last decade of this century, we should not expect that the debates of the coming period will be merely an updated rerun of the more distant past. The Great Society experiments of the 1960s have passed on into history, just as Reaganomics soon will. To restore the American economy to a sustainable long-term path of growth with low inflation, the need is not to generate exciting and bold ideas; but to make the tough choices outlined in these pages—and to make them quickly.

# PART B

# Wrestling
# with the Budget

# 2

# *Probing for Soft Spots in the Budget*

The cynics were right after all. When the Reagan administration arrived in Washington in January 1981, the old-timers pointed out that it was far easier to cut taxes than to reduce government spending. Since then, budget history has demonstrated the federal government's inability to match the huge 1981 tax cuts with spending cuts of similar magnitude. That unfinished task is the focus of this chapter and the three that follow.

In the past, deficits could be reduced fairly easily by a combination of two methods: (1) relying on the automatic growth in revenues as inflation pushed people into higher tax brackets and (2) slowing down or temporarily eliminating the annual increases in various spending programs.

It is now much harder to do either of those things. Since 1985, personal income taxes have been "indexed" for inflation, a procedure that ends the automatic rise of this revenue source with changes in the general price level. On the spending side, the largest civilian programs are similarly indexed for inflation—with the reverse effect on the budget deficit. It has rarely been politically feasible to eliminate or postpone such automatic, built-in increases in expenditures for Social Security and other federally sponsored retirement programs. Thus, deficit reductions now require stepping on some very sensitive fiscal toes, a politically unwise action in the best of times.

It has become fashionable for Republicans to blame an irresponsible Congress for its unwillingness to pay the price for tax cuts—by enacting offsetting decreases in government spending. Simultaneously, Democrats put the onus for the unprecedented mismatch of spending and taxing on the President who was in office at the time. Thus, Washington's favorite parlor game continues to be a variation of "spin the budget" (or, perhaps, "pin the tail on the donkey"—or the elephant).

The truth is that there is enough blame to cover both ends of Pennsylvania Avenue—the Capitol and the White House. It was the President who submitted that string of triple-digit deficits (triple-digit in terms of billions, that is) to the Congress in the early and mid-1980s, thus passing the buck to the legislature to cut them. And, likewise, the Congress talked about those "unacceptably large" deficits—while doing little to reduce them. Either branch of government could have initiated substantial cuts in the deficit, and neither did. For example, the President submitted on February 1, 1984, a budget for the fiscal year 1985 with an estimated deficit of $194 billion. When the fiscal year was over, the actual deficit was $212 billion—Republican and Democratic huffing and puffing notwithstanding.

The annual debate on the budget continues to be a sad spectacle. Decision makers in both political parties and in the legislative as well as the executive branches of the federal government are still not facing up to the fact that the 1981 tax reductions have not been matched by equivalent decreases in expenditures. In a very real sense, those tax cuts have not yet been earned. They can be, however, by reducing the rapid growth of federal outlays.

In the past six years, much effort has gone into cutting back a few of the civilian-oriented programs of the federal government. Howls of anguish are regularly heard from the supporters of "means-tested" programs whose growth was merely slowed down—notably, food stamps and school lunch subsidies. Even though these programs had achieved the status of political sacred cows, it seemed sensible to eliminate the portion that aided middle-class families that qualified simply because their children ate in the school cafeteria. It is not clear why taxpayers must subsidize *all* school lunches in order to help the relatively small portion of students who are from poor families. Nevertheless, in the aggregate, outlays for the various federally funded food and nutrition programs were raised from $16.2 billion in fiscal 1981 to $19.4 billion in 1987.

Some civilian-spending cuts were less controversial, such as eliminating a pamphlet called *Imaginative Ways with Bathrooms,* as well as a coloring book that cost $145,000 and a photo guide to employees of the Bureau of Land Management. Furthermore, the Department of Agriculture found it did not need a recipe book on which it had spent over $33,000—a book that, among other things, instructed taxpayers on how to stuff hard-boiled eggs with crab meat.

The Department of Housing and Urban Development discovered it could reduce the size of its annual report to Congress from four volumes to one and from 1,000 pages to 150, at a saving of over $250,000 a year. The Department of Commerce combined twelve internal employee magazines into an already existing publication—and saved $325,000 a year. The reader should not jump to the conclusion that all silliness has been eliminated from federal civilian spending. In May 1987, Senator William Armstrong described a great many federally financed research projects that, in a period of supposed budget stringency, must lead almost anyone to wonder. They included studies of the following:[1]

- Food-foraging habits of the Ache people in eastern Paraguay
- The formation process of Haitian ethnic organizations
- The lessons learned from older persons saving abandoned buildings
- Late marriage in a village in Spain from 1873 to 1983
- The development of political attitudes of women who graduated from Bennington College in the 1930s
- The social impact of television in rural Brazil
- Private banking institutions in London between 1720 and 1800
- Agriculture and economic development in Russia between 1750 and 1860
- Aggressive behavior in Siamese fighting fish
- Biography formation in Stockholm between 1880 and 1910

All in all, in the past seven years, the overall growth of civilian-oriented programs has been slowed down substantially. However, although it is not fashionable to recognize it, most of that "slowdown" resulted from the reduction of inflation in the economy generally. Moreover, this entire budget-cutting effort was offset by the acceleration in defense spending, farm subsidies, and interest payments. Simultaneously, the growth of what are called entitlement outlays has continued unabated. The counterargument that direct benefit payments for individuals have dropped from 48 percent of the budget in 1982 to 41 percent in 1986 is very deceptive. All that means is that other categories of spending were rising even more rapidly. The share of national defense and interest expanded from 35 percent to 44 percent during the same period.[2] Total federal spending rose by almost 50 percent from 1981 to 1986, substantially in excess of the rate of inflation.

There would probably be far less objection to the magnitude of deficit financing in the United States in recent years if the money had been directed to attractive investments in the future, such as improved schooling of the next generation of citizens or improvements in the "infrastructure" (roads, airports, and so on) needed for a more productive economy. But the fact is that the great bulk of the $1.2 trillion of federal red ink since 1981 arises from financing current consumption—through entitlement, farm subsidy, and interest payments—and operating the military establishment. Unlike those produced by private business debt, the activities financed by the massive run-up of federal debt are unlikely to yield a flow of future income (and hence tax collections).[3]

## The Unfinished Task

Every comprehensive examination of the spending patterns of the federal government reveals an array of waste and inefficiency, and of low-priority and postponable expenditures. The report of the Grace Commission (technically, the President's Private Sector Survey on Cost Control) contains numerous examples.[4] These range from lax controls on mailing lists to legislation preventing government agencies from using competitive bidding to mismanagement of freight traffic. Anyone who has participated in the budget review process knows that attractive candidates for budget tightening exist in every federal department, without exception.

A suitable inspiration for the effort needed is the old motto of the budget office "Good budgeting is the uniform distribution of dissatisfaction." Not enough of the spending agencies are dissatisfied. Far too frequently, pleas for additional spending cuts are brushed aside with the claim that defense is too important to cut, that entitlements are too difficult to change, and that the "all other" category is not big enough to bother with. In reality, opportunities for serious and careful budget pruning abound in each agency, military and civilian, social and economic. To start off the budget process by exempting any major area of spending reflects a basic lack of seriousness of purpose.

## Probing for Soft Spots in the Budget

CUTTING THE ENTITLEMENTS

The first and largest candidate for budget pruning is the area of personal benefits set by statute (the so-called entitlements), which account for two-fifths of total federal spending. This category of the budget, dominated by retirement payments, grew from $163 billion in 1976 to $405 billion in 1986. There is little evidence of budgetary penuriousness here. Moreover, most entitlements are, in the words of former Secretary of Commerce Peter Peterson, "welfare for the middle class."[5]

Unfortunately, the subject of entitlements lends itself to demagoguery. The very term begs the question. Why is anyone inherently "entitled" to benefits from the federal government? A compassionate society like ours may wish to provide assistance to the needy. But, basically, such aid is a voluntary act of generosity on the part of the donor. In the case of federal entitlements, the tables have been turned. The burden of proof is on the donor to explain to the beneficiary why the payments are not increasing more rapidly. This turnabout is at the heart of the problem of controlling "entitlement" outlays.

I still vividly remember the many phone conversations in 1981 and 1982 with my father (whose income consists almost entirely of Social Security payments). The theme of each call was similar: "Murray, why are you Republicans trying to take away my Social Security?"

Of course, the elimination or even the reduction of the monthly benefits being received by Social Security recipients already on the rolls was never proposed—or even contemplated. In fact, Social Security, Medicare, Supplemental Security Income, Head Start, summer youth jobs, and Veterans Administration pensions were all spared budget cuts. These programs were the "thread" of the administration's social "safety net." Table 2-1 shows that cash payments to various beneficiaries increased, rather than declined, during the Reagan tenure.

But it was easy for some political figures to plant the seed of doubt. A case in point was the melodramatic statement the AFL-CIO's president Lane Kirkland made to its annual convention in November 1981. According to Kirkland, the Reagan administration sought "to tear through the safety net woven by the New Deal, the New Frontier and the Great Society, leaving the jobless, the poor and the disadvantaged to the economic jungle."

In any event, the firestorm of opposition engendered by the administration's initial Society Security proposals forced the White House in 1981 to beat a hasty retreat. The lesson was clear: fundamental changes

TABLE 2-1

*Public Income Maintenance Programs, 1980–1986*
*(in billions)*

| Year | Total[1] | Social Security | Veterans Pensions and Compensation | Public Assistance | Supplemental Security Income |
|------|----------|-----------------|-------------------------------------|-------------------|------------------------------|
| 1980 | $228 | $120 | $11 | $12 | $8 |
| 1981 | 241 | 129 | 12 | 13 | 8 |
| 1982 | 283 | 156 | 13 | 13 | 9 |
| 1983 | 299 | 167 | 14 | 14 | 10 |
| 1984 | 309 | 176 | 14 | 15 | 10 |
| 1985 | 325 | 186 | 14 | 15 | 11 |
| 1986 | 365 | 208 | 15 | 18 | 14 |

[1]Includes miscellaneous income support outlays.
SOURCE: *Social Security Bulletin*, various issues.

will not be made in federally sponsored retirement programs until the public recognizes that these "social insurance" programs include large components of subsidy or welfare. Although at least one congressman called for my impeachment when I made this general point during a speech in Washington in 1982, the point deserves to be pursued.

To be specific, the average monthly Social Security check is far larger than it would be if benefits were based solely on employee/employer contributions plus interest on those contributions. In 1986, the average Social Security payment was six times greater than the return a pensioner might have expected from investing in a private annuity. Moreover, the people on Social Security are doing much better than the average worker in terms of the annual increases they receive. As is shown in Table 2-2, the actual levels of Social Security benefits during the past decade have been significantly higher than they would have been if they had grown at the same rate as private wages.[6] In fact, the elderly now enjoy the lowest poverty rate of any age group—less than 3 percent when food stamps and other benefits are counted.[7]

Yet, like my father, the typical Social Security beneficiary is certain that he or she is getting only what was paid for. This pervasive myth constitutes a major challenge to economic education as well as to governmental policy-making. The reality is that a long series of automatic and discretionary increases in benefits has resulted in a situation where the average retiree on Social Security has a higher income than the rest of the population.

# Probing for Soft Spots in the Budget

TABLE 2-2

*The Generosity of Social Security*

| Year | Average Monthly Benefits | | Excess (3) (1)−(2) |
|------|------------------|------------------------|--------|
| | Actual (1) | Assuming Rates Rise with Private Pay (2) | |
| 1976 | $302 | $282 | +$20 |
| 1977 | 332 | 301 | +31 |
| 1978 | 366 | 319 | +47 |
| 1979 | 400 | 345 | +55 |
| 1980 | 450 | 375 | +75 |
| 1981 | 532 | 409 | +123 |
| 1982 | 535 | 450 | +85 |
| 1983 | 553 | 475 | +78 |
| 1984 | 542 | 498 | +44 |
| 1985 | 548 | 500 | +48 |

SOURCE: American Enterprise Institute, *Proposals to Deal with the Social Security Notch Problem,* 1985.

How, then, can significant changes be made in the huge Social Security program? Not easily or readily, of course. Yet, it is useful to analyze the problem in terms of three generations. The first generation is represented by those who are now on Social Security. For most of their working lives, they were told that they were earning a Social Security pension. They point out that the government set up account numbers to record all of their contributions and those of their employers. We may know that those contributions, including the interest earned, do not begin to cover those monthly Social Security checks. But the recipients do not know that, nor do they want to learn the bad news.

Few among us have the nerve to tell our own parents that, each time they cash their monthly Social Security check, they are receiving the economic equivalent of welfare. Why, then, should we expect any elected official to be more foolhardy? The inescapable fact is that this nation has made a moral commitment to those already on the Social Security rolls to pay at least the current level of monthly payments and probably some allowance to cover inflation. Advocates of budget restraint must accept the necessity for making this type of benefit payment not financed by the recipients. It is intriguing to note that, under these circumstances, the most effective way to limit the growth of Social Security spending is by keeping inflation low.

*35*

But the second generation—comprising those who have been in the work force for some years and are not about to retire—is in circumstances that are very different. They have the opportunity to adjust to changes in future Social Security benefits, provided the shifts are phased in gradually. At least some members of that generation are sophisticated enough to understand that retroactive benefits such as annual cost-of-living increases, by their very nature, are not part of an insurance program. Rather, they are a hidden subsidy paid by someone else and thus are the economic equivalent of welfare. Long-term alterations in benefits—to bring them in line with what the beneficiaries have paid in—are feasible but only when those changes are understood by the society in general and are phased in gradually.

The most basic changes can be made in the benefits for the third generation, made up of those who have only recently entered the work force. Retirement benefits are very far from their minds. Provided taxes are not increased in the process, these young people will very likely go along with a great variety of reasonable modifications in the entitlement programs. As a practical matter, many of them doubt they ever will receive the Social Security benefits that they are partially paying for. (Technically, they are correct in terms of expecting a much lower rate of return on their contributions than is being received by earlier generations.)[8] On the positive side, this attitude represents a long-term opportunity to reduce the very large welfare (or intergenerational transfer) aspect of Social Security outlays.

A modest first step is to treat all Social Security payments as ordinary taxable income. Recipients with small amounts of outside income would owe little or no tax. Those with higher incomes already pay tax on one-half of their Social Security benefits. The rationale for exempting half of the monthly check was that the employee half of Social Security contributions supposedly had come out of income that had already been subject to the personal income tax. But, as we have seen, the great bulk of every Social Security check comes not from the taxes paid by the recipients but from the taxes collected from the people who are still working. It would be both fair and sensible to tax such subsidized Social Security income in the same way as the money received by the working population is taxed.

A second step in controlling entitlements is to shift to a more appropriate price index to compute the annual cost-of-living increases. That sounds very technical, but—because of the magnitude of the Social Security program—such a sensible change could have a powerful effect on the entire deficit picture. Traditionally, the consumer price index (CPI) has been used for the purpose. Among economists, however, it is well known that the CPI overstates increases in the cost of living for retired people because their share of income spent on housing is much smaller than that of the middle-aged and younger population.

In that regard, a better measure on which to base the cost-of-living adjustments is the implicit price deflator—the index used to boil inflation out of the GNP numbers. According to John Makin of the American Enterprise Institute, if the GNP deflator had been used instead of the CPI since 1976, the increase in the national debt since 1981 would have been only one-half of the $1.2 trillion that actually occurred.[9] Such a change is overdue and would restore a measure of equity among federal taxpayers and benefit recipients.

More-fundamental reforms of entitlements involve privatization of retirement benefits. An example is the proposal to expand the individual retirement accounts (IRAs) authorized by the 1981 tax law to replace the Social Security payroll deductions for new workers. However, in 1986, the Congress went the other way; it reduced the scope of the IRAs drastically. In the long run, the two major entitlements—Social Security and Medicare—will probably need a fundamental overhaul, whether in the direction of privatization or by some other innovative approach.

Meanwhile, an essential part of any serious deficit reduction effort is for the President and the Congress to refrain from further expanding Social Security benefits. Voting today to expand tomorrow's benefits may seem to be a painless way of rewarding a powerful group of constituents, but it shortchanges their children and grandchildren. Senior citizen organizations would do well to shift from their traditional liberal positions on budget issues to more conservative attitudes that better reflect the substantial improvements in recent years in the general financial condition of older people.

CONTROLLING DEFENSE SPENDING

The second large area of potential budget cuts is defense, an admittedly difficult subject to tackle. "Supply-side" budgeting has made the task especially hazardous during the Reagan administration. Because of the overriding importance of the national security, President Reagan has tended to treat the Defense Department as the ultimate off-budget agency. Thus, for example, a $10 billion increase in defense spending and a $10 billion cut in civilian spending are viewed not as offsetting each other but as a net $10 billion cut in the federal budget.

If this challenges the reader's credulousness, consider the practice of former Budget Director David Stockman, in comparing Carter and Reagan expenditures. He would "adjust" the Carter numbers. Specifically, Stockman increased the Carter projections (such as those contained in his last budget message, the one presented in January 1981) to cover what the Reagan administration considered to be an adequate national defense.

That odd procedure did have its advantages. By assigning the Reagan increases in national defense spending to the Carter administration, the Reagan administration could take credit for its cuts in civilian outlays while ignoring its own increases in military outlays.

Hypocrisy on this subject in the legislative branch should not be ignored either. In 1983, Senator John Tower highlighted this point when he unsuccessfully requested individual senators to suggest military budget cuts in their own states. Tower noted, "[I]n one breath, Senators will argue for reductions in defense, and then, in another breath, will argue just as strongly that such reductions should not be made in programs located in their states."[10]

An example of Senator Tower's concern was provided by the House's action on the military authorization bill for 1987. To lower the spending rate, the House gave voice approval (so that nobody's vote could be recorded) to a financing gimmick whereby payments due to defense contractors during the last twelve days of the fiscal year would not be paid until the next fiscal year. At the same time, the congressional deadbeats voted down an amendment that would have empowered a twelve-member panel to recommend closing unneeded military bases.[11]

Not too surprisingly, the expenditures by the Department of Defense have been growing at a very rapid rate, rising from $88 billion in 1976 to $277 billion in 1986. They now represent 28 percent of total federal outlays, the second-largest category. The accompanying increase in the morale of the armed forces (as measured by quality of enlistments and rates of retention) since 1980 surely is an extremely positive development.[12] That has not come cheaply, nor has the necessary enhancement in military equipment and supplies.

Overall budgetary pressures thus make it important to be a "cheap hawk." The defense establishment should become subject to the same rigorous budget review that civilian agencies regularly undergo. This has not been true during the Reagan administration. That, in turn, has led to various congressional attempts to cut military-spending totals simply out of frustration with the unwillingness of former Secretary of

## Probing for Soft Spots in the Budget

Defense Weinberger to indicate any order of priority in his budget requests. Everything on his shopping list was deemed essential and therefore of equal importance. The most cursory examination of the military budget shows the limitations of his approach.

A report on the Department of Defense's budget problems by the U.S. General Accounting Office (GAO) underscores the point that not every defense expenditure deserves to be given a high priority. Here is a typical quotation from the report. It deals with a major part of the military budget, the tens of billions spent each year on operations and maintenance, or O & M:

> Last year we also reported that DOD did not have a well-planned strategy and priority system for applying increased funding to O & M programs. As a result, funds were applied to some programs in excess of what could be absorbed efficiently and effectively.
>
> DOD still does not have a well-planned strategy for applying increased funding to O & M programs.

The GAO went on to point out specifics:

> - At Fort Lee, $2.7 million was received a few weeks before the end of the fiscal year. The money was used for projects that had not been validated, that were not in the approved backlog, and that were not even in the work plans.
> - At Fort Stewart, year-end funding amounting to $92,000 was used to construct a bicycle path. More mission-related projects were not financed.
> - At Little Creek Naval Amphibious Base, $300,000 was used to resurface tennis courts, widen sidewalks, and paint signs. Roof repair projects went unfinanced.[13]

The GAO uncovered other shortcomings of defense-spending practices. As much as 36 percent of the flying done by Navy tactical and patrol squadrons is for activities other than training. However, the budget is based on training for primary mission readiness.

Each year millions of dollars "migrate"—that is a beautiful phrase, for dollars apparently do have wings—from mission-related programs to real-property maintenance. Because much of these budget transfers occur in the last months of the fiscal year, projects of questionable need are sometimes funded in a frantic attempt to spend the money before year-end. We have seen other reports of the Defense Department's rush to spend all its available money before the end of the fiscal year. Hasty procurement moves included buying 57,600 softballs, a fourteen-month supply of paper, and piles of ice cube makers and videocassette players.[14]

There is no need to put all of the onus for runaway military spending on the executive branch of the government. Despite all of its impassioned rhetoric on excesses in military spending, the Congress has never canceled a single weapon system, no matter how poorly it was performing. Even Secretary Weinberger, who was extremely generous on the subject of adequate military outlays, on occasion terminated an unsuccessful military product, such as the Sergeant York antiaircraft gun abandoned in 1985.

Congress is a notorious protector of special interests. By law, the Department of Defense cannot close down the most obsolete base without notifying Congress well in advance and preparing all sorts of costly and time-consuming "impact" statements. These paperwork requirements serve a sterner purpose; they give Congress an opportunity to veto the base closing. The result is predictable—closing a federal installation is a rarity.

After being berated by Secretary Weinberger, Congress in 1983 eased the paperwork burden on closing installations with fewer than 300 civilian employees—which represent about 90 percent of all military facilities. When asked why the Secretary of Defense had not tried to eliminate any of the smaller bases, a Defense Department spokesman replied, "He knows it's very difficult to close an installation."[15] The leadership of the Pentagon thus shares with Congress the responsibility for keeping open unneeded defense bases.

Many of the 4,000 military installations in the United States were established long before modern communications and jet aircraft rendered them uneconomical and unneeded. The clout of the Illinois congressional delegation keeps Fort Sheridan open even though the Army reports that "no strategic or mobilization mission" has been identified for it. The Defense Department requires $9 million a year to keep this unneeded base open.

Likewise, members of the Virginia congressional delegation have cajoled the Pentagon into continuing to staff 165-year-old Fort Monroe, at an estimated cost of $10 million a year. Its occupants could be shifted to another post just a few miles away.[16] The Grace Commission identified over thirty bases that could be eliminated, at an annual saving of over $2 billion.

Another large example of congressionally mandated waste is the statutory requirement that all military bases convert to coal and that U.S. bases in Western Europe stockpile a year's worth of coal. Those blatant subsidies to the coal industry are estimated to cost the taxpayers more than $5 billion over an eight-year period.[17]

A serious national-defense argument can be developed in favor of slowing down the rapid growth of military procurement. Weapon programs experiencing large cost overruns are precisely those whose unit volumes are cut back the most by a Pentagon forced to meet budgetary constraints. Table 2-3 shows that, in striking contrast, procurement programs that stay close to outlay targets are more likely to be continued as planned. Most programs with cost overruns under 40 percent have been maintained without reduction. Each of the weapon systems with cost increases of more than 40 percent was cut back. The largest reductions occurred in the programs with the greatest overruns.

Perhaps somewhat surprising, a positive conclusion arises from the efforts to cut the waste in military outlays: slowing the growth rate of defense spending to conform more closely to budgetary realities will

TABLE 2-3

*The Price of Military Cost Overruns*

| Weapon System | Overruns in Cost | Cutbacks in Numbers |
|---|---|---|
| *Major Overruns* | | |
| Hellfire missile | 322% | 82% |
| Patriot missile | 154 | 67 |
| SSG-7 ship | 79 | 75 |
| AH64 aircraft | 67 | 43 |
| EA-6B aircraft | 52 | 33 |
| XM-1 tank | 49 | 21 |
| F-18 aircraft | 44 | 40 |
| P-3C aircraft | 43 | 50 |
| *Minor Overruns* | | |
| UH-60 aircraft | 33 | 12 |
| Phoenix missile | 30 | 0 |
| ALCM missile | 27 | 8 |
| EC-130Q aircraft | 26 | 0 |
| SN688 ship | 20 | 0 |
| Pershing II missile | 19 | 0 |
| Harpoon missile | 14 | 0 |
| F-14A aircraft | 9 | 0 |

SOURCE: Based on unpublished Congressional Budget Office analysis, 1980.

both reduce the deficit and make more likely the successful completion of the military buildup. It is not a matter of having to choose between national security and economic factors, because the two go hand in hand.

Tighter reins on defense spending will do more than contribute to a smaller budget deficit. Such improved managerial controls will solidify the necessary public support for the continued high level of military strength that is required for the dangerous world in which we live. A more measured attitude to military preparedness avoids crash programs: it opposes the view that every nickel appropriated must be spent at all costs. We do not promote the national security by showing the Soviet Union how fast the United States can spend money.

Indeed, on occasion, Congress does exercise its responsibility for the public purse, especially in the critical national-security area. For example, after increasing spending authority for defense at a whopping 13 percent average annual rate in the decade ending in 1985, Congress voted to reduce this authority 1 percent in 1986 and 1 percent again in 1987. The main effect, of course, is to force the Pentagon to live off of its fiscal fat, which it can do by reducing the mountain of unused appropriations that it accumulated in the first half of the 1980s. (Such unobligated balances available to the Department of Defense at the end of fiscal 1987 came to approximately $50 billion.)[18]

That sum is more than the total amount used (committed or "obligated") in the entire fiscal year by the Departments of Commerce, Education, Energy, Interior, Justice, Labor, State, and Transportation. There is enough left over to finance all the operations of the Congress, the Judiciary, the Executive Office of the President, the Environmental Protection Agency, the General Services Administration, and the Small Business Administration and over $1 billion of miscellaneous activities.

REDUCING SUBSIDIES

Advocates of smaller federal budgets typically focus on entitlements and defense spending. Any student of the budget quickly discovers a third category: "all other." Contrary to widespread belief, not all the items in this area of the budget are social programs, nor have they been cut to the bone. For example, the complaints of farm lobbyists would lead most observers to conclude that subsidies to agriculture have been on the chopping block. If that is so, they have wiggled away whenever the knife has gotten close. The budgetary data are compelling: outlays for the largest agricultural subsidy, farm price supports, rose from $1 billion in 1976 to $12 billion in 1986. This was the most rapid rise of any major program area among the many financed by Uncle Sam.

Total spending for supporting farmers has now reached a level that would finance a direct gift of more than $16,000 annually to each of the 1.6 million farm families, or an annual payment of over $42,000 for each of the 619,000 commercial farms in the United States. By comparison, median income for all U.S. families is less than $30,000 a year.

Ironically, most farmers get little or no aid from the farm price support program. In 1985, only 34 percent of all American farmers received direct assistance. One-fifth of them obtained almost 70 percent of the total aid. In the cotton program in 1985, some 12 percent of the farmers participating were getting more than one-half of the total, with some getting millions of dollars. In the same year, the fifty largest rice producers each received more than $1 million in price support payments. Still, only half of the farms in financial trouble received any payments at all.[19]

The reason for this illogical distribution of agricultural benefits is that they are based essentially on the annual production of each farm. This means that a large, financially secure farm is eligible for generous subsidies, while a struggling farmer with a small crop winds up receiving very little.

But the farm budget problem is more than a question of waste or unfairness. Federal farm subsidies are counterproductive in two ways. First, high price supports encourage excess production. Second, they discourage consumption, at home and abroad.

The honey price support program furnishes a fascinating case study in how Congress favors particular interests over the general welfare. During World War II, the domestic honey industry increased rapidly because beeswax was needed for the waterproofing of ammunition and equipment. After the war was over, demand dropped sharply. But Congress established a price support program that prevented the price declines that would have encouraged a needed shakeout in the industry. The result is a support level for honey much higher than prices for either U.S.-produced honey or imports.

The inevitable has happened. Domestic producers of honey find it more profitable to sell directly to the federal government. In addition to paying above-market prices for the honey, the government must then pay storage fees on the surplus stuff. Meanwhile, American consumers buy lower-priced imported honey. The honey subsidy thus contributes to two deficits simultaneously—the budget deficit and the trade deficit.[20]

The honey program is not the only "sweetener" in the agriculture budget. To help beet sugar farmers, the domestic price of sugar is maintained artificially at levels three to four times higher than the world price. That induces consumers to switch to other sweeteners. It also forces restrictions on imports of cakes, pancake mixes, and other processed goods that contain large amounts of sugar. It is now profitable to import these items solely to extract the sugar and sell it at the high domestic price.

Some farm programs keep on going even after they run out of farmers who qualify for benefits. Thus, although 99 percent of all U.S. farms are now electrified and 95 percent receive telephone service, the Rural Electrification Administration (REA) is still very much in business. Having achieved its original goals, the agency lives on by offering subsidized loans to electric cooperatives serving prosperous urban and suburban areas. REA loans have financed luxury resorts such as Aspen and Vail, in Colorado, and Hilton Head and Kiawah, in South Carolina.[21]

Moreover, as the Conservation Foundation has pointed out, much soil erosion and consequent water pollution have resulted from the movement to larger and more specialized farms. It is ironic that this trend has been fostered by farm subsidy programs, federal disaster payments, and tax advantages—all of which encouraged movement away from diversified farming and its land conservation practices.

The numerous handouts to farmers—and other producers—are in the budget simply because of the political muscle of these special-interest groups. Given the outlook for continued large deficits, those sacred cows in the federal budget should be taken out of the feedlot and led to slaughter.

There is no need, however, to maintain the pervasive myth that the term *subsidy* must always be preceded by the word *farm*. The federal government provides generous assistance to a great variety of other groups, ranging from homeowners to mining companies and exporters. In many of these instances, federal credit is provided at very low interest rates, far lower than the ones other borrowers have to pay and even lower than the interest rate that the Treasury pays for the money in the first place.

These interest rate subsidies are more than an expensive extra "goody" for groups that the Congress has designated as qualifying for federal lending. The low rates encourage people to get government loans, rather than to look to private credit markets or to their own resources. In 1984, foreign-aid loan programs were charging 3 percent or less and reclamation loans 2 percent; and credit for some foreign military sales was extended at a zero interest rate.[22] The federal government is going to continue to be a popular lender so long as it refuses to charge competitive interest rates.

Although business leaders are often in the forefront among critics of excessive federal expenditure, fairness requires us to remind ourselves of the various federal benefits available to business. Examples of the dispensing agencies and their beneficiaries include the Export-Import Bank and exporters, the Federal Railroad Administration and railroads, the Maritime Administration and ship operators, the Department of Defense and military contractors, the Department of Energy and the energy industry, and the Small Business Administration and a variety of smaller firms.

It is hard for me to forget the business group that came to my office in Washington to urge a new subsidy program for its industry. It was offended by my reply that such action would be the economic equivalent of welfare. As one of them indignantly put it, "Why, Mr. Chairman, welfare is for poor people!"

NOT FORGETTING THE REST OF THE BUDGET

Given the wide variety of federally financed activities, an effective effort at budget restraint must be comprehensive. Sacred cows are not limited to the dairy industry or just to a handful of very large and visible departments of government. The "all other" category of the federal budget contains many rapidly rising outlays, although none of them is in the farmers' league. For example, foreign military aid rose from $2.7 billion in 1976 to $9.2 billion in 1986, a more than threefold increase over the decade. Outlays for general science and basic research (to support agencies such as the National Science Foundation) more than doubled over the ten-year period, rising from $1.0 billion in 1976 to $2.2 billion in 1986. The separate category of health research climbed from $2.3 billion in 1976 to $5.2 billion in 1986, also more than doubling.[23]

The budgets for law enforcement grew from $1.5 billion to $3.6 billion. Meanwhile, those Philistines in Washington (to use one of the kinder epithets that prevail in academia) expanded aid to higher education from $2.8 billion in 1976 to $8.0 billion in 1986, a nearly threefold increase.

Nor should the smaller agencies escape budget scrutiny. The National Endowment for the Humanities is, by Washington standards, a tiny agency, spending "only" about $130 million a year. Given the nature of its mandate, those who urge a cut in that agency's budget surely set themselves up to be criticized as "heavies" who care not a whit for culture. That is not just a theoretical possibility. Because of my participation in budget cutting in 1981–82, I was subject to vehement abuse. After all, as an academic, I should have appreciated the value of the humanities.

But to anyone trained in economic analysis, merely setting forth a praiseworthy objective is not sufficient justification for devoting scarce resources to any specific program. An examination of the details on how the foundation's money is actually being spent is revealing. Take Missouri, my state of residence. The foundation's grants have gone to financing a history of each of the fourteen branches of a municipal library in the eastern part of the state.[24] Surely, the continuing presence of such low-priority expenditures shows that the cuts in civilian-agency budgets have been not too large but far too little.

Of course, the Congress does not do too badly for itself in the allocation of federal funds. The budgets for members of the Senate and House, their staff, and their supporting agencies grew from $678 million in 1976 to $1.4 billion in 1986, a bit more than doubling. But Congress's responsibility for the large deficits is far more basic.

Each federal outlay is made pursuant to an appropriation enacted by Congress. It is discouraging to note the type of responses that Congress makes when instances of wasteful spending are brought to its attention. In answering critics of the many special-interest riders added to a 1987 supplemental appropriations bill, Senator J. Bennett Johnston of Louisiana was quoted as saying, "It is not a perfect bill. If it were, I would have a lot more projects in it."[25]

It turns out that Louisiana did quite well in the competition for favors. The supplemental appropriations bill included $5 million for the Bayou Sauvage National Wildlife Refuge and a year's delay on the rule requiring shrimpers to use special devices to prevent turtles from getting tangled in shrimp nets. Thus, in addition to federal taxpayers, the major losers from this bill were the ten thousand sea turtles that are estimated to die each year in shrimpers' nets.

The 1987 supplemental appropriations bill provides futher elaboration of the theme of waste in government. Congressman Dick Armey, a Texas Republican, described the supplemental as "a bill built on pork, sold with baloney, that allows people to bring home the bacon."[26] An inspection of the bill's details reveals that the congressman's ire was well directed.

The supplemental bill, which is intended to provide for unforeseen and emergency conditions, included $8 million to establish a national center for the study of weeds at North Dakota State University, because Senator Quentin Burdick of North Dakota just happens to be on the Appropriations Committee. The senator also succeeded in inserting a provision to remove the $250,000 limit on federal loans that beekeepers can obtain on their honey. According to the Department of Agriculture, only 20 of America's 200,000 beekeepers would benefit from the rider.

The bill also makes available $750,000 to promote the merits of eating fish. This provision was justified by Senator Robert Stevens, of Alaska, on the ground that the seafood industry "needs a shot in the fin."[27] Other special benefits include $2 million for Iowa State University to establish an international agricultural trade center and $3 million for the Choctaw Regional Industrial Park. Another urgent matter was giving Abilene, Kansas, $50,000 to help plan a celebration of President Eisenhower's one-hundredth birthday in 1990.

There is no need to pick on the Senate. Another example of congressional fiscal behavior was furnished by the House Rules Committee. The members of the committee have been generous in approving trips by members of other committees, but have gone on few themselves. A little while ago, the chairman proposed to remedy this discriminatory state of affairs—at the expense of the taxpayers, of course—by a bus tour across the Potomac to Alexandria, Virginia. That suggestion failed to win sufficient support, but he persevered and succeeded in gaining approval for a trip to South America, Costa Rica, and Jamaica.[28]

I cannot resist offering one last example of federal largess bestowed by the Congress at the expense of the taxpayer. In 1986, Congress added to a lengthy appropriations bill a $200,000 payment to Frederick, Maryland—to reimburse ransom paid to the Confederate Army by the town during the Civil War.[29]

Some may discount these instances of waste in government because of the small amounts of money involved, at least by federal standards. However, I still remember the admonition of a truly wise supervisor in the old Budget Bureau: even if you deal with tens of billions in your day-to-day work, never, never refer to "only 10 (or 5 or 2) million dollars." Sam Cohn is still right. To most taxpayers, $1 million is a great fortune.

To be sure, examples of wasteful government programs come in all sizes. A host of expensive "pork barrel" projects continue to be financed year in and year out. For example, in November 1983 the Senate Committee on Environment and Public Works reported out a list of new

TABLE 2-4

*Proposed Corps of Engineers Projects,*
*Water Resources Development Act of 1983*

| Project | Cost (millions) | Benefit/Cost Ratio |
|---|---|---|
| Rock River, Rockford, Illinois | $28 | 1.1 |
| Green Bay Levee, Iowa | 6 | 1.1 |
| Perry Creek, Iowa | 41 | 1.1 |
| Halstead, Kansas | 8 | 1.1 |
| Bushley Bayou, Louisiana | 43 | 1.1 |
| Quincy Coastal Streams, Massachusetts | 25 | 1.1 |
| South Fork Zumbro River, Minnesota | 88 | 1.1 |
| Robinson's Branch, Rahway, New Jersey | 18 | 1.1 |
| Mamaroneck and Sheldrake Rivers Basin, New York and Connecticut | 59 | 1.0 |
| Saw Mill Run, Pennsylvania | 7 | 1.1 |
| James River Basin, Virginia | 94 | 1.1 |
| St. Johns County, Florida | 9 | 1.1 |
| Atlantic Coast of NYC, New York | 7 | 1.0 |
| Gulfport Harbor, Mississippi | 74 | 1.1 |
| White River, Batesville, Arkansas | 26 | 1.1 |
| TOTAL | 533 | |

SOURCE: Senate Committee on Environment and Public Works, *Water Resources Development Act of 1983,* 1983.

public works projects. At a time when the Treasury was paying approximately 12 percent for its long-term money, the committee and the Corps of Engineers were using the unrealistically low interest rate of 7.75 percent in evaluating these projects. The practical effect was to show a higher ratio of benefits to cost than would result from using a more realistic interest rate. Nevertheless, even with the subsidized interest rate, thirty-one of the projects showed a very marginal ratio of benefits to costs, such as 1.1 and even 1.0.[30] The estimated cost of these uneconomical undertakings exceeded half a billion dollars (see table 2-4).

It is clear that, if a current market rate of interest had been used, these projects would have failed the benefit-cost test; the benefit-to-cost ratio would be substantially less than the minimum 1.0 required by law. In plain English, the Congress has been scraping the bottom of the pork barrel.

In fairness, we ought to pay some attention to the waste in the White House, as well as on Capitol Hill. In recent years, every President has come into office pledging to reduce the swollen White House staff, only to bequeath to his successor an even larger personal establishment. As a practical matter, very few members of the White House staff actually serve the President. Most of them report directly, or through one or two intermediaries, to one of the many designated "special assistants." The special assistants, in turn, usually report to a "deputy assistant." Typically, several deputy assistants report to a bona fide "assistant to the President." Usually (there are exceptions to every generalization concerning the bureaucracy), it is the relatively few "assistants to the President" who work with the man in the Oval Office on a day-to-day basis.

Why the proliferation of staff? From my personal observation over several presidential administrations, it seems that the same normal ego gratification that has led to the buildup of huge corporate staffs is at work in the White House. What is different is the absence of the counterpart to the competitive pressures in the private sector to "restructure" the enterprise by reducing overhead expenses.

It is interesting to contrast the British and the American experiences. The current British prime minister, Margaret Thatcher, reportedly does much of the cooking when she and Mr. Thatcher dine alone. They employ one housekeeper, paid out of their own funds.[31] In contrast, the American first lady has an official staff of about thirty. To be sure, the British support the royal family in a far more lavish style, but it is somewhat discomfiting to justify White House staff outlays by comparing them with those of hereditary royalty.

The President does not have to walk down Pennsylvania Avenue on Inauguration Day to emphasize the need for economy in government. But he has a great opportunity to practice what he preaches in the organization of his own staff. And so do the heads of major departments and agencies. Along the latter lines, I recall from my own days in the Treasury the lament that the department should never have acquiesced to the transfer of the Coast Guard to the Department of Transportation—because of the resultant loss of the captive airplane fleet that used to be available to senior officials of the Treasury Department.

By the way, I did practice what I preach while I held office. I headed virtually the only federal agency that followed the President's instructions in 1982 to reduce its budget by 12 percent. Having the smallest CEA staff in modern memory surely was an inhibition at times, but the Republic survived. I may have overdone the economy effort. Within an hour after his arrival, my successor threw out and replaced the old chairman's chair, which I had carefully repaired with masking tape. But given my enthusiastic participation in the budget-cutting effort, I thought it important to make a personal commitment, no matter how modest it had to be.

# 3

# Solving the Budget Dilemma

Cutting federal expenditures is no easy task for any politician in office—especially one who wants to stay there. Directly or indirectly, every dollar of government outgo represents a dollar of income to some constituent. Playing Scrooge and reducing that flow of benefits is a most difficult undertaking. It is understandable if professional politicians often embrace easy-sounding answers. Let us dispose of two such simple—or simple-minded—solutions before we get down to the serious business of budget cutting.

## Two Simple-Sounding Solutions

### RAISING REVENUES—TOO EASILY

One easy, or at least easy-sounding, answer to the budget deficit is to increase the revenues of the federal government without raising tax rates. And it is true that in the past just a "little bit more" inflation would expand the tax base and hence accelerate the flow of income into the Treasury. As was noted earlier, the "indexing" provisions of the 1981 tax law make that less likely. In any event, a "little bit" of inflation, as we learned so painfully in the 1970s, soon becomes a "little bit more." Escalating inflation eventually results in a tight money policy, which restricts both the economy and the flow of revenue into the Treasury.

A second and more constructive approach to expanding the revenue base is to quicken the growth rate of the American economy. However, if that is done by means of measures that generate inflation—and ultimately anti-inflationary credit restraint—the long-term results can also be counterproductive.

A third approach is to advocate just a "tiny" increase in tax rates. One of the dangers of the 1986 tax reform legislation is that the broader tax base makes it easier for advocates of higher levels of government spending to say that all it takes to finance their latest new spending proposal is just a very small-percentage increase in federal tax rates. "What's so bad about a 1 percent increase in income tax rates, especially if it's limited to top brackets?"

The problem is that, with a two-bracket personal income tax structure, such an increase hits a great proportion of the nation's taxpayers. Moreover, too much solace cannot be taken in the recent decline in federal revenues, from 21 percent of the GNP in 1981 to 19 percent in 1986. That only returns the ratio to the level of 1977 and 1978. But perhaps the main objection to any tax increase is that it diverts attention from the needed task of eliminating the many low-yield activities that remain on the outlay side of the federal budget.

REDEFINING FEDERAL SPENDING

Another easy-sounding approach to reducing budget deficits is to redefine the problem. One common response is to focus only on the nondefense portion of the budget, which has been popular during the Reagan administration. Because the rapid buildup in defense spending offset much of the savings from reductions in civilian programs, the overall budget continued to grow rapidly.

But there is no need to be partisan. In previous administrations, apologists generated variations on this theme by focusing on the "controllable" part of the budget, treating entitlements as uncontrollable. It is true that there is little opportunity to do much about this segment of federal expenditure in the formal review process, because Social Security, Medicare, and many other benefit programs do not require annual appropriations. They are funded by so-called permanent appropriations. But Congress has a great deal of discretion in changing the qualifications for receiving future benefit payments—that is, in changing the terms of those "permanent" appropriations.

Over the years, numerous panaceas have been suggested to improve control over the federal budget, especially in order to reduce the deficit. In the 1960s, a comprehensive planning-programming-budgeting system was developed to improve the process of setting federal priorities. That quickly degenerated into a rationalization of the status quo. Then, in the 1970s, the focus shifted to zero-based budgeting as an effective way of identifying—and, it was hoped, eliminating—obsolete and ineffective federal spending programs. That approach also promised more economic results than it could politically deliver.

With the annual federal deficit stubbornly staying in the neighborhood of $150–200 billion, the latest easy answer is capital budgeting. On the surface, it is an attractive concept. After all, state and local governments typically distinguish between capital outlays, such as those for new buildings and equipment, which are generally used for long periods of time, and current expenditures, such as wages, salaries, and pensions.

Businesses also use that accounting dichotomy, and it makes good sense for them. Charging the cost of a new factory in the year it is built would make the profit-and-loss statement for that fiscal period look very sad—and deceptively good in subsequent years. Moreover, the tax laws require a depreciating of capital items over an extended period of time rather than a writing off of their cost in the year they are acquired.

For the federal government, a capital budget would mean removing capital investments from the unified budget, which would be renamed the "current" or "operating" budget. Only the depreciation of government capital would be recorded in the operating budget. Thus, capital outlays (in excess of current depreciation charges) would no longer be counted in determining the budget surplus or deficit.[1] Clearly, the fact that the reported budget deficit is likely to be lower under the capital-budgeting approach helps explain why this esoteric concept has gained so many enthusiastic adherents. The implications of such a shift deserve careful examination.

There are significant differences between the fiscal situation of the federal government and that of other organizations now using capital budgeting. In the federal government, but not in private companies or smaller units of government, as capital projects are completed in one area, they are undertaken in another. Thus, there is little of the peak-and-valley phenomenon to be smoothed out by means of a capital-budgeting process. Annual federal outlays for physical capital investments fluctuated in the narrow range of $12–15 billion during the fiscal years 1981–85.[2]

There are other, more serious reasons for being wary of adopting a capital budget for the federal government. For example, the experience of state and local governments has shown that, under capital budgeting, funds may be readily available for building new roads (which are classified as capital outlays), but not for fixing potholes in old roads or for rebuilding connecting bridges (which are treated as operating expenses). Similarly, it is often much easier for state universities or local public schools to find the money to construct new buildings (capital outlays) than to pay the teachers who use the buildings competitive salaries (operating expenses).

To the uninitiated, the term *capital investments* conjures up visions of dams, buildings, and similar items that generate flows of benefits or services over a long period of time. In the case of a private company, the original outlay will be repaid out of the profits from that future flow of services. But that is not true of the typical federal expenditure that would be classified as a capital outlay.

For many years, the Office of Management and Budget (OMB) has prepared a special classification that reports capital investments separately from operating expenses. Although most supporters of federal capital budgeting seem bored by such details, it is instructive to examine this already available data base.[3] In the OMB investment analysis, military items—primarily missiles, supersonic aircraft, nuclear carriers, and other weapon systems—represent well over one-third of all capital outlays by the federal government. Putting aside the controversies over the desired size and composition of defense spending, we must acknowledge that there is no reasonable basis for estimating depreciation charges on aircraft, missiles, space vehicles, and the like. How can valid write-off schedules be developed for ICBMs or nuclear submarines, given the rapid changes in military technology and our limited knowledge of Soviet defense capabilities? Some weapon systems, such as the B-58 strategic bomber, are phased in and out of the military arsenal within a few years. Others, such as the B-52 strategic bomber, stay operational for decades.

Another large component of federal investment is grants to state and local governments to help them build roads, airports, schools, and similar items. Nobody quarrels with the states and localities (which wind up owning the assets) for capitalizing them in their budgets. But what would be the basis for the federal government's capitalizing the same assets, when it is only providing some of the financing? After all, General Motors does not capitalize the office buildings of Michigan Blue Cross, even though GM's premium payments constitute a major source of the financing.

A third category of reported federal investment outlays is disbursements that are not considered to be capital outlays when made by either private companies or state and local governments, such as expenditures for education, training, and research and development. However valuable these spending programs may be, they do not generate assets on the part of the federal government and do not belong in a bona fide capital budget.

What is left? By my calculations (see table 3-1), out of the U.S. government's total disbursements of $990 billion in the fiscal year 1986, only $42 billion would truly qualify as federal capital investments. In practice, the number might be much larger because every interest group would try to shield its favorite programs by getting Congress to move them from the operating budget and to reclassify them arbitrarily as "capital."

TABLE 3-1

*Federal Investment Outlays, Fiscal Year 1986*
*(in billions of dollars)*

| Category | Amount | |
|---|---|---|
| *Military assets:* | | |
| Equipment | $77 | |
| Construction | 7 | |
| Inventories | 1 | |
| Subtotal | | $85 |
| *State and local assets:* | | |
| Construction | $26 | 26 |
| *Human resources:* | | |
| Education and training | $24 | |
| Research and development | 53 | |
| Subtotal | | 77 |
| *Federal civilian capital assets:* | | |
| Construction | $8 | |
| Equipment | 3 | |
| Inventories, etc. | 11 | |
| Loans and financial investments | 20 | |
| Subtotal | | 42 |
| TOTAL | | $230 |

SOURCE: *Special Analyses, Budget of the United States Government, Fiscal Year 1988.*

## Solving the Budget Dilemma

Nevertheless, when the Treasury borrows to finance the federal government's operations, it would still have to add together the deficits in both the capital and the operating budgets. Thus, any effective effort to stem the tide of red ink must squarely face the need to cut individual spending programs. Juggling the budget numbers is not an adequate substitute.

## Improving the Tools of Budgeting

The most powerful method of budget control is to say no to a constituent who wants a favor at the taxpayers' expense. It is also the most difficult part of budget cutting. This point can be illustrated by referring to the continuing battle of the budget. I have lost track of how many of my former friends (that term is used advisedly) came to my office at the Council of Economic Advisers in 1981 and 1982 to say how strongly they supported the efforts to cut the budget, *but* . . . The serious message always followed the *but*.

It is not exactly the economic equivalent of man bites dog to note that every business group enthusiastically supports cuts in welfare programs, *but* they insist that maritime or textile or steel subsidies are very different. Those subsidies are essential for economic growth and national prosperity. Nor is it shocking that farm groups are always enthusiastic about cutting urban programs, *but* farm price supports are a very different matter to them. Of course, labor groups are very broad-minded. They are willing simultaneously to support cuts in farm programs and business subsidies, *but* only so long as the social programs are spared.

A basic example of what can be called Pogo economics—"We have met the enemy and they is us"—deals with the very notion of competition and with our strong preference as a nation for depending on the marketplace rather than on government to make economic decisions. Virtually every visitor to my office in Washington paid the most sincere homage to the essential role of competition in the marketplace, *but* . . . Time and again, the visitor's eloquent statement of opposition to government intervention was followed—always reluctantly, of course —by a plea for a very special case of new or increased federal spending, which happened to be the one represented by the visitor.

Those very special cases belonged to a very long list—steel producers, timber companies, the automobile industry, farmers, savings and loan associations, textile firms, mining industries, energy corporations, exporters, regions affected by imports, defense contractors, areas that wanted defense contracts, airlines, railroads, truckers, and, literally, the butcher, the baker, and the candlestick maker. The list of the industries that did not come around for some special help was much shorter.

To put it in a nutshell, it is easy to win applause or even a standing ovation for a general talk about the need for economy in government. But that same audience will not only drag its heels but often strongly oppose specific budget cuts that affect its industry or its locality. Try closing any obsolete government installation. You can predict with 99.9 percent accuracy the reaction in that locality. A solid phalanx of labor people, city government officials, and the chamber of commerce will bitterly oppose this "blow" to the local economy. They will unite in pointing out how essential that Navy yard or Army base is. The generalized support for budget cutting is invariably followed by the plaintive plea "Why pick on us?"

I recall the disingenuous complaint of the Missouri congressional delegates a few years ago. The Air Force was moving its communications unit from a base in Kansas City, Missouri, to one in Belleville, Illinois. The folks from Missouri were greatly concerned about the resultant traffic congestion that would occur in southern Illinois and insisted upon an environmental-impact statement. Apparently, the Missourians were so patriotic that they were willing to put up with the inconvenience but were reluctant to impose a similar burden on Illinois!

Attempting to start a budget-cutting campaign by focusing on the "other" guy's benefits only encourages other interest groups to take the same shortsighted route. The result is that nobody then takes the budget problem seriously.

In 1987, the *Washington Post* and ABC News polled a representative sample of the American public to determine how many supported reducing any specific program of the federal government. The results were discouraging: there was no clear majority support for any single budget cut. This was true even of the food stamp program, which attracted the most negatives—with 26 percent favoring cutting the amount the federal government was spending for this purpose. As is shown in table 3-2, a slightly larger percentage (27 percent) wanted to expand the program, and a plurality (45 percent) indicated no desire to change the current funding pattern.

The public talks about cutting the federal budget, but the really over-

## Solving the Budget Dilemma

TABLE 3-2

*The Limited Public Support for Budget Cuts, January 1987*

| Program | Percentage Favoring Cuts | Percentage Favoring Increases | Percentage Wanting No Change |
|---|---|---|---|
| Food stamps | 26 | 27 | 45 |
| The military | 25 | 31 | 43 |
| Aid to public television and public radio | 25 | 17 | 56 |
| Aid to music and the arts | 24 | 16 | 59 |
| The space program | 23 | 32 | 44 |
| Loans and grants to college students | 14 | 46 | 39 |
| Unemployment insurance | 12 | 33 | 52 |
| Day-care for children of working parents who can't pay | 8 | 57 | 34 |
| Medicaid, free health care to the poor | 6 | 61 | 32 |
| Social Security | 5 | 63 | 31 |
| Medicare, reducing health care costs for elderly | 3 | 74 | 22 |

SOURCE: *Washington Post Weekly,* February 9, 1987.

whelming support is aroused only for specific increases in federal spending. Some 74 percent favor a bigger budget for Medicare; 63 percent, more Social Security spending; 61 percent, larger Medicaid outlays; and 57 percent, more day-care centers. Supposedly, the "other" fellow will pay for the added benefits.

We should understand the ambivalence of public opinion on the question of government. A poll taken about the same time as the one referred to earlier revealed a high level of citizen dissatisfaction with government. A CBS–*New York Times* survey reported that 62 percent of the people surveyed believed that the federal government created more problems than it solved.[4]

## Longer-Run Reforms

In the office of one former budget director, there hung a chart entitled "The Tools of Budgeting." Three items were portrayed—a crystal ball, some dice, and a pair of scissors. These items may still represent the most effective techniques for working on the federal budget. Later in this chapter, I show why I opt for the scissors.

CHANGE THE LEGISLATIVE PROCESS

Because of the great difficulties involved in cutting the federal budget, numerous suggestions have been made over the years to improve the process by which Congress reviews and acts on the President's budget proposals. For example, Congress is rarely able to enact the appropriations bills by October 1, when the government's fiscal year commences.

The result is confusion, waste, and a series of "continuing" resolutions enabling the government to continue operating on a temporary budget. As he was retiring from the Senate, Barry Goldwater vividly described the shortcomings of continuing resolutions:

> [H]undreds of issues are allowed to pass that would never survive in a vigorously debated appropriations bill. As the pressures to adjourn mount, the resolutions become Christmas trees festooned with political favors designed to buy support. . . . [N]othing motivates a legislator like the prospect of adjournment, particularly during an election year.[5]

Occasionally, Congress fails to enact a continuing resolution and federal employees are sent home. Cartoonists and columnists have a field day, but ultimately the employees are paid for the period they did not work. To deal with the problem of not enacting appropriations bills on time, it has been suggested that Congress follow the lead of the twenty-two state governments that have adopted biennial budgeting. In support of that notion, Alice Rivlin, former director of the Congressional Budget Office, says that Congress spends "enormous" amounts of time going over the same decisions year after year.[6]

It is ironic that the basic work for a biennial federal budget already has been done. According to the Office of Management and Budget, the second-year numbers in the President's budget are as precisely worked out as those for the fiscal year at hand. In fact, those preliminary numbers serve as the ceiling for the next year's budget request. In other words, the advance fiscal 1990 estimates in the President's fiscal 1989 budget become the basis for the fiscal 1990 budget. Senator Pete Domenici, former chairman of the Senate Budget Committee, also supports a two-year budget cycle, noting that about 90 percent of the annual appropriations process is a repetition of the preceding year's work.[7] It would surely be difficult to come up with a more convoluted and time-consuming budget system than the one the federal government now uses.

Another reason for the long delays in enacting the annual appropriations is the duplication that results when three different sets of committees in each house of Congress review the federal budget each year. First of all, the House and Senate committees on the budget go over the President's submissions in order to develop resolutions specifying the control totals to guide the other committees involved in approving individual parts of the budget.

Simultaneously, the various "authorization" committees review the budget because, in a great many cases, a new bill authorizing an appropriation must be enacted before the appropriation can be passed. Important authorization committees include Armed Services, Banking and Housing, Commerce and Energy, Public Works and Environment, Labor and Welfare, Agriculture, and Foreign Relations. Finally, the House and Senate Committees on Appropriations propose the various appropriations that require congressional action.

In a lighter moment, the reader might be content with smiling at the mythical tale of a federal inspector. He checked an entire room of government employees, each doing nothing. He went to the next room and found an identical situation. Supposedly, his report was terse: "Duplication."

The duplication in congressional budget review is far more serious. Each committee goes over much of the same ground, but from a different vantage point. This procedure makes it difficult for Congress to take concerted and consistent action on the President's budget proposals. The reason for the continuing overlap among congressional committees may not be obvious until the reader takes a properly cynical approach. Eliminating duplication (or triplication) would mean reducing the power of some of the congressional committees, and especially of their chairmen, ranking members, and subcommittee chairmen.

If the choice is between saving the taxpayer's dollar and retaining a member's perks, the choice is an easy one for the member to make—especially when the taxpayer is mute on such technical issues as the overlapping jurisdiction of congressional committees. A few numbers on the growth of the congressional bureaucracy illustrate the magnitude of the problem. In 1947, congressional committee staffs numbered about 500 and personal staffs of the members another 2,000. By 1986, approximately 3,000 aides worked for Congress's committees and subcommittees, and more than 10,000 were employed by the 535 members.

How do these congressional staffers keep busy? By setting up public "hearings" at which members of the Congress hold forth on some subject. For example, in each of four recent years, Congress scheduled over 1,300 witnesses from the Pentagon to testify before 84 different committees and subcommittees. The number of subcommittees delving into defense matters has tripled over the past fifteen years. The civilian departments of government report very similar experiences.

Again, the solution is apparent in theory: reduce the proliferation of congressional committees and subcommittees. At the last count, there were 47 different committees and 229 subcommittees.[8] It is unlikely that any of the congressional barons will yield his power unless and until the level of public outrage reaches a high decibel range. Under present institutional arrangements, sense will be made of congressional committee work only when challengers can beat incumbents by convincing the public that each current representative shares the responsibility for that string of $200 billion deficits.

Nor should we overlook the financial shenanigans that take place on the floor of the Congress. Our national legislature rarely passes a bill without adding a string of special-interest provisions. The 1986 tax reform law may have set a new high (or low). In its final form, it had over 580 different provisions each benefiting a special person, company, organization, or locality (see chapter 5 for details).

It is more than a matter of delaying the legislative process or wasting the taxpayers' money with special-interest riders, although both are genuine concerns. The preoccupation with helping individual groups deflects the attention of members of Congress from the basic tasks that face them. It is easy to get bad legislation passed when each member is busy attaching an irrelevant section to benefit his or her constituents.

Changing prevailing mores will not be easy. The problem will be solved only when the great majority of the Congress hoot down any member who even tries to tie up a key bill by adding an extraneous or special-interest rider. Of course, that will be a difficult change to make. It will take the understanding and, above all, the strong support of the rank-and-file voter.

Basically, members of Congress want to "do good." Citizens need to understand that it is hard for an elected official—especially one who desires to be reelected—to say no to any constituent's request. But it will be easier when every member of Congress is saying no to all special-interest requests as a matter of principle and because the voters expect and desire that course of action.

## Solving the Budget Dilemma

AMEND THE CONSTITUTION?

Because the self-correction process works so slowly in government, a growing sense of frustration with the results has generated substantial support for the notion of amending the U.S. Constitution to mandate an annually balanced budget.[9] Such a cause is popular among conservatives. However, responses borne of irritation must be viewed with suspicion.

The concern expressed here is not that of a liberal who is opposed to restricting the growth of government, or that of a constitutional lawyer reluctant to "tinker" with the Constitution. Rather, my viewpoint is that of a cynic who infers from all the talk about a constitutional amendment that balancing the budget—or even just reducing those swollen deficits—is an important problem, but one not to be tackled today or even tomorrow.

If that is too circumspect, let me be blunt. In 1986, the federal government ran a triple-digit deficit—in the neighborhood of $220 billion, and that is a tough neighborhood. In 1987, the Treasury financed another triple-digit deficit—in the neighborhood of $150 billion. And, the federal government is likely to run additional triple-digit deficits in 1988, 1989, and 1990. But the balanced-budget amendment, assuming everything happens on schedule, will take effect not in 1988 or in 1989 but probably well after the year 1990.

Advocates of free-market solutions are very good at recognizing shortcomings in the public sector's decision-making process. They have cited the numerous instances in which short-term problems have led to long-term (and relatively permanent) legislative solutions that only created new sets of problems. Also, much bad legislation typically has been enacted because the Congress saw an urgent problem needing attention and glossed over the effectiveness of the specific legislative approach that was proposed. The controlling notion was that, if the problem was severe, the solution on the table should automatically be adopted.

Many conservatives seem to be falling into a similar trap. They are very much aware of the shortcomings of existing measures to control the federal budget. But they possess fragmentary knowledge of the long-term effects of the proposed alternative. For example, very little is known of the likely effects if such a constitutional amendment had been enacted in 1939, just prior to the wartime buildup in the nation's defenses, or in 1986, when the federal deficit exceeded $220 billion.

Given the array of governmental intervention techniques—ranging from off-budget credit programs to imposing financially burdensome requirements on the private sector by regulation—it is also apparent that an arbitrary lid on spending will provide powerful stimulus to rely on nonbudgetary methods of government activity. These subterfuges would quite likely turn out to be even less efficient than direct federal expenditure and more corrosive to individual liberty. Surely, questions such as these should be addressed before, and not after, the enactment of relatively permanent changes in the U.S. Constitution.

Some of the support for amending the Constitution arises from a misinterpretation of recent experience. Because a conservative administration like Ronald Reagan's has been unable to achieve the objective of a balanced budget with conventional means, it is held that only extraordinary measures, such as adoption of a constitutional amendment, will suffice.

On the basis of the facts, plus my own experiences in the Reagan administration, I must reluctantly conclude that constraining the size of the federal government has been primarily a part of the rhetoric of Reaganomics, and not one of its fundamental aims. The record shows that the President has given far greater weight to a shifting of priorities within the public sector—from civilian to military outlays.

In his first term, many opportunities to reduce the growth of federal spending were presented to the President by the Republican leadership in the Congress. But these initiatives were brushed aside because they included some modest slowdown in the projected rapid buildup of military programs. When push came to shove, President Reagan was far more concerned about maintaining the rapid expansion in defense spending than in cutting the budget totals. I attended many meetings in the early years of the Reagan administration in which senior Republican senators left the White House literally with tears in their eyes because the President they admired so much had once again turned down any tough action on the budget.

We may respect or even agree with the President's priorities. Nevertheless, recent experience leads to the conclusion that a comprehensive effort to use existing budget control mechanisms to curb government spending still has not been made. Before enacting an economic version of the ill-fated prohibition amendment to the Constitution—a well-intentioned but unworkable proposal—we owe the public one truly comprehensive effort (that "good old college try") to use existing budget mechanisms to slow down federal spending and reduce the budget deficits substantially.

## Solving the Budget Dilemma

Giving the President a "line item" veto over specific provisions in appropriations bills would help. But we should not expect too much from that approach. It is most unlikely that, had it been available to him, President Reagan would have used the power to cut military projects. Moreover, the largest civilian items (notably, Social Security and Medicare) bypass the budget process entirely and thus are not subject to an item veto.

Another popular proposal should not be confused with a panacea for budgetary problems. The notion of privatization is intrinsically attractive. Many government services can be delivered more efficiently by private enterprises competing for government contracts than by a monopoly civil service. However, many of these "services" should not be paid for by the taxpayer regardless of who performs them. For example, the payment of farm subsidies should not be privatized but eliminated. Privatization is only a second-best solution to the overall budget problem.

## The Long, Tough Road

An economist—perhaps only an economist—would add a word of caution: the continuation of triple-digit deficits in the federal budget does not signify that the end of the world is approaching. Controlling the deficit is an extremely important endeavor, but some cures are worse than the disease. They include reversing the trend toward lower tax burdens by increasing tax rates, on the one hand, and inflating the economy to outgrow the deficits, on the other. In any event, a sensible target is not to achieve a zero deficit but to get the federal budget on a durable path of steady and substantial reductions in deficit financing.

As we have seen, there are no easy answers in dealing with triple-digit budget deficits. Efforts to root out "fraud, waste, and abuse" (the popular litany on the political hustings) are valuable. But they do not suffice, yielding at most billions of dollars of savings when the need is for tens of billions in budget cuts. My experience in federal budgeting, beginning in Harry Truman's administration and extending to Ronald Reagan's, convinces me that there is no substitute for eliminating whole programs.

The really large cuts in federal spending are achieved by closing down entire activities now conducted by the federal government. Here are a few examples of the tough decisions that are needed to get the budget deficits down. It is not essential to endorse each of the "dirty dozen" listed here; but significant progress in reducing the annual tide of federal red ink requires equivalent cuts—and more.

1. *Eliminate VA hospital stays for people whose ailments have nothing to do with their military service.* They should be treated like other citizens. The government should quit building new Veterans Administration hospitals in areas where there is surplus hospital space. Consider the plaintive plea of a former VA official: "Does it make any sense to spend $280 million for a replacement VA hospital in Minneapolis where we've got 2,000 empty beds already there . . . ?"[10]

2. *Terminate the space shuttle program.* The scientific contribution of this activity is modest in relation to the cost. One Air Force official close to the NASA program has been quoted as saying, "No one could design a more expensive way to get things into space even if they tried."[11]

In that light, it is fascinating to recall the original justification provided by the head of NASA: "The basic premise leading to the conclusion that this nation should proceed with the development of a space shuttle system is that the U.S. should and will continue to have an active space program from now on."[12] In other words, the main rationale for the shuttle is that it will keep the space program going.

It is silly to harbor national guilt feelings for the *Challenger* disaster. It would be a far more fitting memorial to provide educational benefits for the survivors' families, and a far smaller burden on the Treasury.[13]

3. *Phase out all farm price supports over the next four years.* Boondoggle is the most accurate term for the many billions of dollars spent each year for agricultural programs that hurt consumers, and farmers, far more than the generous benefits they deliver to a fortunate few. Subsidies to agricultural production clearly encourage excess output and overuse of land resources; simultaneously, the higher prices discourage consumption and make it difficult to be competitive in export markets. The accumulation of farm surpluses is not the result of remediable "poor planning"; it is inevitable. Moreover, as a matter of basic fairness, it is difficult to defend a federal program in which a farmer with cash flow of $400,000 a year states, "We live off the government."[14]

4. *Stop all the pork barrel projects of the Corps of Engineers and the Bureau of Reclamation.* The advocates of economy in government should join forces (at least on this issue) with environmentalists who, on ecological grounds, oppose the big dams and other large-scale con-

struction projects. If the citizens of a locality do not believe that an individual project is worth their paying for it, why should the nation subsidize it?

5. *Reduce the disproportionately generous commitment of foreign-aid money to a few countries.* With smaller amounts of U.S. largess, the nations in the Middle East would have to face their internal problems and try to solve them on their own. In other regions, foreign aid is often merely an ineffective bribe.

6. *Put a cap on the annual increase in Social Security benefits to ensure that retirees are not treated better than working people.* This means telling the recipients of Social Security that they were misinformed by earlier generations of politicians in both parties. Social Security beneficiaries have not paid for the annual cost-of-living increases and therefore are not "entitled" to them. Increases in Social Security benefits to those already retired are gifts from the generation that is currently working.

Action to control Social Security payments will take the kind of political bravery that may shock many voters into supporting such change. We need to recall the warning of Rudolph Penner, former director of the Congressional Budget Office, "Politicians live in abject fear of old ladies and old men. Compared with the political power of the elderly, the clout of the oil lobby seems trivial."[15]

7. *Quit pensioning off able-bodied forty-year-old veterans of the armed forces.* By postponing the payment of retirement benefits for ex-servicemen at least until they reach the age of fifty, the nation would encourage still-young people to find civilian work when they leave military service, as many already do. Of course, the change can be made only for new recruits. It would be unfair to shift the ground rules for those who have served on the old basis.

8. *Stop ignoring the government's generous fringe benefits in computing "comparability" of pay between federal civil servants and private employees.* State and local government employees should also be included in the calculation. The present system biases the calculation of pay standards against the taxpayer.

9. *Repeal federal controls on private construction wages by means of the Davis-Bacon Act.* This rule of the 1930s is an anachronism in the 1980s and should be interred. It needlessly increases the costs of government (by about $3 billion a year for the Department of Defense alone).[16]

10. *Charge competitive, market interest rates for all federally pro-*

*vided loans.* That one change will quickly reduce the many demands for federally subsidized credit.

11. *Abandon the goal of a 600-ship Navy successfully advocated by former Secretary of the Navy John Lehman.* This unjustifiable extravagance should be cut back as quickly as possible to minimize the "sunk" cost generated by the construction work that continues to be performed.

The main rationale for fifteen aircraft carrier battle groups was the "maritime offensive strategy." This called for forays close to the Soviet Union in case of active hostilities. But defense experts contend that even fifteen carriers would not be enough for such an ambitious mission.[17] Moreover, it is contrary to the traditionally more modest, and more realistic, role of the Navy: to secure the sea lanes and to bottle up the Soviet navy. Admittedly, it will be extremely difficult to get the Pentagon to admit that it made a mistake and to cancel the order for building the last two carriers. Similar opportunities for economizing exist in several other major weapon systems—including the Stealth bomber, the rail MX missile, and the Trident II missile—that are entering or nearing the expensive procurement stage.

12. *Eliminate food stamps, public housing, and other noncash "income in kind" that the federal government provides to poor people.* Predictably, we hear howls of outrage from the supporters of these programs whenever any budget cuts are contemplated. But it is fascinating to note how these same advocates of higher federal spending reply when someone wants to include such "income in kind" in the official measurement of the number of people living in poverty.

It is almost incredible, but the proponents of these expensive programs contend that including "income in kind" is unfair. They point out that a dollar of spending for these social programs does not generate a dollar of benefit to the recipients. One champion of these social programs admits that food stamps "certainly aren't worth their face value in cash." He suggests that if these items are included in any measure of poverty, they should be discounted by 20 percent or even 40 percent.[18]

The cynic in me says that we have the makings of a deal here: eliminate food stamps and other "payments in kind," and split the difference. Give the current recipients cash equal to one-half of the government's current cost for these programs, and reduce the budget deficit by the other half. I readily forecast that the major complaints would arise not from the "clients" of these programs but only from the newly unemployed social workers.

The effort to reduce deficit financing and slow the growth of government is not a mere matter of accounting. To the contrary, it should be viewed as part of a larger, more fundamental attempt to shift the focus of economic decision making in the United States away from the public sector. For it is in the private sector where, warts and all, products are created, markets are developed, factories are built, productive jobs are generated, and economic progress is achieved.

# 4

# A Strategy for Controlling Defense Spending

A major paradox of the Reagan administration has been its effort simultaneously to shrink the size and power of government and to increase the military budget more rapidly than in any other peacetime period. The results are more than merely inconsistent. They often have spelled deadlock, as Congress in recent years refused to go along with the defense increases in light of the large budget deficits.

It is also ironic that, at the same time, the modest and useful efforts to reduce the burden of federal regulation generally (to be described in chapter 12) were offset by the expansion of the military market. As we will see, the defense industry is, by far, the most highly regulated part of the U.S. economy. Because that closely controlled sector of business has expanded more rapidly than civilian markets, American industry as a whole has not become less regulated during the Reagan years.

We can, however, develop a strategy that brings the two objectives of strengthening national security and reducing the size of government closer together. That is the primary function of this chapter. But, as lawyers usually note, a necessary foundation must first be built. In this case, we need to understand the uniqueness of federal regulation of defense production as well as the financial and operational benefits of streamlining that process.

## The Regulation of the Defense Industry

When most people think about regulated industries in the United States—if they think about that highly technical subject at all—they have in mind the local electric or gas utility, whose rates are controlled by the state public service commission. In contrast, the defense industry rarely appears on anyone's list of regulated sectors of the American economy.

The reality was best described a few years ago by a senior Pentagon official who asked the heads of two companies—a public utility and a defense subcontractor—about the government rules that were the framework for managing their respective enterprises. From the utility, the request yielded a few pages that spelled out the state-enforced guidelines. The defense subcontractor, in contrast, had to comply with over 450 major specifications, directives, and instructions, weighing several hundred pounds. The federal official concluded, "The reality is that there are infinitely more controls in the so-called free enterprise environment of the major weapons systems contractor than there are in the controlled environment of the public utility."[1]

The same official described enthusiastically his visit to a large defense contractor (it should be noted that each defense plant is under the jurisdiction of a single military service—Army, Navy, or Air Force): "I was impressed with the complete interrelationship of the Service/contractor organizations. They are virtually colocated. . . . The Service is aware of and, in fact, participates in practically every major contractor decision. Both parties join in weekly management meetings."[2]

At a more macroeconomic level, the overall scale of federal involvement in the American economy by way of the defense-contracting process can be appreciated by comparing the size of the total military market ($174 billion in 1986) with important civilian markets ($140 billion for furniture and household equipment or $168 billion for clothing and shoes).

Sheer size makes defense production important, but the specialized nature of many of the items being procured makes any analysis very difficult. The civilian and military economies differ in many important ways. In the civilian sector, the manufacture of durable goods accounts for a modest 19 percent of all nonagricultural production. For defense work, the output of durables is the main show, making up 56 percent of the total. Conversely, services and commerce constitute 57 percent of commercial output and only 23 percent of military production. That the items procured are specialized provides the military with an excuse to bypass the competitive open market.

As a former defense industry executive, I must reluctantly admit that it is hard to overestimate the involvement of Defense Department officials in the internal operations of a typical "private" company producing aircraft or missiles or ships for the armed forces. The military establishment shares the management decision-making functions of its contractors above all through the procurement legislation and through the rules that determine how contracts should be awarded. The military procurement regulations require private suppliers to accept on a "take it or leave it" basis many standard clauses in their contracts, which give the government contracting and surveillance officers numerous powers over the internal operations of these companies. For example, the procurement regulations prohibit charging to government contracts such normal business expenses as interest, civic and charitable contributions, and much of company-initiated research and development.[3]

As of 1987, the regulations governing military procurement from the private sector were over 2,000 pages long, including 500 pages of standard clauses to be inserted into defense contracts and 300 pages of standard forms to be used. This mountain of bureaucratic detail is followed by sixteen more technical appendixes.[4] The military contracting officers, and their defense industry counterparts, must master the intricacies of the massive *Federal Acquisition Regulation* (in reality, a two-volume handbook jointly issued by the Department of Defense, NASA, and the General Services Administration), the even larger Department of Defense *Federal Acquisition Regulation Supplement,* the defense acquisition circulars issued periodically to modify the previous document, and the special instructions issued by the individual services and purchasing commands.

Some insight into both the broad scope of military procurement regulations and their fine level of detail is obtained from a mere perusal of the table of contents of a single defense acquisition circular. The following items are some of the forty-two contained in the issue of August 18, 1986:

> Acquisition of surveying and mapping services
> Acquisition planning
> Agency head approval for completion of construction contracts

> Aircraft ejection seals
> Cancellation of forms
> Distribution of subcontracting overseas
> Field pricing reports
> Foreign weapons evaluation program
> Identification of sources of supply
> Indirect cost certificate
> International traffic in arms
> Investment type contracts
> Logistic support for contractors in South America
> Purchase of commercial publications
> Qualification requirements
> Quality assurance agreement with Australia
> Restrictions on acquisition of critical forging items
> Safety precautions for ammunition and explosives
> Should cost analysis
> Weapon system warranties
> Withdrawal of bid[5]

The result of the do-it-by-the-numbers emphasis is more than a fascinating exercise in bureaucracy. These intricate statements of policy and practice convey a great deal of substantive power. The authority assumed by the government customer includes power to review and veto company decisions regarding which activities to perform in-house and which to subcontract, which firms to use as subcontractors, which products to buy at home rather than abroad, what internal financial reporting systems to set up, what type of industrial engineering system to use, what minimum as well as average wage rates to pay, and how much overtime work to authorize.

Thus, when a business firm enters into a contract to produce weapon systems for the military, it necessarily assumes a quasi-public character. This is implicitly recognized by the firm's being required to conduct itself in many ways as a government agency—to abide by the buy-American, affirmative action, depressed areas, prevailing wage, and similar social requirements. Certain types of purchases must be made from the federal prison industries, others from the blind and the handicapped, and still others from specific federal installations. For example, all jewel bearings must be bought from the government-owned William Langer bearing plant in Rolla, North Dakota. Of course, if such tie-in contracts were made between two private firms, they would run afoul of the antitrust laws.

The unique nature of the military procurement process helps explain why defense contractors have set up special accounting systems and special quality control procedures and why they use special drawings and even special soldering techniques. Many of the federal powers over defense contractors are designed to respond to highly publicized incidents of wasteful practices or to avoid the repetition of scandalous practices that resulted in embarrassing headlines. In contrast, the required social provisions in those contracts are viewed by the Congress as a seemingly costless way of achieving worthwhile objectives, even if not especially relevant to the military mission.

But rarely if ever are the bits and pieces of federal regulation of military production seen as a total process. Table 4-1 presents the results of a study made several years ago by a major aircraft manufacturer, contrasting the required paperwork for the development of a new military plane with that for the development of a jet airliner. The latter included the needs of both the airlines and the Federal Aviation Administration.

The differences between the military and civilian buying procedures are staggering. The 400 pages of specifications required for the commercial market contrast with the 16,000 pages for the military; likewise, the 250 separate commercial data submissions are very modest compared with the 30,000 that the military needed.[6]

The head of contract administration for another major aircraft producer has provided some insight into the shortcomings of the bureaucratic approach, which depends heavily on paperwork in the decision-making process. He referred to "the considerable disparity between the

TABLE 4-1

*Military versus Commercial Paperwork for
Development of New Aircraft*

| Category of Paperwork | Military | Commercial |
|---|---|---|
| Program plans: | | |
| Management systems | 20 | 0 |
| Other | 20 | 1 |
| Specifications | 210 | 9 |
| Data item descriptions | 300 | 0 |
| TOTAL DOCUMENTS | 550 | 10 |
| Paperwork consequences: | | |
| Pages of specifications | 16,000 | 400 |
| Separate data submissions | 30,000 | 250 |

SOURCE: McDonnell Douglas Corporation, *Federal Government Business Aspects Which Entail Unnecessary Expense*, October 27, 1975.

commercial practice which relies so very little on the accumulation of large amounts of data . . . and the reliance instead on the largely subjective evaluations of a smaller number of evaluators and participants in the decision making process."[7]

It is eye-opening to juxtapose the excruciating detail of this important category of federal regulation and the numerous cost overruns and quality deficiencies of weapons production. A generous interpretation of the resulting pattern is that the shortcomings exist despite all the governmental intervention in private-business decision making. A less charitable but far more accurate explanation is that the awesome amount of second-guessing of defense contractors contributes to their poor performance. Surely, the time and effort required to keep abreast of the military's bureaucratic requirements and the resources needed to comply with them are not available for the actual design and production of weapons and other equipment needed by the armed forces.

The trivia included in the military procurement process sometimes border on the ridiculous. For example, the Army has fifteen pages of detailed specifications governing the sugar cookies it purchases for soldiers' desserts. Buying a whistle for the military police means dealing with nineteen pages of specifications and descriptions.[8] Perhaps the most delightful example of military procurement "overkill" is Military Specification MIL-F-1499F. These fourteen pages cover the requirements for fruitcake to be sold to the Pentagon. Only the highlights are contained in table 4-2.

The linkage between such excessive regulation and poor performance provides the basis for my proposing fundamental changes in the relationship between the military establishment and the companies competing for its contracts. Let us first review the major deficiencies in the existing defense production process and then examine the potentials of some proposals for improvement.

## Deficiencies in Defense Production

Reports on defense spending are dominated by tales of $363 hammers, $110 diodes, $640 toilet seat covers, $654 ashtrays, and $3,045 coffee makers. However tenuous the factual basis for these charges (and many of the humorous examples do not hold up to serious analysis), they have

TABLE 4-2

*How to Bake a Fruitcake by the Numbers*
*Excerpts from the Pentagon's Instructions to Private Contractors*

"Vanilla flavoring shall be pure or artificial vanilla in such quantities that its presence can be organoleptically detected, but not to a pronounced degree."

\* \* \*

"The fruitcake batter shall consist of equal parts by weight of cake batter specified in Table I, and fruit and nut blend specified in Table II, blended in such manner as to meet requirements of 3.5."

\* \* \*

"A predetermined weight of the blended fruitcake batter, sufficient to yield the specified weight, shall then be deposited into cans with liners and discs and the lids of the cans shall be clinched on loosely to allow for the escape of moisture and gases evolved during processing. Alternatively, in lieu of paper disk and liner, the can shall have an enamel interior possessing adequate product release characteristics so that not more than 5.0 percent by weight of the product adheres to the interior of the can."

\* \* \*

"Sealing and baking shall be so that the butter portion is heated uniformly throughout to produce a finished product having no raw, stringy or ungelatinized portions."

\* \* \*

"When the cooled product is bisected vertically and horizontally with a sharp knife, it shall not crumble nor show any compression streaks, gummy centers, soggy areas, be excessively dry or overprocessed, and shall display an even grain throughout."

SOURCE: Military Specification MIL-F-1499F.

succeeded in moving the military budget to the front pages and to the evening news. The supposed incompetence of military procurement should be seen in context. For every diode procured at $110 (of which there were two), there were more than 100,000 produced at four cents each. For every hammer bought at $363 (of which there was one), more than 6,000 were bought for less than $8 apiece.[9]

But all that is in reality a sideshow. It is the billions of dollars devoted to specific weapon systems that constitute the real spending pressures that need to be dealt with. Although less dramatic, the news here is not very good. For example, when Lockheed delivered the C-5A transport aircraft with an unstable wing structure, it received an additional $1.6 billion sole-source, or monopoly, contract to restore the wings to their originally promised life.

When the performance on the United Technologies's F-100 engine (used to power the F-15 and F-16 fighter aircraft) proved unreliable in early tests, the Air Force tripled the volume of spare parts ordered from the company. The extra parts were expected to help regain operational status for the aircraft; the prices for the parts were almost all negotiated on a sole-source basis. The deficiencies in the B-1 bomber have added several billions of dollars to the business of Rockwell International, the company producing the inadequate plane.[10] Clearly, the fundamental incentives for efficiency in military design and production are weak—or, worse yet, counterproductive.

Although individual "horror stories" abound, comprehensive information on military procurement costs is hard to come by. Occasionally, it is possible to get a glimpse of unclassified data that show the extent of cost overruns for a given period. The data in table 4-3 are drawn from a 1984 study by the Congressional Budget Office. In absolute magnitudes, the excess over the target price ranged from $929 million for the F-14 aircraft to $2 million for the E-3A aircraft. In relative terms, the largest overrun occurred in the E-6 aircraft (184 percent) and the smallest in the standard missile 2 project (2 percent).[11]

In addition to cost overruns, time overruns—failures to meet production schedules—occur with great frequency. In that same 1984 study, the Congressional Budget Office analyzed forty-nine procurement programs where the delivery schedules had been changed in the preceding year.

TABLE 4-3

*Sample of Cost Overruns in Military Procurement in 1984*

| Program | Total Amount of Overrun (in millions) | Percentage over Target Prices |
|---|---|---|
| F-16 Aircraft | $929 | 1–58% |
| Trident I Submarine | 287 | 7–15 |
| E-6 Aircraft | 183 | 184 |
| AMRAAM Missile | 135 | 32 |
| Aquila Remotely Piloted Vehicle | 132 | 10–37 |
| KC-10 Aircraft | 127 | 88 |
| Inertial Upper Stage Vehicle | 118 | 18 |
| Space Defense System | 109 | 10–28 |
| SSN-688 Submarine | 97 | 2–16 |
| Precision Location Strike System | 59 | 17 |
| MX Missile | 58 | 5–12 |
| NAVSTAR Global Positioning System | 50 | 10–26 |
| Standard Missile 2 | 3 | 2 |
| E-3A Aircraft | 2 | 4 |

SOURCE: Congressional Budget Office, *A Review of the Department of Defense, December 31, 1983, Selected Acquisition Report,* 1984.

Ten of the forty-nine were ahead of schedule, and nineteen were behind schedule. Of the other twenty, the data indicated that the program was on target. In 1987, the General Accounting Office (GAO) reviewed the progress on nineteen major military procurement programs. Only seven were on schedule; the other twelve were lagging. "Schedule slippage" (to use the bureaucratic jargon) ranged from four to fifty-one months, the average delay being seventeen months. The GAO reported that in most cases the delay also increased costs.

The GAO's examination of the advanced medium-range air-to-air missile was revealing. Initially, the Navy had estimated that it would cost about $3.4 billion (in constant dollars) to provide approximately 20,000 missiles. By 1987, the cost (measured in the same dollars of constant purchasing power) had risen to $8.2 billion for 24,335 missiles. The development phase, originally expected to take four and a half years, is now estimated to last more than eight and a half.[12]

These inefficiencies are far more serious than the budget overruns that they produce. In a 1985 study, the GAO found shortages of production machinery that curtailed production on four of the six high-priority weapon systems it was examining. Some of the shortages seemed to be quite serious. Shortages of components and raw materials constrained production on the M1 tank. "Slaving" was resorted to. This expensive practice involves building new tanks around components borrowed from tanks that are already finished. In the interim, the actual degree of military readiness declines.[13]

This incident highlights the intricate relations between cost containment and achievement of national-security objectives as well as the difficulties involved in controlling costs. Simply reducing the number of aircraft or missiles being produced may raise costs, if the production rate falls below the minimum economical rate. For a sample of eighty-five procurements in 1981–86, where the numbers of units bought each year was reduced by 17 percent, the average unit price rose 22 percent.

There are many reasons for cost overruns. One highly experienced military analyst, Richard Stubbing, contends that such overruns occur because only the initial phases (about 10–20 percent) of the total work on weapon programs are subject to competition.[14] That is, the competition to produce a new aircraft or missile—and the rivalry is fierce—centers on design, development, and initial production.

In this environment, contractors face strong incentives to bid very low for the early awards. That is because the winner generally becomes a monopoly supplier and gains lucrative follow-on contracts for the remainder of the production, plus spare parts, for as long as twenty years. Those later contracts for the bulk of the weapon production are negotiated with the government and hardly result from a competitive process. This procedure allows the private contractor considerable leeway in setting the price. The General Accounting Office has described the situation quite succinctly: "Little or no competition exists subsequent to the conceptual developmental phase of weapon procurement. Awarding a developmental contract most often guarantees the award of full-scale development and production contracts."[15]

I find it relatively easy, on the basis of experience, to note which avenues for change should be avoided. Some "improvements" would do much more harm than good. For example, Congress should not institute yet another set of detailed requirements supposedly to "control" some aspects of military procurement costs. Consider section 203 of Public Law 91-441, which regulates how the government reimburses defense contractors for military-related research. The idea was to limit how much contractor-initiated research and development could be included in the overhead costs chargeable to a military contract.

To comply with that law, the Pentagon employs seven technical reviewers, twelve negotiators, eleven on-site reviewers, eighteen technical evaluators, fifteen administrators, six documenters, and seventeen auditors, plus their supporting staff. All that expense, however, is the proverbial frosting on the cake. The really large administrative costs are imposed on the defense contractors, each of whom has a specialized staff to deal with this one set of government requirements.

The Department of Defense is frequently guilty of carrying the do-it-by-the-numbers approach too far. When the Army was ordered to cut in half a ten-inch-thick book of specifications for a new helicopter engine, it initially responded by printing the report on both sides of the page instead of on only one. The entire military procurement process remains an area of fascination to civilians. For example, military contractors reported to a study group of the Harvard Business School that cost underruns are as likely to be penalized as cost overruns:

> The only thing worse than a serious cost overrun is a cost underrun of 15 percent or more. If such an underrun occurred, we would make the Government contracting officer look bad. This in turn would endanger our relationship with him and motivate him to negotiate a lower target price with us on the next contract.[16]

But not all of the onus should be placed on the military procurement officers. The Harvard project also explained the problem of orienting the engineering staffs of the defense firms to cost concerns:

> What if an engineer overruns his budget? Nothing. He gets more money, and gives fifteen reasons why someone else caused the overrun. The top management's motivation to maximize return on investment simply isn't transmitted down the line to our engineers. . . . Never has an engineer been fired for consistently poor budget performance.[17]

## Improving the Status Quo

An important step in controlling defense budgets—without sacrificing important national-security objectives—could be taken by simplifying the way in which the military establishment buys the items it needs. For any business with the size and technological requirements of the Pentagon, the task of procuring goods and services will always be a challenge. Without the guiding economic incentives of the commercial marketplace, the task is especially difficult. Existing procedures that discourage efficiency should be changed. If public policy had really wanted to go the bureaucratic route, there would be no need to use private companies in the first place. But it is precisely to obtain the efficiency and innovation of competitive enterprise that all those defense contracts are awarded to the private sector.

### DEREGULATION

Contrary to the popular perception that defense production takes place with little military oversight, there is—as I described earlier—a great deal of government involvement in the internal operations of defense contractors. For a large defense company, an entire suite of offices is typically assigned to the military's full-time resident inspectors and reviewers. It is hard to imagine any commercially oriented company that is permanently host to customer representatives who regularly participate in the day-to-day running of the organization.

Moreover, the detailed bureaucratic oversight of military production has prevented neither numerous cost overruns nor problems with product quality. The time has come to deregulate many of the formalities of the military procurement process—to strip away the detailed minutiae of the FAR, DAR, DAC, and so on. The potential benefits are awesome. One unpublished study at the Pentagon estimated that meeting regulatory requirements accounted for one-third of all procurement costs.[18] (The much-maligned Postal Service, whose purchases make it second only to the defense establishment in federal buying power, recently reduced its 1,327-page purchasing manual to a modest 460 pages.)[19]

Overregulation is not a merely theoretical possibility. Five competitors for the C-5A cargo plane wrote a total of 240,000 pages of material. Along with supporting documents, the submissions weighed three and a half tons and took several trucks to deliver. The reason for this is onerous regulation. Since the withholding of information on a contract is now a potential felony, defense contractors naturally err on the side of inclusion. However, all that detail did not prevent major cost overruns in the program.

The burdens of the massive paperwork extend beyond the procurement process. So many of the resultant reports and manuals take up valuable space on military missions. The frustration this creates was highlighted by a 1987 statement by Vice-Admiral Joseph Metcalf, "We do not shoot paper at the enemy." He was referring to the twenty tons of paper and filing cabinets that weigh down individual Navy frigates at the expense of weapons and fuel.[20] A substantial degree of deregulation merits a high priority in any effort to reform the military procurement process.

## PRIVATIZATION

Cures for the high cost of military production do not come easy or cheap. The favorite response by former Secretary of Defense Caspar Weinberger to cuts in the military budget—simply to stretch out production schedules—turns out to raise costs over the long run.

But such stretch-outs are not inevitable. According to a Rand Corporation study, much of the increase in unit price arising from a program stretch-out is a consequence of the inflexible production-line technology used by most defense contractors. Defense manufacturing today is not much more flexible than it was in World War II. Then, it was highly successful in producing single designs in quantities often measured in the thousands over long periods of time at low unit costs. However, the national-security environment and U.S. defense policy have changed tremendously since the 1940s. The Department of Defense now procures a new weapon system in the hundreds—or several dozen—with high unit costs and changing designs.

The U.S. defense industry has established world leadership in the design of weapon systems, but this advantage cannot be fully exploited, because it is not supported by modern production facilities. Defense procurement relies on some of the oldest manufacturing plants in the United States, and this helps explain high costs and long lead times.[21] For example, the machinery used by the Grumman Corporation to produce the F-14 fighter aircraft was, on the average, thirty-four years old.

Defense decision makers should take more note of the recent experiences of civilian-oriented manufacturing companies. Hard-pressed by foreign competition, many have shifted to more flexible manufacturing systems based on computer-aided design and manufacturing capabilities (see chapter 7). To obtain today's small buys of weapon systems at reasonable cost, similarly flexible production facilities are needed. The required factories would be able to maintain high utilization rates and low overhead by producing a variety of different items.

The few similar efforts by defense contractors are quite promising. Modernization projects at General Dynamics requiring $226 million of new investments saved $261 million in production costs. A $45 million investment by Westinghouse in a state-of-the-art electronic assembly plant saved the military $37 million in production expense in a recent period.[22]

To provide the incentive for private firms to use their funds for these purposes, private investment in defense work needs to be linked more closely to that politically unpopular but economically essential element—the carrot of profits. That means that contractors would be rewarded with higher profits for work done on time, for meeting promised performance standards, and for delivering goods and services at or below contracted cost. Conversely, penalties in the form of reduced profits would be imposed for poor performance—including late delivery, cost overruns, and substandard work. Total earnings on defense work would not necessarily rise, but the allocation of profits among contractors would be a more powerful tool to achieve better performance.

Under an effective incentive system, a truly successful weapon system program would yield very high profits for its producer, and no congressional committee would greet the results with grandstand displays. But similarly, an inefficient program would result in low profits—or outright losses—and no bailout would follow. A strategy of relying on more private investment and on the profit motive would be an important step to the further privatization of military procurement.

## COMPETITION

Another fundamental approach to raising the efficiency of military procurement is to rely more heavily on competition among potential suppliers. The record of competition in the private marketplace has been impressive over the years, driving down costs and providing efficient production. Substituting economic incentives for detailed surveillance of the operations of government contractors is likely to produce more defense output for the same number of dollars.

Over the years many studies of defense contracting have ratified this commonsense proposition. The Institute for Defense Analysis (IDA) analyzed the effects of competition on twenty defense systems—primarily electronics systems and tactical missiles, all of which had initially been purchased sole-source. The IDA study found that, when the government switched to competitive awards, the average cost saving was 37 percent.

The Army Electronics Command found that savings of 40–50 percent were realized on twenty-two electronics systems when competition was introduced into a sole-source procurement. The Army Procurement Research Office reached similar conclusions on eleven new Army contracts, where savings averaged 50 percent. IDA published a second in-depth report on thirty-one defense items that had been switched from sole-source to competitive procurement. The findings showed average savings of 35 percent.[23] The Tomahawk cruise missile furnishes a cogent example. In 1984, when sole-source procurement was still being used, the missiles were costing about $2 million each. Three years later, with competition between General Dynamics and McDonnell Douglas, the unit cost was down to $1.5 million.[24]

The role of competition in multibillion-dollar military procurements has not been fully appreciated in the current debate on controlling the military budget. The benefits of competition go beyond short-term price advantages. The competitive process provides a means for discovering the various alternatives that are available to meet a particular program need. The most important benefits of competition are often the new ideas, improved designs, advanced technology, earlier delivery, or higher quality that potential contractors are motivated to generate in order to win and hold on to a contract.

Competition could also be encouraged by awarding separate contracts on a competitive basis first for research and development and then for the production phases of weapon programs. This contrasts with the present arrangement, where development and initial production are usually lumped into one negotiated contract, and follow-on production contracts are then awarded to the same company without competitive bidding.

Contracts for a weapon system should be awarded to two or more firms in the early, developmental stages. The government should avoid settling on a single contract for the major production work. This would be especially useful in aircraft and missile programs, where it is feasible for the government to pay for several prototypes that can be tested before it decides on a final version.

The Analytical Sciences Corporation, an important source of outside evaluation for the armed services, reported that cost savings of 30 percent are typical upon introducing dual sourcing. The Army Procurement Research Office reached a less startling conclusion, but nevertheless in the same direction. That agency indicated overall savings of 7 percent for four ammunitions items and an average of almost 11 percent for sixteen missile, electronic, and torpedo systems.[25]

In a few cases, the Pentagon has been moving to adopt dual sourcing, but the efforts have been too modest and incomplete. For example, the Navy initially selected one company to produce the engines for a new helicopter. It implemented the dual-source concept in 1986 by letting the first company choose the firm that would be the second production source.[26] It is nice to be able to pick your own competitor, but that is hardly the way to get the full benefits of two firms going at it head-to-head to win future sales.

Participation in subcontracts should also be broadened so that small companies now oriented toward civilian business have a greater opportunity to get military work. Many of them are scared off by the mountain of paperwork imposed on every company working on these contracts, large or small. Increasing the number of companies involved in defense work would dilute the close and occasionally cozy relationship between the military establishment and a relatively narrow group of industrial suppliers. Surely, the size of the contract being awarded should influence the stringency of management controls imposed by governmental fiat.

### ELIMINATE SUBSIDIES

Another way of improving the current military-industrial relationship is to restore the traditional arm's length relation between government and industry. The performance of the defense industry will improve if it forgoes the advantages of military subsidies in order to shake loose from the accompanying red tape and interference with management.

One major subsidy afforded defense contractors takes the form of government financing through unusually generous progress payments. In recent years, the federal government has been reimbursing the companies for the great bulk (between 75 and 90 percent) of the costs they incur while working on defense contracts. These payments should be drastically reduced, to the much lower levels provided by airlines and other civilian purchasers of comparable types of capital equipment. In 1986, the General Accounting Office reported that progress payments equaled 56 percent of the assets of defense contractors but only 4 percent of nondefense firms' assets. Fairness, however, requires that defense contracts be modified to treat interest on privately obtained working capital as an allowable cost.[27]

The present procedure—whereby the government on the one hand supplies factories, equipment, and working capital to defense contractors and on the other hand attempts to keep down their prices and profits—is inefficient. Encouraging defense contractors to rely more heavily on their own resources by strengthening competitive forces would help bring about a resurgence of the self-regulating mechanism of free enterprise to control costs and spur technological innovation.

AVOID STOP-AND-GO

A related way of enhancing the efficiency of military procurement is to depart from the stop-and-go procedure inherent in the standard practice of awarding production contracts one year at a time. This can be achieved by using multiyear contracting. In the last few years, the Department of Defense has begun to experiment with this hardly radical innovation. In 1986, Congress specifically authorized funding individual major military procurements for as much as five years at a time. There are many reasons for expecting multiyear contracting to produce substantial savings.

First of all, it reduces the chance that production will be stretched out to an uneconomical rate. Second, under multiyear contracting, materials and components can be purchased in more economical quantities. In an analysis of the forty multiyear defense contracts approved from 1982 to 1986, the Congressional Budget Office concluded that costs were 12 percent less than they would have been had the same items been purchased under annual contracts.[28]

The key to making defense contracting more efficient, and thus to controlling military costs more effectively, is an increased reliance on private enterprise. Actually, the Department of Defense has not given it much of a chance. Military contracts are awarded to private companies. But, as we have seen, the contracts require the companies to behave like government agencies.

For the United States to receive the full benefit of the innovation and efficiency that it expects from the private sector, military contractors must be given more freedom from public-sector interference and more exposure to the forces and effects of competition. The ultimate protection to the military customer is the fact that the basic power in the military-industrial relationship is lodged with the military establishment. Every contract it awards provides that the Department of Defense can unilaterally cancel its commitment "for the convenience of the government" and merely repay the allowable costs the company has incurred.

## The Costs of Military Personnel

Procurement of weapon systems is only one of several large areas of defense spending. Many billions of dollars are spent each year on personnel, both those on active duty and those who have retired from the armed services. Opportunities for economy and efficiency abound here too.

The retired-pay question is more appropriately considered together with the civilian entitlement programs covered in chapters 2 and 3. Surely, the ground rules should not be suddenly shifted on men and women who have served for many years on the assumption that they would receive large retirement payments as soon as they left the military service. But, looking ahead, there is little reason to maintain, for the indefinite future, a policy that encourages men and women to retire in their early forties and receive generous pensions while actively working in civilian employment—and simultaneously qualifying for one or more additional pensions.

It costs the federal government three to four times as much to provide a pension to a member of the armed forces retiring at age forty as to someone retiring at age sixty-five[29] (which is approximately the standard in the private sector). In fiscal 1987, the total cost of retired pay equaled 50 percent of the basic pay of the active-duty personnel of the military services.[30]

In the larger category of pay of active-duty forces, the long-established economic principles of wage and salary determination, which operate quite well in the private sector, could be extended to the military establishment. Specifically, the Department of Defense should adopt the sensible practice of paying more for skills in short supply than for those in surplus.

However, I still vividly recall the horrified response of a distinguished military leader when I first made this suggestion as a member of President Reagan's military-manpower commission. Very patiently, the chairman of the Joint Chiefs of Staff explained that business practices are not always appropriate for the nonprofit sector, especially for a career cadre of men and women whose morale is crucial. My response was compelling, but apparently not convincing: as a university professor, I understand the nature of the nonprofit environment. But if the typical university were to follow the approach of the military establishment and pay faculty uniformly for rank and seniority, it very likely would have a great surplus of Latin instructors and a severe shortage of professors of medicine.

On reflection, there is no need to guess at the results of the two contrasting pay systems. For many decades, the public high schools have been using a variation of the "comparable worth" approach to teacher salaries. By paying all teachers, despite their specialties, on the basis of level of education and years of experience, they have created all sorts of anomalies. Year after year, surpluses of physical-education teachers and shortages of math and science teachers are universal in American public school systems.

Another aspect of the military personnel area is the question of personal liberty. The draft, when it was operating, constituted two years of involuntary servitude to the state. As Martin Anderson of the Hoover Institution has pointed out, the concept of the draft is inimical to the basic principles of freedom.[31] Hence, the need to ensure the continued success of the voluntary military services by paying them adequately transcends economic and budgetary concerns.

## Postscript

A perennial question in the debate over the military budget is how much spending for national-security purposes the American economy can afford. There is no simple or generally agreed-on method to measure the burden of defense spending, much less any economic ceiling that may exist on such programs. What is clear is that every serious study of this subject—whether the analyst is liberal or conservative—quickly concludes that the American economy could handle, if necessary, a far higher level of such spending than has existed in recent times.[32]

The total expenditures of the Department of Defense in the fiscal year 1987 came to 6 percent of the GNP. Although a measurable increase from the 5 percent rate of 1980, that ratio is dwarfed by the 15 percent of the GNP devoted to these purposes during the Korean War and the 40 percent during World War II.

However, the long-term growth and prosperity of the United States do not require any particular level of national-security spending. Given a reasonable period of adjustment, the American economy surely could attain prosperity with a greatly reduced defense establishment.[33] Thus, within wide limits, this nation can afford what it needs to spend on national defense, but there is no justification for spending more in a misguided economic pump-priming effort.

The effective limitations on major shifts in military outlays can be seen as inherently political and social. They depend on the willingness of the society to make difficult decisions to do without some civilian needs (in the case of an upturn in military spending) or to take the actions to absorb the resources released by defense cutbacks.

I do not pretend to be an expert on military strategy. I am an economist whose life is devoted to calculations of costs and benefits. National defense is not easily subjected to such calculations. If we go about it efficiently, the more we spend for military purposes, the more secure we can be. Yet, beyond some point, the sacrifices made for defense outweigh the gain from enhancement of the national security. This is a special type of benefit-cost calculation, but it is one made in terms of value judgments, not in terms of dollar prices. We Americans learned during the Vietnam War that we cannot afford everything simultaneously—guns and butter, and fat, too.

You do not have to be an expert on military strategy to note and be concerned about the dramatic reversal in public support of the defense establishment. In 1980, the National Opinion Research Center reported that a majority of the American people—56 percent—believed that too little was being spent on defense. By 1987, after the various reports on waste in the Pentagon had had their effect, the public view had switched completely. The Gallup poll reported that 58 percent believed that the defense budget should be cut back.[34]

Given the continued buildup in the Soviets' armed forces and in their weaponry, the turnabout in the public's attitude is a warning to the military establishment to spend the large amounts of money it receives more wisely. The Pentagon's purse strings need to be tightened in order to serve the goals of maintaining citizen support as well as achieving good management of federal money.

Finally, we need to note a basic influence on the trend of the military budget that is not dealt with here: the changing nature and perception of the national-security threats facing the United States. Although specific actions occur in an erratic fashion, the prospects for negotiated arms reduction seem to be improving. At a lower level of tension, the rate at which new weapons are produced to replace existing inventories can subside. The size of the armed forces may even decline. That desirable state of affairs will not be achieved quickly. The consummation of a nuclear arms control agreement between the United States and the Soviet Union could, at least initially, lead to more spending for conventional (nonnuclear) weapon systems to offset some of the Soviet Union's overwhelming lead in that type of weaponry. Also, monitoring any arms control agreement requires a large amount of expensive surveillance equipment.

Whether real or illusory, the notion of less tension can put a more substantial lid on military spending in the United States than any drive to curb budget deficits. Yet, the underlying need for arms to provide for the national defense will not evaporate. The United States exists in a dangerous world, in an age when war and threats of war are worrisomely common. A high level of military strength, therefore, is essential to deter potential aggressors.

The distinguished historian-philosopher John Nef has provided a pertinent explanation of the need to consider the military establishment in a broad historical framework. In the concluding portion of his monumental study of war and progress, he wrote, "Let us not hoodwink ourselves with notions of perpetual peace and the millennium. These only increase the danger of war, for they rest upon a misunderstanding of human nature. Men and women are not angels."[35]

It is likely that the Department of Defense, for the foreseeable future, will be a major claimant to the resources of the United States. Therefore, the considerations of efficiency that would be enhanced by the suggestions made in this chapter will continue to be extremely relevant.

Achieving an appropriate balance between the needs of national security and the pressures of other priorities is as important as it is difficult. Policymakers have faced this conflict since time immemorial. The Irish economist C. F. Bastable described the problem at the turn of the century in words that remain apt today: "[T]o maintain a due balance between the excessive demands of alarmists and military officials, and the undue reductions in outlay sought by the advocates of economy, is one of the difficult tasks of the statesman."[36]

# 5

# Ending Capital Punishment (by Means of Tax Reform)

The 1986 tax reform law provides a cogent example of the failure of federal government leadership (both executive and legislative branches) to come to grips with the really difficult fiscal problems facing the American economy. The changes made in 1986 increase the magnitude of the budgetary problems that this nation will eventually have to face by discouraging new investment ("punishing capital") and thus lessening the prospects for economic growth.

You have to be a real "heavy" to dump on the notion of tax reform. Nevertheless, a sense of candor impels me to note that in 1985 and 1986 politicians in both parties discovered a clever way of diverting attention from the tough problems involved in cutting the deficit. They initiated a debate on tax reform. It was discouraging to listen to the representatives of both political parties expound on this subject. Democratic spokesmen embraced tax reform in the hope that, in the voters' eyes, it would return the party to the nation's mainstream. But the Republicans were hardly more statesmanlike. They held that the beauty of tax reform was that it would help attract blue-collar families to the Republican party.

It is fascinating to note that, all through the period of the tax reform debate during 1985 and 1986, most public opinion polls reported that large majorities of the nation believed that reducing the budget deficits should receive higher priority than tax reform. A cynic's heart would have been warmed by the actuality: the estimates of the budget deficit were rising all through 1986, almost in tandem with progress on the tax bill.

As would be expected, it turns out that there are many losers as well as winners under the new Internal Revenue Code. But anyone going beyond the label attached to the new tax law quickly discovers its basic characteristic: it reduces federal income taxes paid by voters and increases taxes on nonvoters or business. That is how politicians in Washington, in both parties, can say simultaneously that tax reform is revenue neutral and that most taxpayers are getting tax cuts. It is reminiscent of the mythical salesman who sold gloves that supposedly were bigger on the inside than on the outside. The 1986 version of tax reform also reminds us that, for politicians in office, traditionally the best tax is a hidden tax. Thus, the tax cuts on individuals and families are visible, but the offsetting tax increases on business ultimately push up rents, utility rates, and prices. But the latter are too indirect to be blamed on Congress or the President.

## The Uneasy Impacts of the 1986 Tax Reform

The economic impacts of tax reform—good and bad—are not felt all at once. Some provisions work their way through the economic system over a long period of time. The full effects depend on how people adjust to the changes. Yet, one basic fact dominates the economic adjustments to tax reform: companies do the bulk of the saving and investment, which are the keys to economic growth; families and individuals, by and large, do the consuming. A revenue law that shifts the tax burden from consumption to saving, cutting personal taxes and raising business taxes, is bound to generate considerable economic repercussions. That theme is worthy of development in some detail. Five key points need to be made about the tax changes.

1. *The tax reform law is a major tax increase on American business.* Corporate taxes are being raised by $120 billion over the five-year period 1987–91.[1] But the higher tax payments are not in the form of an across-the-board increase in rates. Actually, the rate table has been reduced for both individual and corporate taxpayers.

# Ending Capital Punishment (by Means of Tax Reform)

The rate cuts are financed by a focus on the politically vulnerable provisions of the old tax code. Various incentives to saving and investment were either eliminated or cut back. Specifically, the investment tax credit was repealed, and many firms now face less generous depreciation schedules.[2] Numerous other changes also hurt savers and investors, notably the termination of the $100 dividend exemption and elimination of tax deductions for most people who contribute to individual retirement accounts (IRAs). On the other hand, the virtual elimination of "shelter" provisions, which enabled many taxpayers to avoid paying their fair share of taxes, is a clear improvement in the Internal Revenue Code. That some of the changes are erratic is shown clearly in table 5-1, which measures the impact of the higher taxes on capital gains. It turns out that the largest increases in capital gains tax rates occur at the middle- and lower-income brackets.

The economics of tax reform may not exactly be brilliant, but the politics are. Elected officials in Washington are crowing about cutting voters' taxes. Later on, they can sympathize with consumers when they gripe about price and rent increases, although those increases will just be the pass-through of higher business taxes. For many taxpayers, the total burden of federal taxation, direct and indirect, is rising (see table 5-2). Not shown in the table is yet another part of the indirect tax increase—the higher tax payments to state and local governments that now collect income taxes on a larger base (because payers of state and local income taxes currently deduct a smaller federal income tax than they did under the old tax laws).[3]

2. *The claim of tax simplification violates the truth-in-labeling law.* For starters, all taxpayers in 1987 had to fill out a new, longer, and far more complicated form for withholding taxes from their paychecks (the "W-4").[4] The W-4 came as a shocker to the many taxpayers who had anticipated tax simplification. For taxpayers who elect to make nondeductible contributions to an IRA (because the interest will continue to be tax-deferred), the new separate Form 8606 requires additional paperwork. Until the taxpayer closes out the IRA, he or she is required to maintain records to verify how much of the account reflects earlier deductible contributions, because they are taxable when withdrawn from the IRA account.

Many taxpayers deducting interest on their home mortgages are now faced with a new two-page form with twenty-four lines of questions, accompanied by four pages of instructions. The chairman of the tax forms committee of the Internal Revenue Service described the situation

TABLE 5-1

*Increase in Capital Gains Tax Rate for a Family of Four*

| Taxable Income | Tax Rate before New Law | Tax Rate under New Law | Increase in Tax |
|---|---|---|---|
| 0–$3,670 | 0.0% | 15% | +15.0% |
| $ 3,670–5,940 | 4.4 | 15 | +10.6 |
| 5,940–8,200 | 4.8 | 15 | +10.2 |
| 8,200–12,840 | 5.6 | 15 | +9.4 |
| 12,840–17,270 | 6.0 | 15 | +9.0 |
| 17,270–21,800 | 7.2 | 15 | +7.8 |
| 21,800–26,550 | 8.8 | 15 | +6.2 |
| 26,550–29,750 | 10.0 | 28 | +18.0 |
| 29,750–32,270 | 10.0 | 28 | +18.0 |
| 32,270–37,980 | 11.2 | 28 | +16.8 |
| 37,980–49,420 | 13.2 | 28 | +14.8 |
| 49,420–64,750 | 15.2 | 28 | +12.8 |
| 64,750–71,900 | 16.8 | 28 | +11.2 |
| 71,900–92,370 | 16.8 | 33 | +16.2 |
| 92,370–118,050 | 18.0 | 33 | +15.0 |
| 118,050–175,250 | 19.6 | 33 | +13.4 |
| 175,250–192,320 | 20.0 | 33 | +13.0 |
| 192,320 and over | 20.0 | 28 | +8.0 |

SOURCE: Pannell Kerr Forster, *Explanation of the Tax Reform Act of 1986*, 1986.

TABLE 5-2

*Estimated Change in Tax Burden in 1988 by Income Brackets*

| Income Class | Change in Total Federal Tax Burden |
|---|---|
| Under $10,000 | −12.5% |
| $10,000–20,000 | −3.1 |
| $20,000–30,000 | −1.8 |
| $30,000–40,000 | −2.0 |
| $40,000–50,000 | −3.1 |
| $50,000–70,000 | +0.4 |
| $70,000–100,000 | +3.9 |
| $100,000–200,000 | +5.0 |
| $200,000 and above | +8.2 |

SOURCE: *Brookings Review*, Winter 1987, p. 6.

very bluntly: "This easy-sounding provision has turned out to be a very difficult one for us to administer."[5]

Another example of the new complexity is the changed rules on travel and entertainment. Taxpayers now can deduct only 80 percent of their business meals and entertainment expenses, such as tickets to sports and cultural events. The 80 percent also applies to meals on the road but not to the room charge. The implications are numerous. The same 80 percent limit hits the intended target—the famous three-martini lunch—no harder than it hits a salesman eating dinner alone in his motel when he is on a business trip. There is one new loophole that has some charm for the author. The 80 percent limit on business meals does not apply to large banquets with a speaker. It may be chalked up to coincidence, but within weeks of the enactment of the tax reform bill, I bought two new suits.

The overall impact of the 1986 tax bill is no laughing matter, however. One former IRS commissioner, Jerome Kurtz, has declared, "I assume error rates will be up significantly."[6] Another former commissioner, Sheldon Cohen, has drawn a broader conclusion from the 1986 tax law: "Congress has enacted statutes that are incomprehensible to the normal human being."[7]

As for the initial impact on business, the following excerpt from a report to a corporate board of directors is typical: "There is no doubt that tax simplification has increased our workload considerably!"[8] During the early stages of the legislative debate, many accountants and tax lawyers worried that tax reform would so simplify the revenue code that they would lose a large portion of their business. That concern has turned to euphoria. Tax reform is, at least at the outset, a bonanza for all the paper pushers. The president of the New York State Society of Certified Public Accountants summed up the result of tax reform perhaps best of all: "It will be quite a boon to our profession."[9]

3. *The tax law is not revenue neutral, because it is not economically neutral.* Several studies show that the 1986 tax revisions are depressing saving and investment, and that reduces economic growth. According to the calculations of the Center for the Study of American Business, at Washington University, the new law lowers real GNP by over 1 percent a year and increases inflation a fraction. By 1991, unemployment is likely to be one million higher than it would be otherwise. Other researchers report close variations on the same theme.[10]

That smaller economy means billions of dollars less revenue into the Treasury. The higher unemployment also generates increased federal spending for unemployment benefits, food stamps, and welfare. Tax reform yields, in effect, a double negative whammy on the federal budget. It simultaneously depresses revenues and increases expenditures. The result, of course, is bigger budget deficits than would otherwise occur. Slower economic growth and larger amounts of deficit financing are two of the costs being incurred to achieve the benefits of tax reform. The Federal Reserve System may be able to offset some of the negative economic effects of the tax change by pumping more money into the economy. But such actions generate added inflationary pressures.

Another reason why the new tax law may depress the future flow of federal revenues (and hence not be "revenue neutral") is the opportunity it leaves for new loopholes to be opened. Take, for example, the change that makes interest on home mortgages the only category of consumer interest payment that remains tax deductible. Even before that provision was signed into law, financial institutions began to gear up to help taxpayers tap the equity in their homes for collateral on new extensions of credit—which can be used for whatever purpose the borrower desires. Second mortgages have become more popular as people finance their purchases of cars, furniture, and major appliances less through traditional installment debt and more through complicated "home equity" lending.[11] The result is less revenue from "loophole closing" than the Congress had anticipated.

Similarly, it would not be surprising to see many hotels react to the new 80 percent limit on the tax deductibility of business meals. One response that might help on-the-road salespeople and other traveling business executives would be to shift away from the European plan, where meals are billed separately and thus subject to the 80 percent limitation, and toward modifications of the American plan, where food is included in the basic room charge, which continues to be 100 percent deductible.

Clearly, the 1986 tax reform law does not mean the end of "cottage industries" specializing in the creation of tax breaks. It does mean many shifts in business activity in order to adjust to the new tax regime.

4. *The claim of fairness is window dressing.* It is hard to explain to the average taxpayer the fairness of eliminating the tax deduction for interest payments on his or her first car while interest on two homes continues to be fully deductible. Also, the amount of federal tax payments that a family makes depends in part on whether its state has a sales tax. That situation results from the ending of the deduction for sales taxes, but not for state and local income and property taxes. Moreover, because income averaging has been eliminated, people with fluctuating

# Ending Capital Punishment (by Means of Tax Reform)

TABLE 5-3

## Some Special Favors in the 1986 Tax Bill
### Language Describing the Beneficiaries

A "state which ratified the United States Constitution on May 29, 1790."

\* \* \*

A company which entered into a binding contract "on October 3, 1984, for the purchase of 6 semi-submersible units at a cost of $425,000,000."

\* \* \*

"Any taxpayer incorporated on September 7, 1978, which is engaged in the trade or business of manufacturing dolls and accessories."

\* \* \*

Any project "which was the subject of a city ordinance numbered 82-115 and adopted on December 2, 1982."

\* \* \*

Any facility where the developer "was selected on April 26, 1985."

\* \* \*

A project to provide a roof or dome for an existing sports facility if "an 11-member task force was appointed by the county executive in June 1985, to further study the feasibility of the project."

\* \* \*

Any project having one of the following Farmers Home Administration Code numbers:
49284553664
4927742022446
49270742276087
490270742387293
4927074218234
49270742244019
51460742345074

\* \* \*

"Any institution of higher education . . . mandated by a state constitution in 1876."

\* \* \*

"A corporation which was incorporated on December 29, 1969, in the State of Delaware. . . ."

\* \* \*

". . . 10 warehouse buildings built between 1906 and 1910 and purchased under a contract dated February 17, 1926."

\* \* \*

"A university established by charter granted by King George II of England on October 31, 1754."

SOURCE: Tax Reform Act of 1986.

incomes now pay more taxes than people with stable incomes. Those are very arbitrary changes made by the writers of the 1986 tax code and are very difficult to reconcile with any effort to increase fairness.

Despite all the talk about equity, the new law also contains numerous new special benefits. It would be a breach of legislative etiquette to designate the lucky recipients by name. Congress describes the "goodies" in words like "a paint and glass project which was approved by the management committee of a company on September 11, 1985." That very language was put into the Internal Revenue Code.

Another special benefit goes to "rental property which was assigned FHA number 023-36602." That is really neat. It is not considered to be special-purpose legislation, because the benefit covers every taxpayer whose FHA number happens to be 023-36602. Here is my favorite: a project that was "the subject of law suits filed on June 22, 1984 and November 21, 1985." That sets an interesting precedent: getting sued now qualifies some people for being included in the tax code. See table 5-3 for other examples of the arbitrary distribution of federal largess in the guise of tax reform.

5. *The 1986 tax changes create lots of losers as well as winners.*
That holds for both corporate and individual taxpayers. As can be seen in table 5-4, over 18 percent of all individual taxpayers (a category that

TABLE 5-4

*Taxpayers with Increases and Decreases in Tax Liability under the New Tax Law*
*(1987 Income Levels)*

| Income Class | Number of Returns with Tax Increase (in thousands) | Number of Returns with Tax Decrease (in thousands) |
|---|---|---|
| $    0–10,000 | 1,701 | 11,970 |
| 10,000–20,000 | 3,391 | 22,025 |
| 20,000–30,000 | 3,095 | 16,981 |
| 30,000–40,000 | 2,597 | 11,320 |
| 40,000–50,000 | 1,472 | 7,052 |
| 50,000–75,000 | 3,148 | 4,777 |
| 75,000–100,000 | 1,021 | 827 |
| 100,000–200,000 | 815 | 859 |
| 200,000 and over | 327 | 319 |
| TOTAL | 17,567 | 76,131 |
| PERCENTAGE OF TOTAL | 19 | 81 |

SOURCE: U.S. Congress, Joint Committee on Taxation, *Estimated Revenue Effects of the Possible Conference Compromise,* 1986.

includes families as well as single people) were estimated to have to pay more federal income taxes in 1987 as a result of the new tax law. What may be most surprising is that there are such "losers" at every income level, including the very lowest. Some other anomalies in the table are fascinating to consider. In the income class of $50,000–$75,000 (which contains many middle-class families in which husband and wife both work), almost as many taxpayers pay more federal income taxes as pay less. And in the upper-income category of $100,000–$200,000, more people experience tax cuts than tax increases!

Not too surprisingly, the battle over tax reform split the business community.[12] During the early stages of the debate, many large companies and business associations lined up in favor of the House of Representatives version of tax reform. An equally impressive number opposed the bill (see table 5-5). However, by the time Congress was getting ready to enact the final version, most business groups who had been vocal on the subject jumped on the bandwagon. (To change the metaphor, many business lobbyists said that they had to get on the tax reform train before it left the station.) Their motives varied from not wanting to be seen as sore losers to making the best of a bad situation by trying to get sympathetic members of the Congress to insert provisions in the bill that would help their company or industry.

The major winners in the 1986 tax reform law included corporations that had been paying close to the highest statutory rates, such as department stores and other retailers, service companies, and small businesses. Other beneficiaries were low-income taxpayers who no longer had to pay federal income taxes and labor-intensive companies that did not feel the loss of the investment incentives, such as high-tech enterprises and makers of consumer goods. The list of winners extended to broadcasters and publishers, American-plan hotels, middle- and high-income taxpayers who had not taken advantage of special tax provisions, and, to be sure, accountants and lawyers.[13]

Numerous groups wound up paying more federal income taxes directly. These included high-income taxpayers who had been in low tax brackets; real estate developers and realtors, because of the loss of tax shelters; heavy industry, because of the reduction of tax incentives for investment; and capital-intensive companies with low tax rates, such as airlines and cable companies. Other losers in the tax reform were promoters of rental housing and tenants, traveling salesmen, and users of tax shelters.

One final point on the impacts of the new tax code: 1986 will not be the last time that Congress acts on tax policy. The cat was let out of the

TABLE 5-5

*The Split in Business Views on Tax Reform*

*Positions Taken on Ways and Means Committee Bill, December 1985*

| Pro[1] | Con[2] |
|---|---|
| Allied-Signal | Aluminum Co. of America |
| American Apparel Manufacturers Association | American Bankers Association |
| American Electronics Association | American Insurance Association |
| American Trucking Association | American Mining Congress |
| Beatrice | American Petroleum Institute |
| Dart & Kraft | AT & T |
| Digital Equipment | Business Roundtable |
| Federated Department Stores | Caterpillar Tractor |
| Food Marketing Institute | Chase Manhattan |
| General Mills | Dow Chemical |
| General Motors | Duke Power |
| Grocery Manufacturers of America | Du Pont |
| IBM | Exxon |
| Levi Strauss | Ford Motor |
| Minnesota Mining & Manufacturing | GTE |
| National Association of Wholesaler-Distributors | Inland Steel |
| National Federation of Independent Business | Mobil |
| National Retail Merchants Association | National Association of Home Builders |
| PepsiCo | National Association of Manufacturers |
| Philip Morris | National Machine Tool Builders Association |
| Procter & Gamble | Rockwell International |
| R. J. Reynolds Industries | Texas Instruments |
| Sara Lee | U.S. Chamber of Commerce |
|  | Weyerhaeuser |

[1]The organizations listed as favoring the tax bill were members of the Tax Reform Action Coalition and the CEO Tax Group.
[2]Those listed as against the bill had signed a letter to the President urging postponement of action on taxation.
SOURCE: *Wall Street Journal,* December 5, 1985, p. 54.

bag by Congressman Dan Rostenkowski, of Illinois, in an off-the-cuff speech given before the ink was dry on the tax bill. The distinguished chairman of the Ways and Means Committee pointed out that the next step in the legislative process would be to reduce the budget deficit by—inevitably—raising taxes.[14]

# Ending Capital Punishment (by Means of Tax Reform)

## A Note on the Tax Burden

Before we consider future changes in the tax burden—up or down—we must deal with a few preliminary matters. One continuing issue is the distribution of the tax burden. A myth has developed in the United States on how little tax business actually pays. As predictable as the spring crocuses is the appearance each year of a widely publicized report claiming that many otherwise profitable businesses avoid federal taxation.

For example, in 1986, an activist organization, Citizens for Tax Justice (CTJ), alleged that forty-four large U.S. corporations paid no federal income taxes in the period 1981–84.[15] These same companies were supposedly the main users of investment tax credits, liberalized depreciation allowances, and other tax incentives to business, yet they were charged with failing to deliver the expected increase in investment and jobs.

To add insult to injury, these forty-four companies were alleged to have received net refunds of federal income taxes totaling $2.1 billion during 1981–84. On the face of it, this situation sounds outrageous. What is the truth of the matter? To resolve the issue, I compared the CTJ report with data issued by Standard and Poor's Compustat Services, the source of corporate statistics that academic researchers use most widely.

The comparison was extremely revealing.[16] It turns out that, rather than receiving net refunds, the companies as a group actually paid more than $1.3 billion in federal income taxes during the four-year period. The discrepancy arises from the fact that CTJ "adjusted" the tax data reported by the companies. In addition to making a few arithmetical errors, the group double counted the various "safe harbor" leasing transactions that many companies entered into during the period studied.

In 1981–82, companies with little or no taxable income could sell their unused tax credits to more profitable ones. The latter could thereby reduce their tax payments. But only one set of companies—the "buyers" of the unused tax credits, not both the buyers and the sellers—got the tax offset. This may sound technical, but billions of dollars were involved, and the results are very different if the correct numbers are used.

An examination of the investment patterns of those forty-four companies is also revealing. The data show that these firms made $102 billion of new investments during 1981–84, more than three times the amount made by CTJ's sample of "high tax" companies.

Also, the group measured the impact of the tax policy changes made in 1981 with a "before and after" analysis. Its report found that companies did not rapidly expand capital investment during 1981 and 1982. By ignoring that a deep and prolonged recession occurred during that period, CTJ could question the effectiveness of the tax changes.

But the proper analysis, as all economics professors explain to their students, is to compare the actual results with what would have happened if the first event (the tax change) had not occurred. Michael Boskin, an economics professor at Stanford University, took such a more comprehensive "with and without" approach. He found that the investment tax credit and liberalized depreciation contributed 20 percent of the net investment in the United States during 1982–84.[17]

The data on the personnel impacts are clear. Job creation has been on a roll in the United States. Between 1981 and 1987, total civilian employment in the private sector rose by more than ten million, making this nation's job creation record the envy of the world. Yet Citizens for Tax Justice claimed that the tax incentives were a "striking failure" in producing more jobs. This misguided notion results from a preoccupation with employment figures limited to the companies that make the capital investments.

A company's increased investment helps create jobs in many other companies as well, notably in those building the new factories and producing the new equipment. The new investment also spurs employment in the manufacturing and service companies that use the products that the investing company makes. For example, the major beneficiaries of a new generation of jet airliners produced by aerospace companies are the traveling public and the additional airline employees hired in response to the greater volume of air travel.

More fundamentally, CTJ and other like-minded tax "reformers" ignore the fact that the investment tax credit and liberalized depreciation schedules were only second-best substitutes for responding to the continuing bias in the tax system against saving and investment. Moreover, neither the old nor the new tax system deals with the effects of inflation on capital assets and corporate earnings.

Still, critics are preoccupied with tax incentives to business, especially for capital formation. They ignore the numerous government expenditures and credit subsidies that are intended to promote capital formation, although their effectiveness is usually lower. Unmentioned are the billions of dollars wasted by the Synthetic Fuels Corporation, the Corps of Engineers, the Bureau of Reclamation, the Small Business Administration, and the Departments of Commerce, Defense, Energy, and Transportation.

The preoccupation may result from the fundamental but neglected distinction between general-purpose tax incentives and closely targeted expenditure and credit subsidies. Under the tax approach, individual companies select an investment project and incur the bulk of the risk involved. Under the government expenditure and credit approaches, a federal agency determines which specific projects are to be financed, with the government bearing all or most of the risk.

The attack on tax incentives is thus an assault on the role of the private sector. Reducing incentives and raising direct subsidies expands the direct role of the federal government in choosing capital investments—and reduces private risk bearing in the process. Such knowledge is useful in planning for any future round of tax reform.

## Another Round of Tax Reform?

Congress frequently changed the federal tax structure during the 1980s. Major bills were passed in 1981 and 1986, and less important but significant laws were enacted in each of the years in between. As a result, there is a widespread feeling that some stability in the Internal Revenue Code would be very welcome. Whatever the shortcomings of the present tax structure, the uncertainty generated by expectations of further near-term changes could have extremely negative effects on investment decisions by home buyers, investors, and business planners.

Let me make myself clear. I do not endorse the hoary proposition that "the best tax is an old tax." Rather, future changes in the revenue system should be carefully constructed, fully considered, and enacted less frequently than in the recent past. This approach is consistent with the notion that interested citizens should begin now to give sustained thought to future changes in the Internal Revenue Code.

Some important points can be made at the outset of such deliberations. The reductions in tax rates contained in the 1986 tax bill were paid for, as we noted earlier, by increasing the tax burden on saving and investment. Although that switch in the burden has made many voters

happy, the economic effects are all negative—less new capital formation, slower economic growth, less job creation, and smaller increases
in American living standards.

## PROMOTING INVESTMENT AND ECONOMIC GROWTH

To many citizens, any discussion of capital formation immediately
brings to mind visions of greedy bankers, wealthy coupon clippers,
and—to use what is to many a pejorative word—capitalists. Nevertheless, capital plays a pivotal role in providing the basis for the future
standard of living of any society. Capital is essential for increasing
productivity and thus providing the basis for rising real incomes.

Educators at times find it amusing when some of their students dis-
cover Maoist economists writing about the necessity to hold down consumption in the Chinese economy in order to free up the capital resources needed to invest in the future growth of that economy. "Why,
they are not even a capitalist society," these students will note in won-
derment.

Then the thought will sink in, sometimes with a little faculty assistance, that a rising stock of capital is necessary for any growing society—capitalist (that is, private-enterprise or market-oriented) or other
(socialist, communist, and so on). It is really a basic matter of how much
we want to eat, drink, and be merry today, and how much we want to
set aside for tomorrow. Boiled down to its fundamentals, assuring an
adequate flow of saving and investment is little more than demonstrating a proper concern for the future.

A slow pace of capital formation in the United States is especially
troublesome at a time of heightened global competition, when modern,
state-of-the-art machinery and equipment are necessary to match foreign firms with low-wage structures. As it turns out, the companies
hardest hit by the 1986 tax law are precisely those capital-intensive
heavy industries that are most vulnerable to foreign competition.

Any doubt about the tendency of the U.S. tax system to be biased in
favor of consumption and against saving can be resolved quickly with
a very simple and straightforward example. Consider three factory
workers, A, B, and C, each of the same age, with the same work experience and size of family, and with the same compensation. Mr. A regularly spends what he earns, no more and no less. Mrs. B, a saver,
deposits a portion of her paycheck into a savings account each week.
Mr. C not only spends everything he earns but also borrows to the hilt,
having bought as expensive a house as he could obtain financing for.

## Ending Capital Punishment (by Means of Tax Reform)

It is interesting to compare the differential tax burden of these three workers. Clearly, Mrs. B, the saver, will have the highest tax bill, for she pays taxes on her wages as well as on the interest that she earns on her savings account. Mr. C winds up with the lowest tax bill, as he receives a tax deduction for the interest he pays on his large mortgage. Actual practice includes many variations in the tax treatment of financial transactions. Yet, for the average citizen, the existing personal income tax structure favors consumption over saving. In addition, many of the government spending programs operate with a similar effect.

Let us assume that A, B, and C all get laid off at the same time and that none of them obtains a new job. Mr. C, the big spender, and Mr. A, the pay-as-you-go man, will quickly be eligible to receive welfare, food stamps, and related benefits. The last to qualify for federal assistance will be Mrs. B, the big saver. Unlike the good Lord, the feds do not seem to help those who help themselves.

All this is no justification for returning to the revenue structure of 1986 and prior years. Surely, the elimination of many tax shelters was a definite plus for the efficiency of the economy, because so many of them had financed investments in uneconomical projects whose major purpose was to generate tax benefits.

CHANGING THE TAX STRUCTURE

Nor is there a need to jump to the conclusion that the investment incentives available under the tax structure of the early 1980s were the most cost-effective way of encouraging capital formation. Nevertheless, one important decision for the 1990s is to consider moving to a tax system that is more favorable to saving and investment, the keys to economic growth and rising living standards. One clearly needed change is to offset the tax increase on capital gains enacted in 1986. The simplest way of doing that is to lower the tax rate on such increases in the value of assets, be they corporate stock, real estate, or other tangible items. But there is no logical rationale for taxing such gains at lower rates than other income.

The economically desirable approach is to correct the basic flaw in the way the Internal Revenue Code measures capital gains, which is to tax real as well as inflationary increases. "Indexing" the reporting of capital gains for income tax purposes—so that only the real gains are subject to taxation—would constitute a true reform of the tax structure.

A far more fundamental tax change would be to substitute an expenditure or a value-added tax for all or a part of the present income taxes.

An expenditure tax would be paid on a similar basis as the individual income tax, except that the annual tax return would focus on the amount of goods and services purchased rather than on the income received. The change from the present system could be made quite readily by allowing each taxpayer to deduct the amount currently saved from reportable income.[18] Many believe that it is much fairer to tax people on what they take from society (as measured by expenditures) than to tax them on the work they perform (as measured by income).

In the manner of collection, a value-added tax (VAT) would be very different from either an income or an expenditure tax.[19] In essence, each business firm would report its sales revenues and deduct its purchases from other firms. The difference—the "value added" by the company— would be its reported tax base. Both the expenditure and the value- added taxes would by definition exempt saving and investment. Both would base the revenue burden on the portion of the national output of goods and services that the taxpayers purchase. As has been amply demonstrated in the public finance literature, an expenditure tax could be made as progressive as an income tax. That would be more difficult in the case of the VAT, but provisions can be enacted that reduce or even eliminate its regressivity.

A consumption-based tax has been described by the American Coun- cil for Capital Formation as the next frontier in U.S. tax policy.[20] It is promoted as an effective mechanism for attacking the twin deficits of budget and trade as well as for moving the entire federal tax structure in a direction that favors saving and investment. Table 5-6 contains estimates of the added revenues the Treasury might obtain from new

TABLE 5-6

*Potential Revenues from New Consumption Taxes*
*Fiscal Year 1988*

| Type of Tax | Revenues (in billions) |
|---|---|
| 5% value-added tax | $104 |
| 5% value-added tax, with exemptions for food, housing, and medical care | 66 |
| $5-per-barrel tax on all oil | 22 |
| 5% tax on all energy consumption | 16 |
| 12¢-per-gallon increase in motor fuel tax | 10 |
| $5-per-barrel tax on oil imports | 9 |

SOURCE: Unpublished data supplied by the Congressional Budget Office.

sales or consumption-type taxes, some broadly constructed and others narrowly based. For example, the Congressional Budget Office estimates that a broad-based value-added tax would yield over $100 billion a year, whereas more narrowly based energy taxes would raise $9–$22 billion annually.

Personally, I cannot generate enthusiasm for imposing a new broad-based tax on the American people, no matter how compelling the rationale offered. The objection is basic: a new revenue source will make it easier to finance increases in government spending.

Thus, with a value-added or other type of national sales tax whose cost would be hidden in product prices, we would wind up with a larger public sector than without such a tax. With any broad-based consumption tax—whether figured on sales transactions or based on annual taxpayer returns—it would become easier to justify an attractive new government program, because it could be financed with just a "tiny" percentage increase in this tax.

A cynic would contend that the natural tendency of the Congress is to change the tax system frequently. It is naive to expect committee members to continue receiving large-scale political contributions if the Senate Finance Committee and the House Ways and Means Committee suddenly stopped working on new tax statutes. But, we can hope that the next round of legislation will do more than merely generate new classes of winners and losers.

In any event, future tax changes cannot be viewed as an alternative to making tough decisions on the spending side of the budget. Having reduced direct tax burdens on many voters in 1986, the Congress must next consider how the future tax system can be modified to strengthen—rather than weaken—the economic system that is looked to for rising income, employment, and living standards, as well as revenues to reduce budget deficits.

In this light, the next round of tax reform, whenever it comes, should be developed on the premise that the 1986 law dealt sufficiently with such questions as equity and fairness. The unfinished agenda for tax reform is to undo the damage on saving, investment, and economic growth.

The Congress has overreacted in its recent effort to close "loopholes." Surely, history shows that narrowly focused tax provisions benefiting small and politically powerful groups in the society are ineffective and an unjustifiable burden on the general taxpayer. But such "loopholes" should not be confused with broadly based incentives designed to improve the performance of the national economy. George Perry of the Brookings Institution has described the needs of policy very clearly: "A high rate of business investment is necessary for strong economic growth and a gradual improvement of living standards. Raising the proportion of GNP devoted to net capital formation, particularly in the manufacturing sector, should be an important aim of policy for the future."[21]

Tax reform should no longer be viewed as merely the modern equivalent of what the Romans called bread and circuses. Carefully constructed changes in the tax system can make an important contribution to the economic health of the United States. Nevertheless, another round of revisions in the federal revenue system should come after, and not before, Congress and the President deal with the pressing issue of controlling federal expenditures. It turns out that the tax committees (the Senate Finance Committee and the House Ways and Means Committee) have responsibility for the largest civilian spending programs in the budget—Social Security, Medicare, Medicaid, and welfare. These key budget areas merit the committee's highest priority.

# PART C

# Helping—or Hindering—
# Business

# 6

# *Responding to the Tide of Imports*

Reducing the extremely large trade deficit (now in excess of $100 billion a year) has become a major preoccupation of many Americans. Yet, as a nation, we remain reluctant to take the kinds of actions that will bring down that massive import imbalance in a constructive and durable fashion.

The concern is genuine, motivated by substantial and often painful changes. Imports have gained unusually large shares of the domestic market, while U.S. exports encounter great resistance overseas. The unemployment resulting from closed steel mills and abandoned textile plants provides mute but powerful testimony to the extent to which the U.S. economy is no longer insulated from foreign forces.

There are many dramatic examples of the success of foreign producers with U.S. consumers. Ten important areas of business have been hit especially hard. The numbers in table 6-1 measure imports as a percentage of domestic consumption in 1986.[1] In many cases, foreign penetration has increased since then.

Moreover, the balance of trade (exports minus imports) has turned negative in many important industries. The 1985 trade gap in food products was $3 billion. In leather products, it was $6 billion. In transportation equipment, which covers autos and aircraft, the imbalance totaled almost $12 billion. In theory, these adverse effects of foreign penetration of some U.S. markets could be offset by rising U.S. penetration of other markets overseas. But that has not happened on a sufficient scale. The U.S. share of world manufacturing exports did rise from 17 percent in

TABLE 6-1

*Imports as a Percentage of U.S. Domestic*
*Consumption in 1986*

| Industry | Foreign Penetration |
| --- | --- |
| Televisions and VCRs | 63% |
| Women's handbags and purses | 60 |
| Semiconductors | 45 |
| Machine tools | 45 |
| Textile machinery | 40 |
| Civilian aircraft | 35 |
| Apparel | 34 |
| Leather products | 32 |
| Automobiles | 28 |
| Steel mill products | 19 |

SOURCE: Department of Commerce, *Industrial Outlook,* 1987.

1976 to 20 percent in 1985. Although this upward trend hardly suggests an uncompetitive economy, the improvement has been too modest to offset the far deeper inroads of imports.

## The Inadequacy of the Current Policy Response

The seriousness of the concern over the trade deficit has not been matched, however, by seriousness of actions. In fact, American public policy has in many ways created or at least increased the massive excess of imports over exports. As was noted in the preceding chapter, the 1986 tax law reduced or eliminated many basic investment incentives; these tax provisions had been heavily used by the capital-intensive manufacturing companies, which are very vulnerable to import competition. This adverse change in the tax law was not accidental. During the 1986 hearings on tax reform, many economists (including me) urged the tax-writing committees to take into account the impact of revenue legislation on U.S. foreign trade. Our views were brushed aside in the haste to enact a politically popular tax reform bill.[2]

More fundamentally, the triple-digit budget deficits, as has been pointed out frequently, have exerted a powerful—and negative—effect on the trade balance of the United States. As Paul McCracken has described it, the trade problem is the budget deficit reflected in a mirror.[3] For any nation, if domestic saving is inadequate to finance both capital formation and government borrowing, an inflow of foreign funds (accompanied by foreign goods and services) will result.

Those budget deficits cannot be blamed on "foreign devils"; they definitely have a made-in-America label. As we have seen, there is a widespread reluctance to do much more than talk about the deficit. It is much easier to berate the "unfairness" of others in their treatment of U.S. goods and services. Despite the budget deficit's powerful impact on the trade position of the United States, we must acknowledge that it is primarily a domestic matter. Action to reduce the budget deficit substantially is not likely to be taken merely to lower the trade deficit.

In the final analysis, these adverse tax and budget effects may be excused or at least accepted because they were not intended to harm U.S. international commerce. Yet, there is a substantial but overlooked category of obstacles to U.S. exports that has been deliberately erected by our own government. These are self-inflicted wounds. It makes us a laughing stock overseas when representatives of the United States urge other countries to lower their trade barriers while we ourselves make it more difficult for our own exporters. Incredible as it may seem, approximately 10 percent of all U.S. exports are now subject to U.S. barriers to exports.[4]

Numerous domestic laws and regulations limit shipments of goods and services from the United States.[5] One statute prohibits the export of oil from North Slope fields in Alaska. Another bans timber exports from federal lands west of the 100th meridian. When restrictions get that specific, the rich aroma of special-interest pressures can readily be detected.

The Export Administration Act provides for controls on exports of goods and technology that would make a "significant contribution" to the military strength of the Soviet Union or other potential adversaries of the United States. That sounds reasonable. But, in practice, the law mandates controls over a great variety of civilian products, including unprocessed red cedar and horses shipped by sea.

A group of former senior defense and intelligence officials chaired by a retired Air Force chief of staff concluded in 1987 that more technologies are controlled under the Export Administration Act than are required by national-security considerations. In their report to the National Academy of Sciences, the group stated that export restrictions are "no longer feasible or necessary" on a wide range of items, including computer memory chips and personal computers. Such technologies are already widely available in the world economy.[6]

In 1980, the Export Administration Act was employed to embargo grain exports to the Soviet Union. It was invoked again in 1981 and 1982 to carry out the ban against U.S. firms participating in the construction of the natural-gas pipeline between the USSR and Western Europe. The ban was lifted after it became clear that the unilateral action by the United States was hurting the NATO alliance far more than the Soviets, who were the intended target.[7]

Export controls do more than limit U.S. international trade for the time they are imposed. These restrictions also call into question the reliability of the United States as a supplier of products to other countries, which are thus encouraged to develop alternative sources.

A clear example is soybeans, hardly a strategic item. Is the Army going to throw beans at the Soviets? Actually, the purpose of the 1974 embargo of soybean exports was to prevent a short-term increase in domestic prices. However, its main effect was to induce Japan to turn to other producing countries, particularly Brazil. Japan proceeded to invest in that country in order to develop alternatives to U.S. production. This effectively and permanently reduced our share of the world soybean market.[8]

Given this array of counterproductive policies, it is not surprising that the U.S. trade deficit has reached all-time highs and that powerful political pressures have developed to restrict imports. Most supporters of trade barriers note their concern about interfering with the flow of international commerce, but they contend that the wishes of their constituents are overwhelming.

While the support of import restrictions helps quell voter discontent, most economists believe that such restrictions are destructive to the well-being of the nation as a whole. In addition to fostering retaliation by foreign countries, import restrictions result in a less efficient economy and thus reduce the wealth and income of the society. Furthermore, the trade deficit is a symptom of a more fundamental disease—the decline of U.S. competitiveness in an increasingly global economy. Attempting to cure the symptom by imposing import restrictions exacerbates the disease by removing the healthy influence of foreign competition.

Are there any responses to the surge of imports that are both politically realistic and economically effective? Let us try to answer that question. Inevitably, we will have to cover quite a bit of ground in order to do so.

*Responding to the Tide of Imports*

## Developing a Constructive Trade Policy

THE PRESSURES FOR PROTECTIONISM

*The First Step Toward Improving Trade Policy is to Learn Why Political Pressures to Regulate Foreign Commerce—to Resort to Protectionism—are So Strong.* Protectionism is a politician's delight because it delivers visible benefits to the protected parties—keeping out some category of imports—while imposing the costs as a hidden tax on the public. Someday the public will learn that too well kept secret that the higher prices that invariably result from the diminished supply of products because of protectionism are paid by American consumers. With many products, such as clothing and shoes, this burden hits most heavily the poorest people in this country.[9] It is hard to deny that protectionism is a means by which small, well-organized groups use the political process to their advantage, at the expense of the American public as a whole.

The balance of political power in the trade debate is uneven because of the limited knowledge that consumers have about these matters. Those who are harmed by the reduced supply of goods and services are generally not aware of the process by which they are hurt. Moreover, any single consumer's stake in the outcome is small. Consequently, resistance at the grass roots level to protectionist measures is much less than pressure for their adoption.

The imbalance of the political forces is worsened by the tendency of organized consumer groups to be mute on the issue; their support from unions favoring protectionism is often a key inhibiting factor. Under the circumstances, associations of retailers have been forced to become a sort of proxy for the consumer interest in the trade debate. But, along with those of the economists, these voices favoring open trade tend to be drowned out by the cries of those in economic sectors believed to have been injured by imports. This requires an effort to raise the information content of the public discourse on free trade versus protectionism.

THE COSTS OF PROTECTIONISM

*The Second Step in Developing a Constructive Trade Policy is to Understand the High Cost of Protectionism.* While the benefits of trade restrictions are received by the protected industries, some costs are shifted to other companies that buy from the protected industries. Ultimately, most of the costs are borne by consumers in the form of

TABLE 6-2

*Estimates of the Cost of Protection to U.S. Consumers*

| Item Subject to Protection | Cost to Consumer |
|---|---|
| Automobiles (for each unit imported from Japan) | $2,500 |
| Dairy products (yearly) | $1.5–$4.9 billion |
| Meat (yearly) | $1.2 billion |
| Motorcycles (for each unit imported) | $400–$600 |
| Peanuts (yearly) | $200 million |
| Radios and TVs (yearly until 1982) | $221 million |
| Shoes (1970–81, for each job protected) | $114,000 |
| Steel (quotas and other similar restraints) | $7.2 billion |
| Sugar (yearly) | $3 billion |
| Textiles and apparel (for 1980) | $19 billion |

SOURCE: *How Much Do Consumers Pay for U.S. Trade Barriers?* (Washington, D.C.: Consumers for World Trade, 1984).

higher prices. With a few exceptions, those costs remain hidden—but substantial. Table 6-2 provides several examples of the high costs of this phenomenon, ranging from $1,900 extra per imported car to $400 for each imported motorcycle. At the macroeconomic level, a study at the Center for the Study of American Business at Washington University estimated the total burden of that hidden tax. In 1980, it came to over $58 billion, or $255 for each American consumer.[10]

The consumer stake in free trade is as striking in other countries as in the United States. The following letter from a Tokyo housewife was published in the *Mainichi Daily News* on January 20, 1983:

Many of us city wives are now fed up with having to pay as much as 500 yen to 700 yen for 100 grams of beef because the government keeps restrictions on its imports. Husbands are asked to buy beef as souvenirs at American or Australian airports on their way home to bring back to their families because beef is much cheaper in those countries. Oranges and grapefruit can also be much cheaper if only our government liberalizes their imports.

The government says it cannot lift the restrictions because the Japanese farmers should be protected. But the Japanese farmers are now the most privileged people. They are paying much less tax than salaried people in the cities. Some of them are even paid for not growing rice in their paddy fields. The farmers are much better off in politics because rural constituencies elect more Diet members than city districts per population. Sometimes a city Diet member represents four times as many electors as a rural MP.

I cannot but suspect that politicians and officials are not so patriotic as they claim, and they seek their own good by spoiling our farmers. Politicians can retain their seats in the parliament and get political funds from the farmers' organizations. Bureaucrats can get key posts in corporations for their own post-retirement jobs. Why should we city people support these farmers (and politicians and bureaucrats) by paying much more for beef and oranges (and rice too) than in other countries?

It is not just a matter of high costs to consumers. Protectionism also turns out to be the most inefficient and regressive welfare program ever designed. If anyone were to identify a government program in which the benefits delivered to the recipients amounted to only 60 or 70 percent of the costs, the public would criticize it as shamefully wasteful. In the case of protectionism, however, the benefits are a much smaller portion of the costs—30 percent, 20 percent, or even less. The total wages of the jobs "saved" are a small fraction of the typical increase in prices resulting from restricting imports. In the case of footwear quotas, the ratio of consumer costs to benefits for the protected workers was nine to one. In the case of steel, the cost/benefit ratio was four to one (see table 6-3). It would have been far cheaper to provide year-long paid vacations to each of the employees involved.

Protectionist measures are a two-edged sword. They can reduce im-

TABLE 6-3

*Estimates of Annual Costs to Consumers per Job Protected by Trade Barriers*
*(in 1980 dollars)*

| Product | Category of Restraint | Average Compensation | Subsidy from Consumer per Job | Ratio of Subsidy to Actual Compensation |
|---------|----------------------|---------------------|-------------------------------|------------------------------------------|
| Apparel | Tariffs | $6,669 | $45,549 | 7 |
| Television receivers | Tariffs, quotas | 12,923 | 74,155 | 6 |
| Footwear | Tariffs, quotas | 8,340 | 77,714 | 9 |
| Carbon steel | Tariffs, quotas | 24,329 | 85,272 | 3 |
| Steel | Trigger pricing | 24,329 | 110,000 | 4 |
| Autos | Domestic content bill (proposed) | 23,566 | 85,400 | 4 |
| Citizens' band transceivers | Tariffs | 8,500 | 85,539 | 10 |

SOURCE: Murray L. Weidenbaum and Michael C. Munger, "Protection at Any Price?" *Regulation*, July–August 1983; Keith E. Maskus, "Rising Protectionism and U.S. International Trade Policy," *Federal Reserve Bank of Kansas City Economic Review*, July–August 1984.

ports from abroad, as when the United States "succeeded" in getting the European Common Market to restrict its exports of steel to this country. But the domestic automobile industry, a major purchaser of steel, bore the burden of higher costs, which in turn made it less competitive. This added pressure to "protect" domestically produced cars. Moreover, the Common Market attempted to offset the loss of the American market by reducing its steel purchases from the Orient. In turn, the Asian countries responded by stepping up their steel exports to the United States.

The indirect costs of trade restriction are especially severe—and often perverse. A report by the Center for the Study of American Business shows that the voluntary export restraints on steel in 1984 saved 14,000 steelworker jobs, but at the cost of 52,000 jobs in the steel-using industries. The higher prices for protected domestic steel resulting from the import restrictions made American automobile and durable-goods products less competitive at home and abroad. The effort to help the steel industry turned out to be a compelling case of adding insult to injury: American consumers were saddled with paying for a high-cost subsidy that resulted in a net loss of 38,000 jobs.[11]

The textile industry furnishes another example of the counterproductive nature of trade restrictions. In 1983, domestic producers succeeded in getting the federal government to establish quotas on imports of textile products from China. The Chinese must have wondered about those "inscrutable" Occidentals, because this country had been enjoying a large and rising trade surplus with them. How was China going to be able to continue being a good customer for American farm and chemical products if Americans did not buy their goods?

Not too surprisingly, the Chinese reacted to the American protectionist action by substantially reducing their imports of agricultural and chemical products from the United States. Once again, the benefits of protection were gained by one special sector of the economy (textiles) and the burden was borne by innocent bystanders (farmers and chemical company workers, managers, and shareholders).[12] Many more American companies can be harmed by our own protectionist actions than the public suspects. Almost 40 percent of all U.S. imports and exports are really transactions between U.S. firms and their foreign affiliates or parents.[13]

The experiences of the textile industry also show the positive effects of import competition. The threat of "brown lung" disease has haunted the industry for years. But the inroads made by imports have forced the textile industry to adopt new technology in its production equipment. The increased mechanization has helped eliminate many dangerous jobs in the industry and, in particular, reduce the incidence of "brown lung" disease. Highly trained operators and technicians working in much cleaner conditions are now replacing the low-skilled people who traditionally have dominated the textile industry work force.[14]

In the protectionist game, there are always winners and losers. Although the list of winners changes, the main losers are invariably the consumers in the country that raises barriers to imports. Thus, it was the American consumers and not the Japanese producers who bore the costs of quotas on imports of Japanese automobiles in the early 1980s. As supposedly visionary economists warned "practical" businessmen, Japanese auto producers responded to the so-called voluntary agreement to limit their sales of motor vehicles in the United States by exporting more-expensive models and loading them with highly profitable extras. As a result, Japanese producers achieved record profits from their sales of automobiles in the United States during the period of the import restraint. While they exported about 30 percent of their auto production to this country, they earned approximately one-half of their profits from U.S. sales.

Moreover, on this side of the Pacific, the dealers for Toyota, Nissan, and so on benefited from the willingness of American buyers to pay substantially more than the sticker price in order to obtain the then relatively scarce Japanese product. In the aggregate, American auto buyers paid about $5 billion a year more for cars than they would have in the absence of the import restraints.[15] When we stop to think about it, that is the result to be expected. Reducing the supply without changing demand results in higher prices. Unfortunately, $5 billion is a high price to pay for economic illiteracy on the part of U.S. government policymakers. Yet, to a politician, the best tax is a hidden tax. No member of the Congress would have voted a $5 billion bailout to the auto industry financed by a visible sales tax. Protectionism was an "easy" way out.

THE PANOPLY OF PANACEAS

*The Third Step in Developing a Better Policy on Trade Issues is to See the Shortcomings of the Popular Panaceas.*   It is not surprising that the unprecedented trade deficits have generated urgent pressures for the federal government to "do something," especially to keep out "unfair" competition. Proponents of trade "protection" are apt to cite low costs of production in many foreign countries and government-subsidized exports in others as good reasons for this country to abandon its formal policy of open international commerce.

The challenge is to separate hard facts from soft opinions in the heated debate on free trade versus protectionism. It is clear, as we have seen, that imports have displaced a substantial portion of American production. As a nation, the United States in recent years literally has been consuming far more than it has been producing. What is not as clear is why this has occurred.

One reason frequently given for the U.S. trade deficit is the lower pay scales overseas. But that is nothing new. Foreign wages were much lower, both absolutely and relatively, in the 1970s and 1960s when U.S. firms maintained stronger competitive positions at home and abroad and we enjoyed trade surpluses. American markets are not now being flooded by low-wage imports. The numbers show the reverse. In 1960, two-thirds of all U.S. manufacturing imports came from countries with wage rates less than half our level. By 1985, less than one-third of such imports came from those countries.

The United States has been losing its position in world markets to producers in other high-wage nations. Textile machinery furnishes a good example. Although the United States was once the world's leading producer of textile machinery, by 1982 it had lost this market, not to Taiwan or South Korea, but to West Germany and other European nations.[16]

Moreover, the basic productivity and effectiveness of American industry, and of its work force, have not been eroded over the past several years. U.S. wages are generally higher than elsewhere because American workers are more productive (although the gap has been narrowing). A good example is the aerospace industry, where employee compensation is substantially above the average for industrial workers, but productivity growth is strong. U.S. jet airplanes remain the leaders in world markets.

On the other hand, poor production practices in the United States cannot be blamed on foreigners. It is no tribute to either managerial leadership or worker conscientiousness when a large U.S. manufacturing company has to give a bonus each time a blue-collar employee puts in a full work week.[17] That is akin to a teacher's having to give an apple to each student who comes to class on time! It is no surprise that the company (Caterpillar) has been losing its share of world markets.

Comparisons of domestic and foreign production experiences are a real eye-opener. Studies of U.S. and Japanese industries find that Japan's absenteeism rate is much lower than ours. Likewise, our labor turnover is much higher.[18] Such poor performance cannot be blamed on low foreign wage rates or on subsidies by foreign governments. Management and labor practices here at home need to be improved. As is shown in the next chapter, many American firms are taking that message to heart. They are making the painful changes necessary to restore competitiveness. But we need to understand the basic reason for the recent loss of foreign markets, and for that we have to look to the public sector.

## THE TWIN DEFICITS

*The Fourth Step to Improving Our Trade Policy is to Understand the Economic Origins of the Trade Deficit.* There is a great tendency to focus on Japan as the source of the foreign-trade problems of the U.S. economy. It is true that Japan maintains an intricate variety of obstacles to imports that compete with its own products—and that its government seems to reduce those obstacles only in response to constant pressure from other nations. Furthermore, the U.S. trade deficit with Japan, about $59 billion in 1986, is far greater than with any other country. In fact, trade with Japan accounted for nearly one-third of our entire merchandise deficit that year.

But some perspective is essential. Americans must face the painful fact that, even if Japan did no foreign trade at all, the United States would still be suffering a record excess of imports over exports. Without Japan, the total U.S. trade deficit in 1986 would have been about $111 billion.

In this connection, it is intriguing to note the changes in U.S. trade with other parts of the world. This country's traditional export surplus with Western Europe has turned into a trade deficit. Our trade accounts with Canada and Mexico are also in the red. In fact, the United States has been experiencing an excess of imports over exports with almost every nation in the non-Communist world, and it has had such deficits for some years.[19] It is unrealistic to contend that everyone is out of step but us. In fact, few nations (except the United States) have been moving toward protectionism during the 1980s.

But something important has changed dramatically and relatively recently. It is the value of the dollar in world currency markets. The unprecedented increase in the foreign-exchange power of the dollar from late 1980 to early 1985 (over 50 percent) raised very substantially the price of American-produced goods and services to foreigners.[20] Simultaneously, the strong dollar reduced the price of foreign goods to Americans. This, in turn, caused the volume of U.S. exports to decline while merchandise imports rose by about one-half. Thus, our traditional surplus of exports of goods and services over imports reversed dramatically and sharply.

To be sure, other factors contribute to the unusual rise in the U.S. trade deficit since 1980. For example, as a result of the changes made in the economic system of China, the productivity of its agriculture improved and reduced that nation's need for food imports from the United States. At about the same time, the debt problems facing the Latin-American countries forced them to reduce their imports, and the United States had been a major supplier to them.

Nevertheless, the run-up in the dollar was the major cause of the trade deficit. Moreover, this cause can be traced to our own domestic policies. The sharp rise in the dollar began in late 1980 and early 1981 when the shift to a policy of monetary restraint signaled that the era of accelerating double-digit inflation of the 1970s was drawing to a close.[21]

But it was the prospect of massive and continuing budget deficits in the United States that caused the sustained rise in long-term interest rates and the accompanying increase in the value of the dollar. The budget deficit rose from 2.5 percent of the GNP in 1980 to 5.3 percent of the GNP in 1986. Financing those large deficits would have absorbed virtually all of the domestic saving generated by the American economy—and that surely would have ended the recovery in the national economy—had it not been for the increased number of dollars available from foreigners (dollars they earned from selling us more than they bought from us).

The interactions are complicated but very important to an understanding of the relation between the trade deficit and the budget deficit. As a result of the sharp rise in borrowing by the federal government, the real rate of interest (real rate equals market rate minus inflation) on long-term bonds rose sharply. Market interest rates on those bonds were as high in 1983 as they had been in 1980, even though the inflation rate had fallen from 12 percent in 1980 to less than 4 percent in 1983. This sharp increase in real long-term interest rates attracted funds from overseas to be invested in dollar securities. This increased demand for dollars to be invested in the U.S. raised the exchange value of the dollar. Thus, in a sense, the U.S. budget deficit was self-financed. Financing the deficits set in motion forces that led foreign investors to buy a large part of the increase in Treasury issues of bonds (as well as shorter-term investments like notes and bills).[22]

Since early 1985, the underlying situation has improved. Congress has taken a variety of actions designed to slow down the growth in federal spending and to reduce the budget deficits. Although the precise target of zero deficit in the fiscal year 1993 (embodied in the revised Gramm-Rudman-Hollings deficit reduction law) is not likely to be achieved, participants in financial markets do foresee substantial reductions in federal deficit financing in the years ahead.

Coupled with other favorable factors, such as the growth in Western European economies and the decline in oil prices, the value of the dollar dropped in foreign-exchange markets by over one-third between early 1985 and late 1987. This change has been gradually reflected in the relative prices of U.S. imports and exports. However, once markets are lost to overseas competitors—and new business relations are developed—it is difficult to win those customers back, and to do so quickly. Many American consumers have developed new tastes for foreign products, and foreign producers are often shaving their profit margins in order to keep their newly won markets in the United States.

In any event, the decline in the dollar has thus far helped reduce this nation's large and persistent trade deficits. A lower dollar, however, generates serious side effects. It means that American consumers are paying more for imports, as well as for the domestically produced goods with which they compete. Paying the interest and dividends on the large investments that foreigners have been making in U.S. stocks and bonds will mean that eventually a portion of the potential increase in American living standards will be deferred. Professor Martin Feldstein of Harvard University estimates that, during the 1990s, more than 1 percent of each year's GNP will be given to foreigners in payment of interest on the indebtedness incurred to finance the high level of imports of the 1980s.[23]

Meanwhile, further substantial trade deficits are likely to occur in the United States for the next several years. Individual industries will continue to face substantial import competition. Thus, the debate over free trade versus protectionism is likely to persist and remain heated.

OUR OWN TRADE BARRIERS

*The Fifth Step in Developing a More Realistic Trade Policy is for Americans to Drop the Pretense That This Nation Is an Island of Free Trade in a World of Protectionism.* For example, Congressman Tony Coelho, a Democrat from California, has described the United States as "a free trade patsy for a protectionist world."[24] That line may play well on the political hustings, but it bears little resemblance to reality. It would clear the air both in domestic debates and in our negotiations with other nations if Americans would acknowledge that not all of their country's actions are on the side of the angels.

Despite the lip service that our fellow citizens pay to the virtues of free trade, the United States has in recent years been moving toward protectionism. There is universal agreement—at least in the United States—on the urgency of eliminating "their" barriers to our exports. But we Americans rarely even acknowledge our barriers to "their" exports.

In 1986, the United States started a small trade war with Canada by slapping a 35 percent tariff on shakes and shingles, the cedar wood products used in the housing industry. Canada responded by placing a 10 percent tariff on books, magazines, and computer products.[25] Although the later action was rescinded the following year, the whole incident left a residue of bitterness, which a proposed free-trade agreement between the two nations is designed to deal with.

The U.S. tariff on cedar products, however, is no exception. The United States has erected many barriers to inhibit imports from other countries. Many "Buy American" statutes give absolute preference to domestic producers in federal, state, and local government procurement. The Buy American Act of 1933 requires federal agencies purchasing commodities for use within the United States to pay up to a 6 percent differential for domestically produced goods. As much as a 50 percent differential is paid for military goods produced at home. In addition, the Surface Transportation Assistance Act of 1978 requires that, in building mass-transit systems, American materials and products be used. Yet another federal law requires that U.S. ships must transport at least one-half of the gross tonnage of all commodities financed with U.S. foreign-aid money.

In addition, many states have enacted various forms of Buy American laws. New York requires state agencies to buy American steel. New Jersey requires that all state cars be domestically produced. Arizona gives preference to other states with "Buy State" laws, if the product is not available in Arizona. Missouri requires state agencies to purchase domestic goods unless they cost more than 10 percent more than available imports. In addition, numerous states and municipal authorities require the use of American materials in privately owned as well as government-owned utilities.[26]

U.S. discrimination against foreign suppliers is extensive. The federal government's Jones Act (technically, the Merchant Marine Act of 1936) entails the opposite of keeping up with the Joneses. It prohibits foreign ships from competing for commerce between American ports. The perverse effects of such laws are much greater than might be expected. Because timber from Oregon meant to be sold in southern California must be shipped in high-cost U.S. vessels, Canadian lumber transported by Japanese-flag vessels has at times undersold domestic timber in that major domestic market. In such cases, both the American merchant marine and the American timber industry suffer. Although the U.S. merchant marine is the intended beneficiary of the Jones Act, it is foreigners who benefit from this attempt to "protect" a domestic industry.[27]

Also, agricultural laws limit imports of many products, such as sugar, beef, peanuts, cotton, dairy goods, and mandarin oranges. From time to time, the federal government has imposed quotas on shoes and autos. The restriction on Japanese cars was informal, but no less binding. A more elaborate set of import restraints covers textiles. In that realm, the United States has entered into a series of interrelated bilateral agreements with the major textile exporters and importers to restrict the import of textiles to and from various nations.[28]

Finally, the escape clause of the Trade Act of 1974 provides for temporary relief from "low" U.S. tariffs for domestic industries that can show serious injury, or threat of injury, from imports. That procedure was used in 1984 to increase the tariff on motorcycles tenfold.

Nonetheless, it is a common belief that U.S. tariff rates are low. In practice, they are almost as low as Japan's! Actually, the United States does levy high tariffs on quite a few items. Tariffs on textiles average 20 percent. Duties on fruit juices are over 27 percent; even clothespins are hit with a 17 percent levy. The proportion of imports covered by tariffs is growing. In 1950, the United States allowed 54 percent of all imports to enter duty-free. Despite all our talk about being the only country that practices free trade, by 1984 only 32 percent of the goods entering the United States were allowed in without any tariff. Moreover, at least one-third of the U.S. market for manufactured goods is covered by voluntary quotas and other quantitative restrictions.[29]

In addition, there are numerous nontariff barriers to international trade.[30] Local construction codes are a popular device for keeping out foreign-produced building supplies. They often specify arbitrary product characteristics based on those of existing domestic products. This is done not because of safety or quality considerations but to rule out foreign-product designs. Provisions governing the use of ceramic tile are a pertinent example. After imports captured much of the U.S. market for floor tile in the 1960s, many building codes were revised to screen out imported wall tile by requiring a thickness of one-fourth inch. That rule disallowed the import of tile produced in Japan and Western Europe, which had a standard 5/32 inch thickness.[31]

The federal government also restricts, and at times prohibits, foreign companies and citizens of other countries from investing in specific sectors of our economy. Some of these provisions are clearly needed: foreign corporations are effectively barred from defense contracts and atomic energy facilities because of security considerations. Other curbs are more arbitrary: the chief executives of fishing companies and dredging firms must be U.S. citizens; foreigners may not hold more than 25 percent of the stock of domestic airlines or more than 20 percent of that of TV and radio stations.[32]

By no means is the United States the only nation with trade barriers. Every nation has them.[33] But the United States is the world's largest exporter, as well as the largest importer. This nation has a vital stake in the continued health of the international trading system. The concerns of domestic manufacturers and of the consuming public alike are better served by responding to the underlying problems that generate both the trade deficits and the pressures for protectionism. The answer surely is not to retaliate against the nations with which we do business. That would open the way for a return to the trade wars of the 1930s, which exacerbated the great depression of that decade.

Citizens of the advanced industrialized nations—and not just of the United States—also have to realize that the economies of the developing countries are beginning to catch up to them. Traditional shares of world trade are changing in a lasting way. In retrospect, that is to be expected in view of the generous aid extended to them by the advanced societies through the World Bank and its related agencies (the Asian Development Bank, the Inter-American Development Bank, and so on).

In many cases, the less-developed countries now possess significant competitive advantages. Their cost levels for producing standardized items are a small fraction of those prevalent in the developed world. Their technology in many production processes is now close or equal to the technology available in the United States. In fact, much of their capital equipment is newer. Also, few of them have felt the need for enacting antitrust laws and similar restrictions on business.

While the exports of such advanced economies as the United States and West Germany rose by 10–11 percent from 1978 to 1985, several developing countries doubled their volume of world trade during that same period of time—Brazil, China, Taiwan, Hong Kong, South Korea, Malaysia, Mexico, Singapore, and Turkey, among others.

In any event, the problem of import competition, especially our large trade deficit with Japan, may have been solved several years ago by an unusual economic analyst, the humorist Russell Baker. Back in 1983, during the controversy about limiting the imports of Japanese cars, Baker noted that the Japanese auto industry had a productive capacity far in excess of its domestic requirements. He reported, too, that the United States was producing far more lawyers than it needed.

Unencumbered by econometric analysis or weighty theory, Baker recommended a simple swap of Japanese cars for American lawyers. He was not concerned about an ensuing flood of foreign-produced motor vehicles or denuding this country of its supply of attorneys. Rather, he saw this type of tied trade as possessing self-limiting features.

As American lawyers entered the Japanese economy, he reasoned, the ensuing expanded litigation would erode that nation's productivity. In contrast, the exodus of legal specialists from the United States would contribute to a rise in the efficiency of this nation's economy. Eventually, the economic competitiveness of the two nations would equalize. Baker felt so strongly about his plan that he suggested that the United States start the process by sending the Japanese a hundred thousand lawyers on the cuff.[34] Would that our trade problems could be solved so simply!

## A Positive Approach

The United States does not have to choose between counterproductive protectionism or a do-nothing response to the large trade deficits. A positive approach, far more satisfactory than a restricting of international commerce, is to improve the competitiveness of American industry. Our large trade deficit did not develop overnight, and no panacea will cure the problem quickly. In fact, the deficit will not fall below $100 billion a year by 1990 even if exports rise at the rapid rate of 12 percent a year and imports rise imperceptibly at a modest 2 percent annual pace.

Nevertheless, six constructive sets of actions will help increase domestic productivity and thus reduce the attractiveness of imports and enhance our export potential.

1. *Reduce the budget deficit.* There are two extreme positions on this issue, neither of which needs to be accepted. One polar alternative blames the trade deficit entirely on the budget deficit, while the other absolves it completely. As noted earlier, the financing of large deficits pushed up real interest rates and the value of the dollar in world currency markets. This in turn made it easier for foreign companies to compete against American companies, both in our home markets and overseas. However, many other factors, such as monetary policy, will continue to influence our foreign-trade position. But a reduction in the budget deficit is inherently desirable for purely domestic reasons.

2. *Gear tax reform to enhance productivity and competitiveness.* Recent changes in the tax law have ignored the repercussions on international trade. Future tax policy needs to emphasize incentives for the items important to enhancing international competitiveness—saving, investment, and research and development. In rewriting the Internal Revenue Code, we should learn from the experiences of the past. Narrowly focused tax preferences geared to one industry or region are ineffective and unfair. We need broad-based incentives aimed at encouraging saving and investment generally.

3. *Renew the regulatory reform effort.* The costs of producing goods and services in the United States can be reduced by launching a new effort to reform government regulation of business (see chapter 12 for details). The elimination of some economic regulation has reduced the cost of transportation. Closer attention to the tremendous costs imposed by the EPA, OSHA, and other social regulatory agencies would help restore industrial competitiveness. The present high cost of compliance with many of these regulations bears little relation to the modest benefits that are achieved.

4. *Reduce U.S. barriers to U.S. exports.* Restraints on the export of strategic goods should be administered with common sense. It does not contribute to national security to prevent American companies from selling overseas items that are readily available from foreign competitors. Efforts to dismantle our own trade barriers would supplement existing pressure on other nations to open their markets to our products and services. In any event, unlike protectionist actions, the reduction of federal government barriers to our own exports does not generate retaliation.

5. *American business and labor must face the challenge of increasing productivity.* Poor production practices in the United States cannot be blamed on foreigners. The answer is not to prop up industries

with import restrictions or government subsidies—or to play King Canute and try to prevent, by law, businesses from closing down or "running away." Rather, labor and management in each company need to face the challenge of enhancing their competitiveness. The sooner we confront this problem, the stronger will be the prospects for solving it. The "quick fix" of import restrictions only delays the inevitable.

Management can show the way. In many companies, cutting back on the proliferation of staff activities and layers of executives is creating an operating environment in which labor is more likely to accept changes in costly factory work rules. Protectionism is counterproductive since it lessens the pressure on management and labor to make the painful but necessary changes that enhance productivity. Foreign competition is the most effective spur to greater productivity.

On occasion, albeit reluctantly, the necessary changes are being made. In both Weirton, West Virginia, and Johnstown, Pennsylvania, unprofitable steel plants were sold to employees. In the face of economic disaster and unemployment, tough decisions were made. Wages and benefits, which were approximately 90 percent above the average for factory workers, were brought closer to competitive reality. Layers of management were eliminated. Work rules were streamlined. Both plants are now operating in the black, despite the strong dollar and powerful foreign competition.

This approach is not easy to carry out. But it is a constructive response to our trade problems, and a far more economically sound approach than another burst of trade restriction. Fundamentally, the future of American industry will be settled not by government directives from Tokyo or Washington but by decisions made in business offices and on production floors in Boston, Detroit, Chicago, Pittsburgh, Los Angeles, St. Louis, and other major cities throughout the nation.

6. *We need to encourage the positive role of multinational corporations in the world economy.* Multinationals adapt to change more readily and are less likely to plead for protection than other companies.[35] With their ample supply of capital and technological ability, they are also the private-sector alternative to foreign aid and other types of government intervention intended to encourage the growth of developing nations. This helps explain why so-called transnational enterprises are a conspicuous target for criticism by advocates of an enhanced role for government and especially why they are increasingly subject to regulation by the United Nations.[36]

Surely, the trend toward more detailed rule making over business activities that is now so evident in the UN's specialized agencies should be reversed. It is ironic that an organization originally set up to promote world peace and prosperity may be undermining one of the most realistic means of achieving those goals.

Viewed in the most fundamental light, international trade is not a narrow matter of business or economics but a basic aspect of foreign policy. In this broader context, the resurgence of protectionism is troublesome because it raises tensions between the nations of the world. The potential for strained political relations is greatly increased by heightened economic tensions. Conversely, open trade provides opportunities for improving relations among nations and their peoples.

Sooner or later, the United States must adjust to the fact that it has become a far more open economy. We can neither ignore nor insulate ourselves from developments abroad.[37] It is useful to reflect on some words of Ralph Waldo Emerson: "The historian will see that trade was the principle of Liberty; that trade planted America and destroyed Feudalism; that it makes peace and keeps peace."

Government policy on international commerce will not remain static. The choice is between a creeping protectionism and a concerted effort to remove trade barriers. The longer the United States waits, the more firmly the obstacles to trade will be in place and the more difficult it will be to deal with them.

# 7

# *Avoiding a Hamburger Economy*

Are America's basic manufacturing companies, pressured by overwhelming import competition, becoming an anachronistic "rust belt"? Must government step in to assure the survival of older, heavy industries, especially in the Midwest? Is the United States becoming a service economy focusing on information, hamburgers, and repair shops? Because of the close relations between the public and private sectors, the way we answer these questions will help determine the future direction of the American economy.

The truth of the matter is that some of this nation's heavy industries are in the process of shrinking in size and importance; steel, textiles, and automobile companies have reported the most dramatic cutbacks. In autos and textiles, the painful changes have returned the companies involved to substantial growth and profitability. In steel, a growing new subsector is dwarfed by an ailing conventional subsector. But, on balance, the answer to each of the three questions posed above is a clear no.

Any "rust belt" is in the eye of the beholder; the survival of the American industrial economy does not depend on either luck or a new set of federal bailouts. The American economy remains far more diversified than many people realize.[1] The facts are compelling.

American manufacturing companies—producers of hard goods and soft goods alike—are holding their own after coming out of the severe downturn that occurred in the early 1980s. As can be readily seen in figure 7-1, manufacturing in the United States has fully recovered from recession. By late 1983, total industrial production had attained a new peak. That widely used measure of physical output has continued to rise, albeit at a slower rate, through 1987. In fact, since 1980, industrial production has grown more rapidly in the United States than in any other major country in the world.

In view of these facts, how do we account for the gloom-and-doom talk about the supposedly sad prospects for U.S. manufacturing industries? There are several reasons. First of all, some casual observers tend to generalize from a few highly publicized instances of true distress. Moreover, Gresham's law seems to be working with a vengeance in the media: bad news drives out good. The positive side of economic events is rarely considered newsworthy and thus escapes widespread public attention.

But, perhaps most important, the authors of the new gospel of industrial policy—as well as other "megatrend" thinkers—have fallen into one of the oldest analytical traps. They have drawn grandiose and long-term conclusions from the most recent data that they have seen. Many of the doom-and-gloom soothsayers were doing their writing in

FIGURE 7-1
*Industrial Production, 1971–1987 Ratio Scale, 1977 = 100*

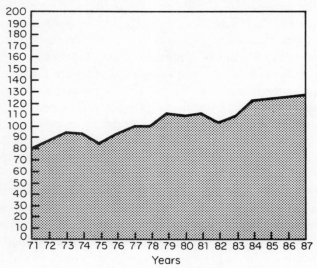

Years

Source: *Federal Reserve Bulletin,* various issues.

## Avoiding a Hamburger Economy

1981 and 1982, when the economy was declining, and, in a simpleminded fashion, they merely extrapolated that decline into the future. An example of such thinking was provided by Ira Magaziner and Robert Reich in 1982. They wrote in *Minding America's Business,* "The U.S. economy is in crisis. . . . In the absence of new strategic directions, the crisis can only deepen."[2]

In October 1982, Lester Thurow wrote, "The engines of economic growth have shut down and they are likely to stay that way for years to come. . . ."[3] The chief executive of a major chemical corporation embellished this negative statement when he described the competitive environment as "a zero-sum global economy."[4] In his view, this means that if individual companies expect to grow, they will increasingly have to do it at someone else's expense. Ironically, these statements were published just as the economy began the longest peacetime recovery in American history.

In each of these cases, the implicit forecasting approach used was to extrapolate naively from the most recent experience. Yet, U.S. economic history clearly shows that Americans do not live in a linear world. Important feedback effects occur. During periods of extremely rapid growth, marginal resources are brought into production, lowering productivity while raising costs. This contributes to inflationary pressures, which lead to changes in economic policy—notably, a move to restraint—that halt the expansion.

During "hard times," in contrast, steps are taken that provide the basis for future expansion. These include those cost-cutting, product and process innovations, and other productivity-raising moves that help to turn the tide. Thus, rapid growth in the first half of the 1950s (with an average annual increase in the real GNP of 5 percent) was followed by a slower pace in the second half of the decade (3 percent yearly). Similarly, strong growth in the 1960s, when the real GNP increased at an average of 4 percent a year, was followed by the slower growth of 3 percent in the 1970s. More recently, the sharp decline in the American economy that occurred in 1981–82 was followed by a strong recovery in 1983–84, which has continued at least through 1987, albeit at a slower pace.

To treat the downside of a business cycle as a fundamental and lasting new development is, of course, as silly as reacting with euphoria to news of the upturn. It is intriguing to note that some observers at the conservative end of the political spectrum have done just that. The prediction of a runaway boom in the late 1980s, however, is as misleading as the counsel of despair, because it sets up unattainable expectations.

TABLE 7-1

*Production of Manufacturing Industries*
*(1977 = 100)*

| Industry Group | 1970 | 1975 | 1980 | 1981 | 1982 | 1983 | 1984 | 1985 | 1986 |
|---|---|---|---|---|---|---|---|---|---|
| Primary metals | 95 | 88 | 90 | 95 | 66 | 73 | 82 | 80 | 76 |
| Fabricated metal products | 82 | 83 | 102 | 102 | 87 | 89 | 103 | 107 | 107 |
| Electrical machinery | 69 | 77 | 130 | 134 | 128 | 144 | 173 | 168 | 166 |
| Nonelectrical machinery | 73 | 85 | 123 | 130 | 116 | 118 | 142 | 145 | 142 |
| Transportation equipment | 75 | 81 | 97 | 95 | 88 | 99 | 114 | 121 | 126 |
| Instruments | 60 | 81 | 122 | 126 | 125 | 123 | 137 | 139 | 141 |
| Total Durable Goods | 78 | 83 | 109 | 111 | 100 | 108 | 125 | 127 | 128 |
| All Manufacturing | 77 | 83 | 108 | 110 | 102 | 110 | 124 | 127 | 129 |
| Total Industrial Production | 78 | 85 | 109 | 111 | 103 | 109 | 122 | 124 | 125 |

SOURCE: *Federal Reserve Bulletin,* various issues.

It is useful to examine the trend of output in key sectors of the American economy. As is shown in table 7-1, almost every heavy industry group has snapped back from the recession. The only exception is primary metals, mainly steel, which is still operating below its level of output during the 1970s. Taking full account of the variations among industries, we see that the decline in manufacturing industries that was so noticeable in 1982 did not represent the adverse, long-term trend that the doom peddlers have advertised. Rather, the decline was primarily the result of a severe but short-term cyclical contraction. For the most part, those negative effects are behind us. As the economist Paul McCracken has noted, "U.S. manufacturing is not a rust heap sinking into the weeds."[5]

## Employment Trends

Up to now, we have been focusing on production as the prime indicator of economic performance. But it is the high levels of unemployment that often exacerbate pressures for restricting imports and for providing government handouts to domestic corporations.

One widely held myth is that imports are the main cause of unemployment in steel, textiles, and other key industries. The data simply do not support this contention. The granting of generous wage increases—far in excess of the average wage gains by other factory workers—has been the largest single reason for the lack of competitiveness and, thus, for the loss of jobs in American steel companies.[6] Also, rapidly improving productivity is the main reason for declining employment in the American textile industry.[7]

Another myth that needs to be demolished is that all the new jobs being created are in high-tech industries, and only a small part of the U.S. labor force is trained for those new positions. A preoccupation with percentages can be extremely misleading. It is true that, over the coming decade, the most rapid rates of growth in job creation are expected to occur in such occupations as data-processing mechanics, computer operators and programmers, and servicers of office machines. On reflection, you can easily achieve a large percentage increase when you start from a small base for making comparisons.

It is in the more traditional job areas that by far the largest absolute increases in the number of new jobs will occur in the remainder of the twentieth century. The U.S. Labor Department's estimate that 335,000 new computer programmers will be needed in the years 1986–2000 is impressive. (It will constitute a 70 percent increase.) But those numbers are overwhelmed by the estimated demand for an additional 3 million people to staff eating, drinking, and lodging places during the same period. Likewise, the anticipated increase in computer systems analysts (251,000, or 76 percent) represents a fraction of the 890,000 construction workers expected to be added to the nation's work force. And the 882,000 new nurses and nurses' aides contrast with the 56,000 added computer repairers (an 80 percent rise over the period).[8]

Despite the talk about high-flying technology, the great bulk of the jobs in the United States will continue to be conventional. The skill qualifications for many of these positions will be enhanced. In general, machines will not replace the trained, literate people who operate and maintain the equipment. But that is hardly a revolutionary development on the labor scene.

Nevertheless, we need to reconcile manufacturing's declining share of total U.S. employment with its stable portion of total production. That situation results not from long-term weakness in the industrial sector of our economy but from its greater efficiency. Those two different relationships reflect the fact that the growth of productivity in manufacturing usually exceeds that in the rest of the economy. This point is worthy of some explanation.

Public discussions rarely acknowledge the complicated links between production, job creation, and productivity. In an economy with rising productivity (technically, increasing output per worker hour), employment would be expected to rise more slowly than output. In fact, declining employment might occur simultaneously with slowly growing or stable production. Thus, a loss of jobs does not inevitably imply declining production; it may merely reflect a more efficient method of production. Many people forget the economic fundamentals: the health of an industry is determined not by its demand for inputs (labor, capital, and so on) but by its supply of output—by its contribution of goods and services to the society's standard of living. By that measure, most U.S. industries are in good shape.

The generation of employment, though important, is fundamentally a by-product. Because of the interest in the subject of employment (and the related question of unemployment), it is useful to examine the job data in a historical context. It turns out that, since 1970, the total number of workers in manufacturing companies in the United States has fluctuated in the narrow range of 18 million to 20 million. The decline in employment in 1982 was followed, in every major hard-goods sector, by an expansion in 1983 and in subsequent years. In most cases, the rise continued through 1987, when manufacturing employment averaged a little over 19 million.[9] As in the case of the production data, variation among industry groups is substantial. The statistics do not support a feeling of elation, but neither do they justify a counsel of despair for job opportunities in U.S. manufacturing.

Recent research shows that the total employment of production workers in the United States is continuing to rise. The point overlooked by most analysts is that the fastest growth in openings for production workers is occurring in the service sector of the economy. In large measure, this results from the trend toward less vertical integration among manufacturing firms. Manufacturers are performing a smaller range of activities in-house and contracting out other work to subcontractors and suppliers, many of whom are classified as being in the service sector.[10] This occurs, for example, when an industrial firm contracts out its trucking operation; drivers, mechanics, and other employees who continue to do the same work are reported as service rather than manufacturing workers.

In any event, the industrial sector of the American economy is not in the sad shape that we read about so often. Manufacturing's share of the real GNP has held steady for the last thirty years, at about 21 percent (see figure 7-2).[11] Manufacturing in the United States is not going "down

FIGURE 7-2

*Manufacturing's Share of Real Gross National Product, 1947–1986*

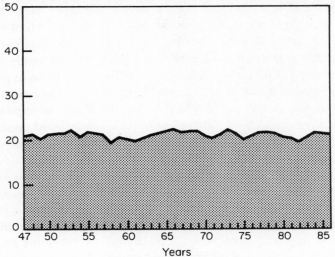

Years

SOURCE: Department of Commerce.

the tube," nor are we becoming a nation whose major employers are barbershops and gasoline stations. It is true that more people are employed producing services than goods. But that has been true since late in the nineteenth century.[12]

## A Growth Industry in the Rust Belt

It is useful to look below the aggregate statistics. For example, there are lessons to be learned from the rapid rise of the steel minimills, which are a growth industry in the midst of the sickest part of old-line heavy industry, the so-called rust belt. Even as the use of steel had been declining around the world, the minimills doubled their output in the United States in the decade from 1975 to 1985.[13]

The minimills are a dynamic group of young firms, smaller than the traditional giants and using simplified techniques of production. Each produces a narrow product line at low costs, often even lower than the foreign competition's. For example, the number of worker hours required to produce a ton of wire rods in a typical U.S. minimill is half of

*135*

that in a traditional domestic integrated steel mill and 60 percent of that in a Japanese integrated facility.

Since minimills are scattered around the country, often in small towns in the West and the South, their wage rates are considerably lower than those at the major integrated companies. In 1985, wages and fringe benefits at the major minimills averaged $17.50 an hour, compared with approximately $22.80 for the larger steel mills.

The high productivity of U.S. minimills enables them to compensate their workers at levels far above those of the steel industries in the Orient, and yet match their costs. In 1985, the average hourly compensation in the U.S. industry ($17.50) was substantially higher than that in Japan's ($11.70) or that in South Korea's ($2.40). Yet, total costs per ton of finished product came to $250 in the United States versus an estimated $258 in the two Asian nations.

What accounts for the different experiences in steel and other U.S. industries in countering foreign competition? In the domestic steel industry, new firms with new managements emerged to challenge foreign producers. Moreover, the minimills were not bound by the high cost of traditional labor contracts or the burdensome work rules that accompanied them. They could create new jobs in a difficult global competitive environment, and they did that without government subsidy.

## Are Smokestack Industries Passé?

As we saw in earlier chapters, serious economic problems continue to bedevil the United States—stubbornly large budget deficits, historically huge trade deficits, and unusually high real interest rates. Important parts of the economy especially sensitive to high interest rates and foreign competition, such as portions of the farm belt and primary metal manufacturing, are truly hurting.

But there is no need to join the professional doomsayers, who have been enjoying a field day. Their litany is predictable: "We are becoming a knowledge and information society. Traditional smokestack industries are passé. Service and high tech are the wave of the future."

The economist must play the role of the heavy and ask, "What are the facts?" The fact is that important shifts in emphasis from traditional to high-tech manufacturing are occurring in virtually every industry—steel and automotive as well as electronics and scientific instruments. If industrial giants of the past like Andrew Carnegie and Harvey Firestone were to visit their old companies, they would be surprised by the array of high technology now in use: industrial robots, sophisticated process control, laser inspection, flexible manufacturing systems (FMS), automated material handling, and CAD/CAM (computer-aided design along with computer-aided manufacturing).[14] They would very likely be impressed by the extensive retooling that now enables production changes to be made literally in minutes rather than in days or hours.

Deere & Company's sprawling tractor works provides a good example. The facility includes four FMS installations and sixteen machining centers—groups of totally automated machines and conveyors linked to a computer. In addition, visitors can see robotic welding and robotic spray painting, computers providing a total integration of conveyors, towlines, monorails, cranes, and automated storage and retrieval systems. There is hardly a conventional forklift truck in sight.

Many companies have adopted "flexible manufacturing," a high-tech marriage of robots and computers. Deere's plant can turn out tractors in more than five thousand different configurations. General Electric now makes two thousand versions of its basic electric meter at a single, small plant. In a new facility, General Motors has installed a robot system that paints its cars. In the textile industry, new-generation machines clean cotton and other fibers ten times faster than was possible a decade ago. Looms produce a hundred yards of cloth an hour, twice as rapidly as ten years ago. The man-machine interface is being redefined. Manual operations using gears, pulleys, and belts have often been replaced by microprocessors, keyboards, electronic switches, and cathode-ray tubes. Indeed, traditional or low-tech companies are the best customers of the high-tech industries.[15]

Why, then, is so much heard about the decline of U.S. manufacturing? For one thing, prospering companies are too busy to say much, but those that are still hurting let everyone know. A more basic factor is at work: a bull market for "big thinkers" who express their thoughts in glib and dramatic absolutes. In widely circulated books and magazines, they blithely report that the industrial era is over, that Americans live in an economy based only on the creation and distribution of information. Taking such overstatements at face value is silly. Are we going to eat, wear, and house ourselves in information?

Of course, the so-called knowledge industries are key growth sectors of the economy. But decades before Americans learned the buzzword *high tech,* these were already the dynamic parts of U.S. society. Yet, the production of goods will not wither away. Major nonmanufacturing industries, what are usually called the "service" sectors, are important customers for the products of manufacturing companies. Utilities, airlines, and agriculture are key examples of extremely capital-intensive, nonmanufacturing operations.

Those who fear for their business future should discount the bloated vocabulary of the big thinkers who peddle such vacuous nonsense as "Yesterday is over."[16] That is not terribly profound. Here is another: "We have two separate economies—sunrise industries and sunset industries."[17] That simple dichotomy brings to mind the old psychology professor who said that there are two kinds of people in the world—those who think there are two kinds of people in the world and those who do not.

A realistic appraisal of the future leads to the conclusion that the total number of jobs in manufacturing is not likely to grow much in the coming decade, but that their complexity—and pay—will continue to rise. Flexible automated systems will continually restructure production technology in order to keep American firms competitive in world markets. A decade from now, most viable manufacturing operations will be more fully automated than they are today. They will have converted to flexible systems that can be continually reprogrammed to make a large variety of products while maintaining necessary economies of scale.

The United States possesses the basic capabilities necessary to recapture leadership in many industrial areas, especially by relying on the advanced technology in sensors, computers, and software. No other nation devotes as many resources ($15 billion in 1987) to basic research year in, year out. R & D performed in the United States each year exceeds the combined totals of Japan, West Germany, France, the United Kingdom, and Sweden. No other economy contains a comparable depth, breadth, or scope of technical-industrial infrastructure that can translate basic discoveries into useful products and processes in a relatively short time.[18] In the words of Lord Harold Lever, a former economic adviser to several British prime ministers, ". . . the U.S. economy remains not only the most powerful economy in the world, but one of the most virile, flexible and productive. . . ."[19]

Moreover, the United States is the world's largest market with a common language and a strong entrepreneurial culture. The domestic availability of capital resources to finance new investment should not be underestimated. Not too many years ago, it became fashionable in the United States to bemoan the loss of our technological initiative just when the entrepreneurs in the Silicon Valley in California were making their greatest progress.

While the wailing goes on about the supposed erosion of our manufacturing base, three forces are emerging that make a period of sustained prosperity more likely in the years ahead:

1. Numerous company actions that reduce the cost of producing goods and services in the United States
2. A new awareness of their personal responsibility for the quality of what they produce on the part of American workers and managers
3. A rapid growth of private investment in R & D, the basic fuel for innovation and technical progress

Let us examine the increased importance of each of these factors.[20]

## Reducing the Cost of Production

For a variety of compelling reasons—most notably, to keep up with foreign competition and to fend off potential takeover threats—many American business firms have been reducing their costs of production. These actions have been taken by companies in the automobile, steel, chemicals, textiles, machinery, and almost every other sector of manufacturing. The specific responses they have made range from simple changes in production methods to a basic restructuring of the entire business. A 1987 report by the American Management Association revealed that about half of the firms surveyed downsized their operations between January 1986 and June 1987.[21]

Where do they start? Because the compensation of employees constitutes about two-thirds of the cost of producing the nation's output, labor costs are a natural for cutting. The measurable improvements occurring in the labor market are dramatic. Strike activity—whether measured by number of strikes or number of people out on strike—is at one of the lowest points since the Labor Department first started collecting the numbers. Over the period 1983–86, the number of work stoppages involving 1,000 employees or more averaged 66 a year, compared with 301 a decade earlier. Despite the growth in the labor force, the average of 535,000 workers idled by strikes in the mid-1980s was a fraction of the comparable number during the 1970s—1.4 million.[22]

Competitiveness also has been enhanced by the substantial slowing of the rise in wage costs. In 1980, the average U.S. worker in the private sector received a 9 percent wage boost. By 1986, the average annual increase was down below 4 percent. In some industries, workers actually are "giving back" prior wage and benefit increases.[23] The reader should not be confused about motivations. Givebacks do not arise because workers are suddenly worried about stockholders. Rather, their new attitude reflects rough on-the-job economic education in the new competitive reality, especially on the part of workers in companies that in the past were unusually generous in granting increases in wages and fringe benefits.

While management negotiations with unions are stabilizing labor costs, import penetration has sparked a war on other costs. By improving productivity, firms are getting more for their labor dollars. They are accomplishing this goal with more-flexible work rules and improved worker attitudes. Loosened work rules generate important savings in the production process. The traditional way was to have narrow job classifications, each employee performing one task. With new agreements to have workers perform several different tasks, fewer are required or the same number can produce more. Also, downtime is reduced when it is no longer necessary to wait for a worker with the right classification.

A Chrysler plant in Indiana reduced labor costs 30 percent by getting workers to agree to perform tasks outside their crafts. Goodyear has signed a pact that allows the 429 craftsmen at its Alabama plant to work outside their trade as much as 25 percent of the time. General Motors successfully negotiated with its Manville, Ohio, union to eliminate jobs such as machinists' "tool chasers." Having machinists get their own tools and other changes raised productivity in one stamping plant by 26 percent.

Changes in work rules also save money in the petroleum industry, where refiners report that output per worker has been increasing by more than 10 percent in recent years. One oil company merged six classifications into two at one refinery, cutting its work force by 25 percent.[24]

On the reasonable assumption that better-motivated workers do better work, some companies have attempted to improve worker attitudes. At Jones & Laughlin, a major steel maker in Aliquippa, Pennsylvania, a joint labor-management participation team analyzes production problems and suggests ways of improving efficiency. In one recent year, the company saved $75 million largely because of employee suggestions and work force cutbacks that resulted in the remaining workers' being assigned more duties.

Several American companies have adopted the Japanese just-in-time (JIT) inventory system. Under the JIT system, components are provided as needed instead of having large batches made in advance and stored. Harley-Davidson reports that the system freed $22 million previously tied up in inventory at one plant alone. JIT also dramatically reduced reorder lead times. Using JIT effectively requires better sales forecasting and delivery planning than many American companies have been accustomed to.[25]

The Chrysler plant in Fenton, Missouri, also shifted to the just-in-time approach. That change cut its inventory from $29 million to $20 million, resulting in savings of $1 million a year in interest costs. Reduced inventory may also mean less damage to parts from overcrowded storage conditions. One of the most ambitious production improvement efforts to date is the General Motors Flint Assembly project. GM has converted a sixty-year-old complex of unrelated component manufacturing and auto assembly plants into a 500-acre integrated production facility.

The Flint Assembly complex builds under one roof the major components needed for front-wheel-drive vehicles. The products worked on include engines, transmission components, and complete bodies. When the project is fully under way, steel blanks for body construction will enter at one end of the plant and finished cars leave at the other. Previously, partially completed automobile bodies were built at a body plant on one side of town and shipped to the final assembly location at the other side. The complex operates without the usual inventory "safety net" in a conscious effort to force discipline into the manufacturing system. Formerly, GM operated with convenient, but expensive, fallback positions.[26]

American firms respond to import pressures primarily through price reductions that force cost containment. But they often also rely simultaneously on more-technical approaches to meet foreign competition. In the auto-manufacturing industry, operations were traditionally based on achieving economies of scale by means of high-volume, long-running production. Product specifications were fairly rigid. Because economies of scale meant large factories and standard product design, changes in the product were expensive. Today, as a result of a shift to computer-based design and manufacturing (the CAD/CAM approach described earlier), production can be based on economies of scope. This newer approach allows for low-cost, flexible manufacture of a variety of products on the same automated equipment.

An extension of this economizing strategy is leading to important structural changes in a great many of the larger American corporations. The horizontally integrated firm, producing virtually every product in the markets in which it operates, is becoming less prevalent. Many companies are finding it preferable to specialize, focusing on specific product niches that are more secure against foreign competition.[27] This is to be expected as U.S. firms find themselves competing more fully in a global economy. Fewer domestic markets can be now thought of as being part of a closed economy.

In one of the most ambitious restructuring efforts, General Electric raised over $7 billion in the years 1983–87 by selling off more than 150 of its divisions. Among them were GE's well-known small-appliance operation, seven radio and TV stations, and its consumer electronics division. The company's new strategy is to move gradually away from traditional manufacturing and to focus instead on growth industries like electronics, financial services, and medical equipment. The proceeds from its restructuring activities helped finance its acquisition of RCA, Kidder Peabody & Co., and the medical equipment business of Thomson S. A. of France.[28]

The Union Carbide Corporation, a firm that is under severe pressure for many reasons in addition to foreign competition, also has undergone extensive restructuring. It has divested $500 million in what it now views as "nonstrategic" assets and businesses. This includes its commodity-metals business and its European bulk-chemicals, plastics, and polyethylene businesses and its battery division, which it sold to Ralston Purina.

In addition, a rapid rate of product innovation has been emphasized by many U.S. firms. American shoe companies like Timberland, Reebok, and Rockport have responded with stylish footwear to ward off foreign competition. Apparel manufacturing, one of the most import-affected industries, is using style to compete with low-cost foreign products. Companies like RJMJ continue to earn a profit by making women's pants and shorts through improved timing and greater flexibility of production. Foreign apparel makers need at least six months' lead time to coordinate manufacturing with retail sales. RJMJ's president says his company can turn on a dime: "We can get piece goods to [our plants] in a day or two and produce products for the shelves in three to four weeks. That enables us to catch a trend."[29]

*142*

## Improving Product Quality

The inroads of foreign competition into U.S. domestic markets have frequently been caused by the superior quality of the import rather than just its lower cost. As a result, unprecedented pressure has been generated for improving the quality of products that American businesses manufacture.

The payoff from higher quality is larger than is generally realized. It comes from the savings realized by doing the job right the first time and avoiding the costs of reworking defective products and replacing defective parts. Failures are much more expensive to fix after a unit has been assembled than before. Westinghouse Electric is an example of a corporation that can show benefits from an emphasis on quality. It has established 2,000 quality circles, involving 20,000 employees, and a quality college for training management in this field. The company has averaged productivity gains of 7 percent a year for three years in a row. This means that every ten years the company doubles its output without adding any resources.[30]

At Harley-Davidson, a motorcycle producer, employees receive forty hours of training to enable them to measure the quality of their output, a move that has resulted in a rise in defect-free motorcycles coming off the assembly line. Five years ago, one-half of the motorcycles coming off the assembly line contained defects; 99 percent are now reported to be flawless. The Ford Motor Company provides another example of progress. The company reduced its rejection rate of sheet steel from its domestic suppliers from as much as 9 percent in 1979–81 to under 2 percent in 1985.[31]

One way of improving quality is to iron out the bugs in the assembly process before the product is shipped to the dealers. GM took this step in its new Wentzville, Missouri, facility. It halted production on a new model until it met quality standards. This move was unusual because the company's—and the industry's—previous practice was to work on these problems while continuing production. To avoid the huge costs of halting production, quality problems in the past were thus passed on to dealers and customers.

A similar thing occurred in Ford's automotive operations in Dearborn, Michigan. Production was delayed because the rear doors were not meeting the rear fenders correctly. One Ford executive said, "Ten years ago, confronted with the same problem, we would have built on the appointed day. Today we start when we meet the standard."[32]

The enhanced concern with improving quality in American industry has not been primarily a matter of setting up new quality-control departments or even of expanding existing ones. Companies in the United States traditionally devote more resources to quality-control efforts than do their foreign counterparts. But quality assurance means more than just a collection of expensive professional personnel who check, review, and improve production practices. To produce defect-free products, it is necessary to emphasize quality manufacturing throughout the firm.

A study of the air-conditioner industry confirms this point. By means of such innovations as internal customer review boards to evaluate products, Japanese companies pay more attention to quality than do most of their American competitors. The Japanese foster quality by having top management hold daily review meetings on the subject. In contrast, American firms with the lowest rates of assembly defects meet about ten times a month; the U.S. companies with the highest rates of defective products average only four such meetings each month.

Management's message is also reflected on the front lines of production. First-line supervisors at four out of the six Japanese air-conditioner manufacturers surveyed say quality is most important to management; their counterpart at nine of eleven U.S. companies studied reply that meeting the production schedule is the highest priority.[33]

Management can communicate its emphasis on quality by paying more attention to details. National Steel now requires workers to clean their work stations instead of leaving the task for janitors. The Japanese co-owners, who suggested the policy, reasoned that if workers have enough pride to take care of their work stations, they may also care more for their product. Many comparisons between the United States and Japan focus on the greater sense of responsibility of Japanese workers and managers. But the differences cannot be assigned to genetic or other inherent characteristics.[34]

The most effective quality controls involve a shift in the locus of responsibility—from the inspectors in the quality-control department to the people who actually do the work.

## Avoiding a Hamburger Economy

### The Growth of R & D

"Don't confuse me with the facts" may be an old and trite expression, but it accurately describes the attitude of some of the latest big thinkers. In *Tales of a New America*, Robert Reich tells of the failure of American industry to invest in research and development (R & D).[35] The facts clearly show that to be a very tall tale indeed—and simply not true.

Since 1981, the number of scientists and engineers in American industry who have Ph.D.'s has risen from 344,000 to over 400,000. In the past decade, industry spending on R & D has risen at an average of 5.3 percent a year. The private sector is emerging as a more important channel than the federal government for financing and promoting R & D. During the period 1981–87, private industry each year spent more of its own money on R & D than did all federal agencies combined.[36]

Promising indicators of the effects of the stepped-up investments in R & D are available. More than 15,000 companies make high-tech equipment in the eight states bordering on the Great Lakes. At least 100 new companies specializing in biomedicine and computer software have located within fifty miles of the Mayo Clinic in Rochester, Minnesota.[37] Historical experience suggests that recent investments in research and development will create new product lines and perhaps even new industries.

Investments in R & D constitute an important way in which American industry can hold its own in the face of tough foreign competition. Domestic products that incorporate substantial amounts of R & D are competitive, whereas more mature items are increasingly replaced by imports. In 1985, the U.S. trade surplus in high-tech products was $3.6 billion, while non-high-tech manufacturers suffered a trade deficit in excess of $100 billion.[38]

The huge buildup of defense spending begun in 1981 has ended the slowdown of federal R & D outlays that occurred in the 1970s. In recent years, the largest dollar increases in federal expenditures have been budgeted for the Pentagon, a part of the government that spends more than twice the proportion of its budget on R & D than does the typical civilian agency (see table 7-2).

When the Department of Defense devotes an additional $100 billion to applications of science and engineering in half a decade, there is an excellent chance that more product and process innovation will occur

*145*

TABLE 7-2

*Federal Agency R & D and Total Outlays in 1986*

| Department or Agency | R & D Outlays (in billions) | Total Outlays (in billions) | R & D Percentage of Total |
|---|---|---|---|
| *Above-average R & D Ratios* | | | |
| National Science Foundation | $ 1.3 | $ 1.5 | 93.3 % |
| NASA | 3.4 | 7.4 | 45.9 |
| Energy Department | 4.7 | 11.0 | 42.7 |
| Commerce Department | .4 | 2.1 | 19.0 |
| Agency for International Development | .2 | 1.3 | 15.4 |
| Defense Department (military) | 33.3 | 265.6 | 12.5 |
| Interior Department | .4 | 4.7 | 8.5 |
| Environmental Protection Agency | .3 | 4.6 | 6.5 |
| *Below-average R & D Ratios* | | | |
| Health and Human Services Department | 5.5 | 333.9 | 1.7 |
| Agriculture Department | .9 | 58.7 | 1.5 |
| Transportation Department | .4 | 27.9 | 1.4 |
| Veterans Administration | .2 | 26.1 | 0.7 |
| All other | .5 | 283.2 | 0.2 |
| TOTAL, FEDERAL GOVERNMENT | 51.5 | 989.8 | 5.2 |

SOURCE: Compiled from data prepared by the Office of Management and Budget.

in the years ahead. That possibility is reinforced by the Pentagon's current tendency to support technological advancement in areas having civilian applications—that of computers, for example.

The Department of Defense recently awarded Carnegie-Mellon University a $102 million contract to develop and operate the Software Engineering Institute. The bulk of the institute's work will be unclassified research, including development of better education processes for teaching software. Although the main customers will be defense contractors, a second tier will include companies that build such commercial items as telecommunications and air traffic control systems.[39]

## The Three Factors Together

These three factors—cost cutting or quality improvements or expanded research and development—rarely yield quick and dramatic changes. Yet, their cumulative effects are likely to endure and to reinforce each other. All three factors work in the same direction—toward developing new and better products that will result in more orders, production, employment, income, and profits. These changes will not prevent imports from continuing to threaten individual companies. But they make for a brighter industrial outlook for the United States as a whole.

Solid evidence is already available. The average manufacturing company in the United States has become more productive during the 1980s, in the conventional terms of how much it produces per worker per hour. From 1973 to 1981, domestic manufacturing firms averaged a subnormal increase in productivity of 1.5 percent yearly. From 1981 to 1986, the average rate of productivity growth more than doubled, to 3.8 percent a year (that is also comfortably higher than the average rise of 2.7 percent a year during the period 1948–73).[40]

Thus, there is a reasonable basis for expecting that the ability of American firms to compete in world markets in the years ahead is being substantially improved. Likewise, the relative attractiveness of domestically produced products to American consumers should increase significantly.

There also are lessons to be learned from the experiences of Japanese-owned firms operating in the United States. Typically, they outperform their American competitors. Those Japanese-owned firms put a heavy emphasis on production quality, customer service, and employee involvement.[41] Their rate of absenteeism is generally low. About half of them report less than 1 percent absenteeism; the rest have less than 5 percent. "Percent defective" (the portion of goods produced that are deemed unsatisfactory) is generally at a modest 5 percent. This rate is much lower than that for comparable American firms. To underscore the emphasis on teamwork and the notion of the company as one big family, the president of one Japanese-owned company puts on work clothes and gets his hands dirty on what are considered to be low-level jobs. Another chief executive has lunch, individually, with each of his fifty-five workers.[42]

A word of warning is in order: these positive developments in American industry do not guarantee success in the future. Overseas competitors can heat up while U.S. companies try to catch up. South Korean construction companies, which have increasingly been giving their American counterparts tough competition in bidding on overseas projects, are now complaining about the even-lower-cost rivalry from Turkish and Indian firms.[43]

The chances of an improved economy in the 1990s may also be hurt by unhelpful changes in public policy. Pressures to reduce the budget deficit can result in further increases in the tax burden on saving and investment. The continued large budget deficits are a constant source of pressure for Congress to introduce new revenue-raising devices.

Should protectionist pressures succeed in the erection of additional trade barriers, much of the burden would be borne in the form of higher costs imposed on the industries using the higher-priced protected products. U.S. export industries would be especially vulnerable to retaliation.

A new round of burdensome domestic government regulation would both raise the cost of compliance and deter companies from investment and innovation. Moreover, another shift in federal budget priorities—from defense to transfer payments—could dampen the upward trend of R & D spending.

Domestic producers also continue to face private challenges. The concerns of consumers about shoddy products cannot be ignored for long, but the underlying consumer attitudes are brighter than many people realize. A survey by the American Society for Quality Control reveals many important product areas where American consumers consider U.S.-produced goods to be superior. For furniture, the margin is 84 to 4; for large appliances, 78 to 6; and for clothing, 70 to 13. As is shown in table 7-3, the only major product area where foreign quality is deemed superior is consumer electronics (TVs, radios, VCRs, and the like).

The positive developments to date are not guarantees of future per-

TABLE 7-3

*U.S. Consumers' Views on Product Quality*
*July–August 1985 Survey*

| Item | Percentage Viewing U.S. Goods as Higher in Quality | Percentage Viewing Foreign Goods as Higher in Quality | Percentage Reporting No Difference |
|---|---|---|---|
| Furniture | 84% | 4% | 12% |
| Major appliances | 78 | 6 | 16 |
| Clothing | 70 | 13 | 17 |
| Small appliances | 58 | 19 | 23 |
| Automobiles | 46 | 38 | 16 |
| Personal computers | 41 | 22 | 37 |
| TVs, radios, VCRs, etc. | 40 | 45 | 15 |
| Weighted average | 53% | 14% | 33% |

SOURCE: American Society for Quality Control.

formance. Foreign competitors can improve on their current strategies. Yet, the key forces in the private sector that make for enhanced competitiveness on the part of American business have developed considerable momentum.

This upbeat conclusion relies on the power of feedback effects. The prospects for the 1990s look good because downward trends are, after a while, reversed in the nonlinear American economy. Economic events do not move in a straight line for long periods of time. Changes in one direction sooner or later generate counterpressures. Thus, we also need to recognize the tendency of expansionary periods to breed the complacency that erodes the progress made during harder times. This crosscurrent of economic forces underscores a far more basic point: in change, there is both challenge and opportunity.

# 8

# *Handling the Rise of Takeovers*

A competitive business system is central to the vibrant economy needed to provide the resources to meet the many public and private demands of Americans. In that regard, some concerns must be raised about the powerful pressures to "do something" to prevent hostile takeovers of private corporations. Reducing the competition for ownership and control of American business would very likely have the same kinds of adverse effects that flowed from earlier efforts of government to contain the natural forces of competition.

Experience with existing regulation of private business provides a warning against hasty action. Too often, Congress devoted 90 percent or more of its time to discussing a specific problem of public policy and 10 percent or less to examining the proposed legislative solution. Nobody ever asks whether the proposed new law will work or whether another approach will work better.

A clear case in point was the 1974 pension reform law—the Employee Retirement Income Security Act, or ERISA. The objective of the law was noble, to protect worker pension rights. However, the numerous paperwork requirements were so onerous that thousands of companies, especially small businesses, threw up their hands and simply abandoned their pension programs. Such unintended side effects left many workers worse off than they were before Congress passed ERISA.[1]

## Handling the Rise of Takeovers

In the light of such experiences, a careful examination of the complicated issues involved in developing public policy on takeovers surely is required. Newspapers, magazines, and television news programs are all devoting substantial attention—often in a very dramatic form—to the new form of business combat known as the hostile takeover. The coverage of these events is dominated by such colorful terms as *poison pills, shark repellents, junk bonds, raiders, white knights, wolf packs,* and *greenmail.*

In 1985, more than fifty bills were introduced in the Congress to deal with mergers and acquisitions; more than twenty hearings on the subject were held by nine different committees.[2] Follow-on hearings were held in 1986 and 1987. However, there is hardly a meeting of minds on this cluster of controversial issues. Several states have responded with legislation, but no standard approach has emerged. Serious questions of substance have been raised about the methods proposed and the ends to be achieved. For example, Lane Kirkland, president of the AFL-CIO, takes the side of the managements that try to fight off unsolicited tender offers: "I think corporate raids are an outrage and a bloody scandal. . . . I see no virtue in it at all." The investor Irwin Jacobs responds, "We're really not a bunch of big, bad wolves. Mergers and acquisitions have created a great deal of value."[3]

Clearly, opinions vary sharply on many aspects of corporate takeovers, and especially those made by new shareholders who oppose existing managements. Many economists and other scholars welcome the efforts to replace the corporate management, contending that this process enhances shareholder value. In contrast, executives of these same firms, as well as many other observers, contend that these hostile attempts to change corporate control reduce business productivity and performance. They view such efforts as a diversion of executive attention and corporate resources from the serious business of producing and distributing goods and services.

These opposite reactions to corporate takeovers generate fundamentally different ideas on what is desirable public policy in the field of corporate governance. Thus, the specific policy proposals that various groups advocate follow from their views on the effects of takeovers. Let us examine these positions, but with the skepticism that is appropriate when we encounter any special pleading.

## The Effects of Takeovers

Supporters of greater regulation of corporate takeovers believe that such involuntary changes in corporate control are socially, economically, and financially detrimental. In the words of the investor Warren Buffet, "American industry should not be restructured by the people who can sell the most junk bonds."[4] Hostile takeovers are viewed as leading to forced liquidations or to the restructuring of viable companies by "raiders" who reap considerable profit. Moreover, the process is supposed to leave the companies in weakened and highly leveraged positions (that is, with far greater indebtedness), with stockholders becoming mere possessors of risky (for example, "junk") bonds.

The groups initiating hostile takeovers are considered to be only financiers and speculators, who are not serious about the operations of the companies and who are out solely for quick profits. In this view, takeover threats force corporate officials to look to the short term in order to keep their stock prices high. This diverts attention from longer-term investment potential and growth. Fending off raiders is also seen as forcing management to take time away from managing the business.

Alfred D. Chandler, Jr., the distinguished business historian at the Harvard Business School, worries about the rising trend of unfriendly takeovers: "How can anyone justify it? It provides no productivity, services, or function. . . . While our managers are fighting takeovers, the Japanese are finding it easier to take over their markets."[5] The economist Edward Denison of the Brookings Institution, a leading authority on productivity, makes a similar point, stating that the current takeover wave is distracting management from its duties of production and "making them think about raiding instead."[6]

The investment banker Felix Rohatyn presents a somewhat wider view in his negative evaluation of takeovers: "Large corporations can be treated like artichokes and simply torn apart without any regard for employees, communities, or customers, solely in order to pay off speculative debt." Peter Drucker has echoed this theme: "The new wave of hostile takeovers has already profoundly altered the contours and landmarks of the American economy. It has become a dominant force . . . in the behavior and actions of American managements and, almost certainly, a major factor in the erosion of American competitive and technological leadership."[7]

## Handling the Rise of Takeovers

The standard response of economists is that there is little demonstrable connection between the pace of takeovers and the economic maladies that Drucker and others bemoan. Moreover, the stock market's valuation of takeover efforts, they contend, is very positive. Numerous studies show that the stock of the target firm goes up quickly on the mere announcement of a tender offer.[8]

Because markets are considered to be efficient, that run-up in stock prices is viewed by many scholars as reflecting potential new economic gains in economies of scale, better management, and more productive use of labor and capital. The very threat of a takeover is supposed to provide a discipline on inefficient management. There may be an especially good economic rationale for restructuring in mature industries, where demand has fallen off considerably, overcapacity exists, and research and development and other investment prospects are currently less attractive. In the words of John D. Williams, "IBM isn't a candidate for takeover because it's an exquisitely run company."[9]

The prevailing school of thought among economists acknowledges that the redeploying of assets in restructured companies may cause some unemployment and community dislocation, but the assets do not disappear from the economy. The new investors have a strong economic incentive to put them to productive use. Hostile takeovers are thus seen as creating real value for shareholders.[10]

Given the vast discrepancy between these two viewpoints, the average citizen may wonder where the truth lies. Personally, I am reminded of the words of an old song, "My name is Sammy Hall and I hate youse one and all!" The explanation of the impacts of hostile takeovers surely is more complicated than either proponents or detractors are willing to admit. Although the shares of the companies taken over usually rise, it is premature to jump to the conclusion that stockholders generally benefit from takeovers. First of all, it is no wonder that the stock market value of the target company almost invariably increases during the takeover battle. No raider would make a bid for a company below its current market value. As we teach in Economics 101, an increase in demand for an item, without a commensurate increase in its supply, will result in a higher price.

An equally important question is what happens to the stock of the firm that makes the acquisition. The answer is downplayed by the proponents of takeovers, perhaps in the spirit of the sloppy housekeeper who sweeps some unwanted dirt under the rug. Study after study shows that the stock of the acquiring firm declines in the period following the

TABLE 8-1

*Changes in Stock Prices of Acquiring Firms after Announcement of Takeover (adjusted for marketwide stock price change)*

| Study | Length of Period Studied | Percentage Decline in Stock Prices |
|---|---|---|
| Asquith, 1983 | 299 days | −7.2 |
| Asquith et al., 1983 | 20 days | −0.2 |
| Dodd, 1980 | 40 days | −0.2 |
| Dodd and Ruback, 1977 | 1 year | −1.3 |
| Firth, 1980 | 1 year | +0.5 |
| Langetieg, 1978 | 1 year | −6.2 |
| Malatesta, 1983 | 150 days | −5.4 |
| Mandelker, 1974 | 40 months | −1.5 |
| Mueller and Magenheim, 1984 | 39 months | −42.2 |
| Eger, 1983 | 20 days | −3.1 |

SOURCE: These ten studies are described in Murray Weidenbaum and Stephen Vogt, "Takeovers and Stockholders: Winners and Losers," *California Management Review*, Summer 1987.

announcement of the merger (see table 8-1). It is clear that the owners of the stock evaluate the takeover announcement negatively. Thus, there are both winners and losers in each takeover. Ironically, the winners are usually the owners of the company being taken over and the losers are the owners of the firm doing the taking over.

It is not clear at all that the takeover process generates positive gains to society. Of the studies that show the dollar amounts of the gains and losses to both groups of shareholders, several show net gains and several show net losses, but few of these results are statistically different from zero.[11] Thus, for the nation as a whole, little net benefit is seen to accrue from the entire takeover process—not even when we use the changes in stock prices as a measure of the overall economic effect. The cold, hard reality is that we have little organized data available to affirm the synergy or efficiency hypothesis. It is difficult to reconcile that hypothesis with the large number of "postmerger divorces"—up to 40 percent of the acquisitions of the 1970s, according to the data published by W. T. Grimm.[12]

Professor F. M. Scherer of Swarthmore University, who studied the actual data available in corporate annual reports, has concluded that leaders of takeovers do not manage the businesses they acquire any more profitably than do their industry peers. Nor do they achieve significant profitability improvements relative to the pretakeover situation.[13] Other empirical studies reach similar conclusions.

## Handling the Rise of Takeovers

The staff of the Federal Reserve Board reported that a sample of banks acquired by holding companies during 1968–78 did not perform any differently, either before or after acquisition, from the way other banks performed. On a broader basis, of the twenty-five major acquisitions of 1965, only thirteen were still part of the acquirers or their successors by early 1986. Ten others were divested, one was dissolved, and still another was up for sale.[14]

Moreover, the conventional wisdom that takeover targets are characteristically poor performers—and hence attractive candidates for a change in management—does not appear to be true on any broad scale. A sample of seventy-seven target firms during 1950–76 had just about the same income/asset ratios as the average manufacturing corporation.[15]

There is an alternative response to the "efficient market" argument. Even if there is a gain in the share value of the merged company, that increase does not necessarily prove that expectations of increases in operating effectiveness are responsible. The key factor at work may be a reduction in tax liability. Thus, the Congressional Joint Committee on Taxation discounts the efficiency gains from mergers, noting that a large portion of the stock price gain may be due to the capitalization of tax benefits arising from the merger.[16] If tax benefits explain the increase in stock price, then it cannot be concluded, from that evidence alone, that mergers increase efficiency.

To sum up, the controversy about takeovers generates fascinating, and contradictory, conclusions. On the positive side, we do know that the shareholders of the target firm usually benefit, especially in the short run. But, on the negative side, we have learned that the shareholders of the acquiring firm generally suffer. There is a sleeper here: this latter point implies that the takeover effort on the part of the acquiring management must reflect a lack of concern about the interests of their own shareholders. That point, often neglected in conventional writings on the subject, is worthy of some attention.

## The Motivations of Managers

What does motivate the managements of the raiders? In theory, they are agents of their shareholders and are paid to protect the interests of the owners of the business. But a realistic approach must clearly go beyond mere theory. On the other hand, we can dismiss out of hand the visionary notion that the raiders are such idealists that they are willing to use the resources of their own companies, at the expense of their shareholders, in order to liberate the downtrodden owners of some other company. We are left, therefore, with a more cynical but a more credible explanation—there must be extraordinary gains to be gotten from controlling and managing large enterprises. Let us reflect on that point for a moment.

Corporate managers are not fundamentally different from other individuals. Self-interest should be expected to dominate their decision making. The same factors that encourage managers to be generous to themselves in allocating corporate resources (the widely discussed case of the entrenched management) may also be the driving force behind corporate acquisitions (the raider case). After all, acquisitions do increase the amount of corporate resources in the winning management's span of control.

A 1986 study by the Conference Board confirms with telling statistics what most people instinctively know: top executives in larger companies are paid more than their counterparts in smaller companies (see table 8-2).[17] To be sure, profitability and other factors also help determine management pay and fringe benefits. But, on average, the chief executive of a ten-billion-dollar company gets paid much more than the head of a firm whose annual sales volume is only five billion dollars. Moreover, in many sectors of business (ranging from manufacturing to banking and retailing), bonuses tend to be a greater percentage of salary, the larger the size of the company. In plain English, the bigger the company, the larger the rewards to top management.

It is logical that, in order to obtain such special gains, the raiders are

TABLE 8-2

*Portion of CEO Compensation Explained*
*by Company Size, 1985*

| Type of Business | Total Compensation | Base Salary |
| --- | --- | --- |
| Commercial banking | 66% | 60% |
| Manufacturing | 64 | 66 |
| Life insurance | 63 | 57 |
| Gas and electric utilities | 56 | 58 |
| Retail trade | 55 | 58 |
| Property and casualty insurance | 46 | 54 |
| Diversified services | 37 | 61 |

SOURCE: Charles A. Peck, *Top Executive Compensation*, 1986.

willing to offer above-market prices for the shares of the target company. The management of the acquiring firm winds up sharing its rewards with the stockholders of the target firm—but, ironically, not with the owners of the firm that employs it.

The academic supporters of takeovers look down at the existing managements of target firms because of their supposed lack of concern for their shareholders. This attitude toward the owners is surely conveyed, from time to time, by the top executives of some of the most successful firms. A 1983 study at the Harvard Business School reported that none of the top executives of twelve successful American companies was very concerned about the current market value of the company's stock. One CEO stated this position very clearly: "The highest priority with me is perpetuation of the enterprise. I'd like to leave this joint in better shape than when someone passed me the baton. I have to take care of the shareholders in this, but I don't sweat the shareholders too much. Most investors in our industry are passive."[18]

Another CEO expressed a similar viewpoint to a researcher for the Conference Board: "A year from now, 70% of my stockholders will have changed. On that basis, I put my customers, and my employees, way ahead of them."[19]

The Harvard researchers concluded that the primary goal of the CEOs is the survival of the corporation in which they have invested so much of themselves psychologically and professionally.[20]

Yet, it is equally hard to deify the managements of the "sharks," who, as we have seen, have little more regard for their own shareholders. This somewhat cynical approach also helps explain why researchers have found it so difficult to identify the actual improvements in management that are supposed to justify the run-up in the market value of the stock of target firms. In any event, it is hard to make a convincing case that takeovers in general generate substantial net benefits—or substantial net losses. From the vantage point of the economy as a whole, the results seem to be a draw.

## Takeovers and Financial Markets[21]

A different argument in favor of more federal control of corporate takeovers is that credit markets are hurt by "nonproductive" merger activity. Speaking at the time for the Federal Reserve System, former Chairman

Paul Volcker said, "I . . . have concerns about the potential risks associated with mergers and takeovers when these transactions involve unusual amounts of leveraging." After acknowledging that many, but not all, mergers may have positive social effects, Volcker warned that "these potential benefits clearly are diminished if the mergers are accompanied by more fragile balance sheets or more precarious loan portfolios."[22]

Private-sector financial executives use even stronger language. In talking about the takeover boom, Thomas S. Johnson, president of Chemical Bank, has stated, "I'm worried about what this leveraging up will do. . . . I'm worried that the aggregate of all these things, including leveraged buy-outs, is simply a perverse result of greed and not a logical, rational thing. I don't know how all this debt will be serviced." Felix Rohatyn of Lazard Freres has described the financing of corporate takeovers by means of high-yield "junk" bonds as follows: "It says something about where we are in our financial system when impeccable institutions buy something that calls itself 'junk' up front."[23] The responses to these arguments take many forms. The basic rejoinder is that the credit devoted to takeovers is not used up but recycled in the economy.

The pace of mergers has been increasing rapidly in recent years, from 2,326 in 1981 to 4,024 in 1986. As can be seen in table 8-3, both the numbers and dollar volume of takeovers reached record highs in 1986. Despite the large amounts of money involved, bank lending for takeovers has so far not been a cause for great concern. For example, merger-related loans for 1984 totaled $32 billion (including $25 billion from American banks). This may seem large from the viewpoint of any

TABLE 8-3

*The Rising Pace of Corporate Takeovers*

| Year | Number of Deals Recorded[1] | Deals in Which Value Was Disclosed | Dollar Amount (in billions) |
|------|------|------|------|
| 1981 | 2,326 | 1,212 | $67 |
| 1982 | 2,326 | 1,159 | 60 |
| 1983 | 2,385 | 1,041 | 52 |
| 1984 | 3,142 | 1,502 | 126 |
| 1985 | 3,397 | 1,618 | 144 |
| 1986 | 4,024 | 1,450 | 190 |

[1]Includes takeovers valued at $1 million or more.
SOURCE: *Mergers and Acquisitions*, various issues.

individual or company, but it was only about 2 percent of the total loans outstanding at U.S. banks in December 1984. Moreover, many merger-related bank loans are paid down fairly quickly with funds raised by sales of assets or with proceeds from the issue of commercial paper or long-term securities. About two-thirds of the bank loans extended in 1984 for larger mergers were repaid by the beginning of May 1985.[24]

Another way of gauging the impact of takeovers on financial markets is to examine the high-yield securities that are often issued to finance them (so-called junk bonds, to whose creditworthiness credit agencies give very low or no ratings). In 1985, $6 billion worth of junk bonds were issued for mergers. However, that was only 5 percent of that year's acquisitions (both hostile and friendly), suggesting that the rise of junk bonds is not a driving force behind the current wave of mergers. Moreover, $10 billion of junk bonds were used for purposes unrelated to takeovers, an amount greater than the total issue of these bonds in any year prior to 1984. Clearly, junk bonds are not simply a device for acquiring companies cheaply. Nor do junk bonds play a major financing role in hostile takeovers. In 1984, only 2 percent of the hostile takeovers were financed with junk bonds.[25]

In fact, takeovers are a small part of corporate restructuring. In the eighteen months from January 1984 to mid-1985, nearly 400 of the 850 largest corporations underwent some type of restructuring—acquisition, divestiture, spinoff, or stock buyback. Yet only 52 of these moves, or about one-eighth, were either direct or indirect results of takeover threats.[26] Some of the others may have been defensive reactions in response to general fears brought on by the high level of takeover activity.

However, a less optimistic view emerges from the balance sheets of particular companies. Many firms that have fought off unsolicited takeover efforts have greatly increased their debt loads. According to Standard & Poor's, 31 percent of their credit downgrades in 1985 resulted from corporate restructurings. Table 8-4 gives four extreme examples of the changing pattern of indebtedness before and after repelling unwanted suitors.[27]

During any future recession, some of these firms may find their capital cushions to be inadequate. In recession, debt/equity ratios based on market values rise, interest rates fall, cash flow is reduced, and the rate of bankruptcies grows. Some companies that have recently gone private are so highly leveraged that recessionary conditions might well push them into bankruptcy.

Indeed, the large amounts of corporate debt outstanding may make

TABLE 8-4

*Total Debt and Preferred Stock as Percentage*
*of Total Capitalization*

|  | Before Takeover Attempt | After Takeover Attempt |
|---|---|---|
| Phillips Petroleum | 39% | 84% |
| Unocal | 21 | 78 |
| CBS | 20 | 76 |
| Union Carbide | 35 | 88 |

SOURCE: Louis Perlmutter, "Takeovers: The Current Outlook," 1986.

the next recession more severe. The economy as a whole has been "leveraged up"—and not just those companies that have been involved in takeover battles. There will be a thinner cushion to withstand a severe jolt, on the part of both corporate borrowers and the financial institutions that lend to them. If the Federal Reserve System decides to relieve the pressure on debtors by turning to an excessively easy money policy, that could lead to a new round of inflation. But those problems would arise primarily from factors other than battles over corporate control. Although with some trepidation, I conclude that the role of takeover debt is marginal when viewed in the context of the total size of U.S. financial markets. If public policy makers turn to the issue of the huge indebtedness of the American economy, it should be for reasons other than takeover activity.

## Approaches to Public Policy

Under the circumstances, let us see what changes in public policy, if any, are needed to deal with the issue of corporate takeovers. There is no shortage of suggestions to consider. Proposed responses range from laissez-faire to tough new legislation designed to correct the perceived market failures. The following are the five key alternative approaches that have been suggested.

1. *No problem exists, and therefore no "solution" is necessary.* As we have seen, the prevailing academic view is that the market for corporate control is functioning reasonably well. Given the passive roles of many boards of directors, hostile takeovers are considered to

be helpful in keeping companies on their toes and in replacing inefficient, entrenched managements. In this view, if there is any role for
public policy, it is to prevent the boards and managements of target
firms from thwarting the will of the shareholders by means of "greenmail" payments and similar self-serving practices.

The proponents of freedom for takeovers note that recent legal
changes have strengthened the position of existing managements. For
example, the Delaware Supreme Court validated the "poison pill" used
by Household International, making it very expensive for a raider to
merge with the target company. More recently, the U.S. Supreme Court
upheld an Indiana law that restricts takeovers by, in effect, disenfran-
chising the purchasers of large blocks of stock.[28]

2. *There is a problem with regard to hostile takeovers, but it will
cure itself.* The substitution of debt for equity and the increasingly
short-term orientation of many American corporations are viewed with
some concern. These factors are emphasized as a result of the increasingly global context in which U.S. firms compete.

However, those in this second category believe that the hostile-take-
over phenomenon will cool substantially when the next recession
reduces the earnings of the highly leveraged companies. Many corporations that have been restructured to a far riskier mode as a result of
leveraged buyouts are expected to go "belly up." Such negative experiences would dampen the ardor of other potential hostile suitors and,
more pertinent, reduce the funding available to them. One Washington
attorney has summed up the matter very succinctly: "[T]he one thing
that would stop the takeover boom the quickest is the insolvency of a
financial institution that has invested heavily in junk bonds."[29]

In this second view, the takeover wave will subside as a result of
natural causes, and no change in public policy is warranted. Moreover,
the best-intentioned changes in legislation, it is contended, will benefit
only one side of the takeover battles and thus generate pressure for
another round of government intervention to even the score.

3. *There is a continuing problem, but it can be handled with further
changes in tax policy.* Because the tax deductibility of interest is a key
element in hostile takeovers, this group contends that all that is needed
is a change in the tax provisions that favor debt over equity.

They point out that interest charges are tax deductible while dividends are taxed twice, once when the money is earned at the corporate
level and again after the funds are received by the individual shareholder. The 1986 tax reform legislation reduced the differential tax treat-

ment by removing capital-gains advantages for equity financing. More-over, the cuts in corporate and individual tax rates reduced the overall tax differentials between debt and equity.

A more direct approach, proposed by some members of the Congress, is to reduce or eliminate tax deductions of interest for designated "un-productive" purposes, such as hostile takeovers, and to terminate tax deductions for payments of "greenmail." Such changes, in effect, would have the government determine the merit of individual business transactions.

4. *Additional regulatory devices should be resorted to.* Some want the Securities and Exchange Commission to crack down on trading "abuses," such as manipulation of stock prices through false rumors, leaks, and other sharp arbitrageur practices. The SEC's 1986–87 investigation of illegal "insider" trading was such a response. The resultant jail sentences to those investment bankers and stock arbitrageurs who were breaking the securities law discouraged several potential takeovers. One prominent attorney describes the situation that the SEC is dealing with as "the era of a two-tier, front-end-loaded, bootstrap, bust-up, junk-bond takeover."[30] In this view, the free flow of information has been impeded and the relative economic power of bidders and management altered.

Several dramatic cases, such as the Ivan Boesky scandal, have focused renewed attention on specific practices that can be considered to be "abuses." One is the ability to start a takeover without having binding financial commitments in place. Such conditional bids have a headline-grabbing effect and stampede the shares of the company into the hands of arbitrageurs and speculators. The second abuse involves the tactic of putting a company into "play." Seemingly deliberate leaks drive the company's shares into the hands of short-term speculators.

5. *The takeover problem is so serious that tough new legislation is required.* The aim is to make it more difficult for shareholder groups to make tender offers for the company's stock that are not endorsed by the company's board of directors. Virtually all the bills introduced in Congress to regulate corporate acquisitions are designed to protect target companies. Former Supreme Court Justice Arthur Goldberg, who served on the SEC Advisory Committee on Tender Offers, has suggested an ambitious agenda for legislative change that includes most of the specific proposals that have been put forward.[31]

He would outlaw "greenmail," a device used by target companies to fend off raiders by buying back their holdings at substantial premiums above the going market price. One antigreenmail bill introduced in the One-hundredth Congress would prohibit a corporation from paying more than the market price if the raider owns more than 3 percent of the stock and has held the stock for less than two years. This prohibition would be waived if the greenmail payment was approved by a vote of the stockholders (which thus far has never or rarely happened). Studies of greenmail payments almost invariably show that the action resulted in substantial declines in the value of the stock of the other shareholders.[32]

Goldberg also would have "golden parachutes" declared illegal. These are special and usually very generous payments assured to top management in case of a takeover. The rationale for the "parachutes" is that they encourage top executives to stay and fight a takeover without having to worry about the financial consequences of being fired by the new management.

In addition, Goldberg would prohibit "poison pills"—the adoption by the board of directors (without shareholder endorsement) of technical changes in shareholder rights. Poison pills try to make a takeover not approved by the target company's board prohibitively expensive. Their use and effectiveness have been heatedly debated by specialists in the area.

The former Supreme Court justice would also make it more difficult for corporate raiders by requiring them to disclose purchases of 5 percent or more of a public company within two days. Under the current rules, such large stockholders have ten days to report to the SEC. He would, furthermore, extend the time which a target company has to respond to an unsolicited offer to acquire the company. He notes that British law provides for a six-month freeze. In sum, the Goldberg proposals would constitute a major expansion of federal regulation of corporate governance. They constitute a comprehensive agenda for public consideration.

Some practices, such as paying greenmail and voting poison pills, do clearly hurt the individual shareholder. The serious question is whether a new federal law outlawing these devices would open the door to a massive wave of federal intervention in corporate governance. It certainly has been true in other areas of government involvement that regulation begets more regulation: public policy makers strive to correct the inevitable shortcomings of any new law with yet another statute, while interest groups vie for special advantage in the legislative process.

## The Case against More Regulation

Takeovers are not without costs or dangers. Not every takeover succeeds in achieving the intended benefits. Indeed, the volume of subsequent divestitures shows that, in hindsight, many were misguided. In fact, about one-third of the number and dollar amount of all recent merger and acquisition transactions are divestitures. The same lack of universal success, of course, might be attributed to any other corporate investment.

Moreover, many efforts at regulation are also ineffective. In 1986, the Federal Reserve System attempted to limit corporate takeovers that use junk bonds. Its new rule limited to 50 percent the portion of a hostile takeover that could be financed with debt if a "shell company" (one without significant assets or operations) was used. Following the issuance of the new Fed regulation, many raiders simply shifted to offering preferred stock, which has many of the characteristics of debt but counts as equity. Some companies avoided the governmental restriction by converting the equity into debt after the merger agreement was announced.[33]

In other cases, the attacking company used a shell that had a modest amount of assets and activities. For example, Pantry Pride was the corporate vehicle used to acquire Revlon, notwithstanding that its annual revenues of $110 million paled in comparison with Revlon's $2.4 billion. The experience with the Fed's junk-bond rule illustrates the futility of much governmental intervention because, in competitive markets like those typical of battles for corporate control, people often can adjust to governmental action without really changing their ways of doing business.

Several large and contentious contests for corporate control have focused national attention on the subject of hostile takeovers. However, these highly visible transactions are only a small fraction of the changes in control of American corporations carried out each year. Hostile takeovers represented only 1.2 percent of all mergers and acquisitions in 1986.[34] Most takeovers continue to be friendly and approved by the boards of both companies involved.

For well-financed groups to attempt hostile takeovers of private corporations is legitimate. But to claim they are promoting the public interest is stretching the point too much. The new breed of multimillionaire corporate raiders contend that they are the champions of the small stockholder. But more modestly—and more accurately—one highly visible raider has described the group as "acting in pursuit of personal financial gain and not out of altruism," adding, "I do it to make money."[35]

Perhaps the most significant factor to take into account in evaluating proposals for government to "do something" about hostile takeovers is historical. The experience of government in business decision making is not impressive. Whether that intervention is made by the judicial, legislative, or executive branches, government often does more harm than good when it interferes in private economic matters. The real gainers are the regulated firms rather than the public that regulation is designed to protect. As is shown in chapter 12, consumers have benefited from deregulation in the airline, trucking, railroad, telecommunications, and energy markets.

The presence of some shortcoming in the private business system (often called "market failure") is not sufficient cause for government to intervene. In recent years, we have learned painfully and repeatedly about "government failure." To justify added government regulation of the market for corporate control, it is necessary to demonstrate that the various costs associated with government intervention are less than the benefits it is expected to generate.

Much government regulation fails to meet this type of elementary but necessary benefit-cost test.[36] As a result, such a strong supporter of corporate takeover efforts as President Reagan's Council of Economic Advisers has concluded that "it is preferable to allow individual companies to decide whether and how they want to protect themselves than to have the Federal Government dictate an inflexible nationwide policy."[37]

There is little evidence that current law is inadequate to deal with investor crimes, such as those arising from the stock trading based on "insider" information. A crime spree that is followed by the criminals' being caught and punished is not a justification for more laws, but a vindication of existing legislation. Some members of Congress are always advocating closer federal control of business. They have been using the Boesky scandal to promote their traditional agenda. It is reminiscent of an old Steve Allen routine: "Here is the answer; now what was the question?"

As has been demonstrated, there are many pros and cons on each side of the controversy over hostile takeovers of U.S. corporations. The traditional "business judgment rule"—the presumption that the decisions of a board of directors will not be disturbed if they can be attributed to a rational business purpose—remains the most desirable approach to corporate governance. It is not necessary to conclude that the status quo produces the best of all possible worlds. It is sufficient to acknowledge that current policy constitutes a workable compromise between the desires of existing managements and those of the people who would wrest corporate control from them.

The balance between management's need to act expeditiously in the interest of the corporation and the shareholder's right to call that action into account should be resolved at the level closest to the problem and the relevant facts—by the corporation, its owners, and its managers in the first instance; by state law if necessary; and by federal law only as a last resort. This does not mean that inequities in the battle between management and the tenderers created by tax biases or existing regulations should be ignored. But the basic task of ensuring that the market for corporate control serves investors, employees, and other interested parties ultimately lies outside of government. There is an important private-sector role to be performed.

On reflection, it appears that if the raiders are opportunists, it is the board of directors and senior executives who have given them the opportunity. Too many CEOs and boards have focused on the theater and the opera as the epitome of a corporation's responsibility to society. They seem to forget that a business is an economic institution, designed to provide goods and services for consumers in order to benefit the shareholders.

The irony is that some of the problems of the takeover "targets" have arisen from their desire to be more socially responsible. The modern business literature tells management to balance the desires of employees, customers, suppliers, public-interest groups, and shareholders. The Committee for Economic Development, in its influential report on the social responsibility of business, states that the professional manager regards himself as a "trustee" balancing the interests of many diverse participants and constituents in the enterprise. Shareholders are listed only as one among those worthy groups—and they are listed last.[38]

Where does all this leave public policy on corporate takeovers? Since neither takeover forces nor defending managements can lay sole claim to the moral high ground and since there appears to be no obvious "market failure," there seems to be no compelling reason for expanding the federal government's role in these matters. If anything, it is the responsibility of the boards of directors of the acquiring firms to safe-guard their shareholders' interests more carefully. But if corporate boards do not fully exercise their responsibility for protecting the interests of the shareholders, then pressures for more government involvement in corporate governance will continue to mount—and the odds of Congress's responding will rise.

## A Positive Response to Takeover Threats

The heart of a positive response to unsolicited takeovers is not poison pills or shark repellents, nor is it government restraints on raiders. That often neglected force is the company's own board of directors.[39]

Under law, all corporate power is exercised by or under the authority of the board. The directors are elected to represent the shareholders. But the complaisant or rubber-stamp director has not totally vanished from the boardroom. Too many boards still view their prime task as supporting the management. Surely, the outside directors and the senior management who typically serve as inside directors should develop good working relationships. But they need to understand that, at times, their interests may diverge.

Responding more fully to the desires of the owners of the business is the key to repelling takeover threats. Corporate officials, both board members and officers, often forget until the company's stock is in play that shareholders continually vote with their dollars.

The most important, and rarely performed, duty of the corporate board is to learn how to say no. It often falls on the outside directors to favor a dividend increase over a marginal project even if the latter is the pet of a key manager. A supergenerous corporate donation to the ballet may do wonders for the social life of the chief executive officer, but it hardly benefits the shareholders. And it is up to the board to oppose a prospective merger that would, over the long run, dilute the earnings of existing shareholders and, in the short run, reduce the market value of their shareholdings. Similarly, it is the responsibility of the board of the target firm to decide when an offer for the corporation's shares is sufficiently attractive to be accepted over the protestations of the existing management.

Given the chemistry of corporate board meetings, it will continue to be difficult for the outside directors to exert such independence so long as an inside director (typically the CEO) remains as chairman of the board and is in charge of the agenda, the information flow, and the board proceedings. A useful precedent to follow is that of the numerous universities, hospitals, museums, and other nonprofit institutions whose boards are chaired by outside directors. Many West European companies and some venture-capital firms in the United States also follow this practice of separation of powers in the private sector. Of course, no committee (and that is the organizational nature of a board) can run an organization. That task clearly resides in the chief executive—and no competing power center should be created.

Nevertheless, the outside directors must assert themselves, especially in light of the increased liability that is imposed on them in the form of stockholder derivative suits. Although some may question the voluntary approach I am suggesting here, it is based on experience. It should be recalled that, in the 1960s and 1970s, many writers proposed changes in federal statutes mandating that a specified majority of the board members of the larger U.S. corporations be outside directors.[40] Because of the reluctance to involve the federal government in such a detailed aspect of corporate governance, neither the Congress nor the Securities and Exchange Commission acted on the matter.

Yet, important progress was made. Acting entirely on their own, most of the larger and many of the medium-size corporations are now electing a majority of outside directors (that is, those not members of the company's own management) to their boards of directors. By 1984, the typical board of the larger companies contained nine outside directors and four inside directors. The larger the firm, the more likely is the predominance of outside directors.[41]

The board has a pivotal position in the market for corporate control. If the board will not make the tough decisions that enhance the value of the corporation, the takeover artists will. Takeover mania is not a cause but a symptom of that unmet challenge. The 1986 tax reform bill underscores the point that the challenge to many boards is to pay out more cash for shareholders and to reduce outlays for low-yield projects. By equalizing the tax rates on capital gains and dividends, the new Internal Revenue Code deprives management of a traditional justification for retaining earnings in order to finance marginal projects.

What is really needed is corporate directors who use the full authority the law gives them. Outside directors are the heart of the critical third force in contests for corporate control. They need to bear in mind that the future of the corporation is in their hands—as long as they serve the desires of the shareholders. According to the traditional view, the key role of corporate boards is to deal with the succession problem. Surely, cultivating and selecting the firm's future chief executive is a fundamental task. But the key responsibility of board members, and one frequently unfulfilled, is to know when to say no to the management—on takeovers, investments, and other strategic issues. An active board is a vital form of preventive medicine. It reduces the likelihood of another expansion of government regulation of corporate governance.

# 9

# Coping with
# Business Bailouts

The continued high level of imports has been accompanied by ever more urgent pleas for some type of "industrial policy" to restore the competitiveness of the American economy. By guiding investment into expanding areas and out of declining markets, a new federal "growth policy" (the euphemisms are endless) will supposedly restore the competitiveness of American business at home and abroad. Especially fascinating about this development is the large number of business executives who are joining in this chorus for more governmental intervention. These are men and women who normally champion private enterprise and oppose large deficits or a bigger role for Uncle Sam in business decision making. To be sure, the dirty word *bailout* never appears in their suggestions.

## The Competitiveness Fad

The newest buzzword in Washington is *competitiveness*. After all, who is against making America more competitive? Consider the recent statement entitled *Promoting Economic Growth and Competitiveness.*[1] It is sponsored by a fascinating trio: Felix Rohatyn of Lazard Freres, the king of bailouts, Lane Kirkland, president of the AFL-CIO, and Irving Shapiro, retired CEO of Du Pont and former President Carter's favorite businessman. The contents of their package of panaceas follow predictable lines.

THE PLANNING AGENCY

For starters, they would promote economic growth and competitiveness by establishing a tripartite Industrial Development Board. Composed of business, union, and government leaders, the board would be charged with developing "cooperative" strategies to promote industrial expansion. That would supposedly help ensure that government efforts do not work at cross-purposes with private efforts. The board would also identify key sectors of the economy that deserve "special consideration." Now, that's getting down to business—the usual business of government planning, trying to pick winners and losers.

The competitiveness statement contains an open invitation for bailouts: "The initiative for governmental assistance would come generally from the industry itself. . . ." The board would be far more than an advisory study group, however. "Through negotiation among all affected interests," it would be charged with developing packages of "mutually reinforcing actions" designed to improve the competitiveness of specific industries. The inherent power of the "advisory" board is referred to explicitly: "The stature of its members and its access to the President would give it influence to marshall the resources of the executive branch." Of course, in theory, it would be just a voluntary committee. But a tripartite commission of private citizens that could marshal the resources of the federal government sounds as if it would have far more power than the run-of-the-mill committee of thinkers.

The historical record on governmentally established tripartite (business-labor-public) commissions is not auspicious. They have invariably been unable to reach a consensus on polarizing issues and have usually avoided difficult questions altogether. But they have experienced little difficulty in generating plans for using the resources of taxpayers and consumers to benefit their particular interests.

The 1979–81 Steel Tripartite Advisory Committee, for example, did not deal with the vital subject of concessions by labor and management required to make the steel industry more cost competitive. Rather, it focused on government aid to the industry. President Kennedy's Advisory Committee on Labor-Management Policy never issued recommendations on wages or prices, although those were the issues that the panel was charged to address. The low point in tripartite boards was reached in the 1970s. The Economic Revitalization Board, established by President Carter, never met.[2] Nevertheless, suggestions for tripartite commissions continue to proliferate.

SHADES OF THE RFC

A second predictable proposal in any competitiveness package is a financing agency—the outfit that directly provides the bailouts. Rohatyn-Kirkland-Shapiro call their version the Industrial Finance Administration (IFA). It would be, they contend, a "more flexible" agency for providing financial assistance to business. Its aid would be available only to industries designated by the tripartite Industrial Development Board. The board would set the policy for the financing agency and oversee its operations. How's that for real power for a group of part-time volunteers!

The IFA would be funded initially by a $5 billion subscription drawn from a combination of congressional appropriations and undesignated "other sources." It would have the authority to borrow a multiple of its initial capital. It would also fulfill a role private banks do not always assume—that of "an active lender helping to restructure U.S. industry."

To those with long memories—or a working knowledge of American history—that Industrial Finance Administration conjures up visions of the Reconstruction Finance Corporation (RFC), which lasted from Herbert Hoover's presidency to the early part of the Eisenhower administration. That the RFC was an "active lender" is beyond question. Its positive contribution to the structure of American industry is a very different matter.

A creature of the depression of the 1930s, the RFC grew rapidly during and following World War II.[3] A brief review of its activities is instructive. President Hoover originally recommended a two-year life for the new federal agency. Under the original act passed in 1932, Congress granted the RFC very modest lending powers, limited to railroads and financial institutions. During the next six years, the agency's authority was steadily broadened. By 1938, it had the power to buy the securities of any business enterprise. Although it was useful during the depression and World War II, the RFC made most of its loans to business (both in numbers and in dollar volume) in the postwar boom period of the late 1940s and early 1950s—when it really was not needed. Adequate financing was available from commercial lending institutions in the private sector.

## Coping with Business Bailouts

By 1949, rumors circulated that knowing influential people in Washington was often the real criterion for getting a loan approved by the RFC. Congressional hearings disclosed numerous examples of favoritism in granting loans. Two of the RFC's five directors and one of President Harry Truman's closest advisers were charged with influence peddling. The chief executive of one of the agency's "customers" (the Lustron Corporation) charged that an RFC director repeatedly tried to transfer control of the company to some of his friends and associates. Ultimately, Lustron went bankrupt.

In 1953, Congress ended the life of what was by then a discredited agency. The history of the RFC shows that government subsidy of business encourages and perpetuates a misallocation of resources. The agency's loans included such "high priority" ventures as distillers, brewers, drive-in theaters, hotels, motels, and bars (see table 9-1). The RFC experience also demonstrates that a government program can develop a life of its own and persist long after the problems for which it was created have been solved.

Clearly, *Promoting Economic Growth and Competitiveness* is hardly an innocuous call for Americans to work harder and invest more. Rather, it is a plan for a substantial expansion of the role of the public

TABLE 9-1

*Selected RFC Business Loans Outstanding, 1950*

| Loan Recipient | Amount Outstanding |
|---|---|
| United Distillers of America, New York, N.Y. | $331,500 |
| James Distillery, Inc., Baltimore, Md. | 315,000 |
| Harvard Brewing Co., Lowell, Mass. | 300,000 |
| Bluebeard's Castle Hotel Corp., St. Thomas, Virgin Islands | 250,000 |
| Morello Winery, Kerman, Calif. | 200,000 |
| Coast Drive-In Theaters, Calif. | 164,669 |
| Shore Club Lodge, Inc., Boise, Idaho | 164,500 |
| Saratoga Hotel Co., Saratoga, Wyo. | 125,000 |
| Coast View Winery, Inc., Fresno, Calif. | 117,750 |
| Gold Front Bar, Gold Front Theatre, Gold Front Recreation, Sheboygan, Wis. | 85,000 |
| Wooden Shoe Brewing Co., Minster, Ohio | 65,040 |
| Plymouth Rock Bar, Detroit, Mich. | 39,500 |
| Sandpiper Inn, Fort Walton, Fla. | 32,000 |
| Cactus Courts, Carlsbad, N. Mex. | 11,446 |

SOURCE: Senate Committee on Banking and Currency, *Hearings on S. 514, S. 1329, S. 1376, and S. J. Res. 44* (Washington, D.C.: Government Printing Office, 1951).

sector in private economic and financial matters. The proposed Industrial Development Board, for example, would also be charged with evaluating the idea of creating a new government agency to expand the commitment to technological R & D.

That the public and private sectors are both financing unparalleled levels of R & D does not deter the impulse for more federal intervention in internal business decision making. The panel raises the notion that industrial firms may be "too close" to immediate market decisions to explore adequately the many promising avenues of applied research. Supposedly, the more detached (or perhaps uninformed) views of government officials would be superior. So far, a comprehensive industrial policy for the United States has not been legislated by the Congress. But, as the Rohatyn-Kirkland-Shapiro plan attests, the idea continues to be supported by a variety of interest groups and prominent individuals.

## Rationales for Government Aid to Business

The reader may wonder why so many business executives flirt with expanding the supporting role of government in the private-enterprise system. Six different but overlapping reasons pervade the public discussion.

1. *The specific bailout proposal under consideration supposedly does not involve federal control over business, just some helpful government assistance.* It is fascinating to see how many otherwise smart, tough corporate chief executives think they can obtain generous benefits from the U.S. Treasury without any government strings attached. Any business manager who is so naive should not be let out alone at night, much less let loose in Washington.

In a burst of bipartisanship, let us quote Senator William Proxmire, a Democrat from Wisconsin, on this topic: "Money will go where the political power is. Anyone who thinks government funds will be allocated to firms according to merit has not lived or served in Washington very long."[4]

2. *Government action will be more fair and logical than unplanned competition in the marketplace.* Following up Senator Proxmire, neither logic nor fairness dominates political decision making. The truth is that the future is underrepresented politically. New and growing firms

are economically strong but politically weak. They lack either a track record of extended financial contributions to political candidates or the detailed knowledge of lobbying techniques. Moreover, the successful ones are too busy making and selling their products to devote their time and energy to politics.

In contrast, the past is overrepresented politically. Old firms may be economically weak, but they are politically strong. They possess well-developed relationships with key political figures (the much vaunted "access," which is the goal of much of the PAC contributions). The "sickies" also have the incentive to lobby. The result is a very uneven contest: the political process tends to favor old-line business over new enterprises. If that sounds too theoretical, just consider the actions taken in any recent session of Congress. After paying all due homage to the virtues of high-tech industries, the committees regularly report out bills appropriating large sums for agriculture, mining, fisheries, ship-building, and other old sectors of the economy that already are over-invested.

3. *The federal government has all sorts of policies in place to help business.* That has been true from the beginning of the Republic. In his *Report on Manufactures,* Alexander Hamilton argued for a strong government role in the encouragement of American industry. He noted in 1792 that other nations were offering subsidies and inducements to their manufacturers and that this inhibited free competition.

The sad fact is that proponents of bailouts try to justify them by pointing to the substantial largess that the federal government already provides to many parts of the economy. They are correct. Over the years, the Congress has been all too willing to "do something" for worthy constituents. Once again, we find that it is easier for elected officials to say yes to a request for assistance than to play Scrooge and turn down the plea. Is it too cynical to conclude that it is exhilarating (and easy) to do good with other people's money?

Few nations use as extensive an array of assistance to private enterprise as does the United States. The aid ranges from loans and grants to import quotas, tax subsidies, and research assistance.[5] The list of federal subsidies is almost endless, and it continues to grow.[6]

Table 9-2 contains a sampling of just one type of subsidy—federal credit that is provided at low interest rates. The federal government lends out its money at below-market rates to farmers, defense contractors, small businesses, electric and telephone companies, housing developers, shipbuilders, exporters, overseas investors, companies operating

TABLE 9-2

*Federal Subsidies to Borrowers in 1986*

| Federal Agency and Program | Market Interest Rate[1] (1) | Subsidized Interest Rate[2] (2) | Subsidy (1)–(2) |
|---|---|---|---|
| Department of Agriculture: | | | |
| Farm ownership | 14.5% | 10.4 % | 4.1 % |
| Emergency disaster relief | 15.3 | 5.0 | 10.3 |
| Farm labor housing | 14.0 | 1.0 | 13.0 |
| Farm home ownership | 14.0 | 3.0 | 11.0 |
| Farm exports | 14.9 | 11.5 | 3.4 |
| Commodity loans | 13.8 | 10.6 | 3.2 |
| Rural electrification | 14.6 | 11.6 | 3.0 |
| Rural telephones | 14.4 | 5.0 | 9.4 |
| Department of Education: | | | |
| Students | 18.5 | 5.0 | 13.5 |
| College housing | 12.8 | 3.0 | 9.8 |
| Department of Housing and Urban Development: | | | |
| Housing for elderly, handicapped | 13.1 | 9.0 | 4.1 |
| Low-rent public housing | 16.9 | 10.7 | 6.2 |
| Housing rehabilitation | 15.2 | 4.7 | 10.5 |
| Department of the Interior: | | | |
| Reclamation | 15.1 | 2.0 | 13.1 |
| Department of Transportation: | | | |
| Highway rights-of-way | 12.9 | 0.0 | 12.9 |
| Ship financing | 17.4 | 13.1 | 4.3 |
| NASA | 14.2 | 12.7 | 1.5 |
| Export-Import Bank | 15.2 | 11.2 | 4.0 |
| Small Business Administration: | | | |
| Disasters | 17.8 | 4.0 | 13.8 |
| General business | 17.8 | 13.5 | 4.3 |
| Tennessee Valley Authority | 13.6 | 10.1 | 3.5 |
| Other Agencies: | | | |
| Foreign economic aid | 15.3 | 2.8 | 12.5 |
| Foreign military aid | 14.6 | 6.2[3] | 8.4[3] |
| Credit unions | 11.0 | 9.9 | 1.1 |
| D.C. government | 13.5 | 12.2 | 1.3 |

[1] Interest rate available from banks and other private lenders.
[2] Interest rate actually charged by the federal government.
[3] Midpoint of range.
SOURCE: *Special Analyses, Budget of the United States Government, Fiscal Year 1988*, Special Analysis F.

in rural areas, hospitals, health maintenance organizations, credit unions, students, Indians, the elderly, the handicapped, veterans, railroads, banks, savings banks, savings and loan associations, local governments, developers of new energy sources, and installers of pollution equipment.[7] The beneficiaries do not include the proverbial "butcher, baker, and candlestick maker," but the providers of the raw materials (meat, wheat, and so on) do benefit from federal aid!

Some credit subsidies are modest, such as providing loans to credit unions at 9.4 percent when the prevailing commercial rate is 11 percent. In other cases, the subsidies are extremely generous. Thus, home mortgages to farmers are provided at 3 percent when the going private rate is 14 percent. On some foreign sales of military equipment, no interest is charged at all.

Not every government action affecting business is benign. Many existing government policies adversely affect industry in important ways. Government intervention has often contributed to the difficulties faced by the private sector. These negative impacts of government action are, in the main, side effects of laws designed for other purposes. The federal government does not mean to discourage investment; it just wants to provide a more equitable tax structure. Uncle Sam does not intend to discourage private saving; he just wants to use the public purse to generate a fairer distribution of income and wealth. Likewise, the feds do not want to burden American industry and reduce its competitiveness; they just desire to enhance the quality of life, improve the physical environment, increase the coverage of private health insurance, and so forth.

Table 9-3 shows the rapidly rising trend in the cost of federally mandated benefits. In 1960, employer payments for Social Security, unemployment compensation, and workers' compensation came to $10 billion, a sum equal to 4 percent of total wages and salaries. By 1986, hospital insurance and supplementary medical insurance had been added to the list of required fringe benefits. The total cost of all compulsory company payments had grown to $155 billion, or 9 percent of all wages and salaries. Government-required fringe benefits have become a veritable growth industry, expanding far faster than the value of the goods and services being produced by the employees receiving the benefits.

Intentionally or not, many government policies have weakened the industrial sector of the economy, either by increasing its costs or by reducing the amount of capital available for expansion and new-prod-

TABLE 9-3

*Rising Costs to Private Employers of Required Fringe Benefits*
*($ in billions)*

| Benefit | 1950 | 1955 | 1960 | 1965 | 1970 | 1975 | 1980 | 1985 | 1986 |
|---|---|---|---|---|---|---|---|---|---|
| Social Security[a] | $2 | $3 | $6 | $9 | $17 | $31 | $57 | $93 | $98 |
| Hospital insurance[b] | - | - | - | - | 2 | 6 | 12 | 23 | 26 |
| Unemployment Benefits[c] | 2 | 2 | 3 | 4 | 4 | 12 | 16 | 25 | 27 |
| Workers' compensation | 1 | 1 | 2 | 2 | 4 | 2 | 4 | 4 | 5 |
| Total | $4 | $6 | $10 | $15 | $27 | $50 | $89 | $146 | $155 |
| Wages and salaries | $124 | $175 | $277 | $290 | $427 | $639 | $1,112 | $1,594 | $1,698 |
| Fringe benefits as percent of wages and salaries | 3% | 3% | 4% | 5% | 6% | 9% | 9% | 9% | 9% |

[a]Includes railroad retirement.
[b]Includes cash sickness compensation.
[c]Includes railroad unemployment insurance.
Detail may not add to totals because of rounding.
SOURCE: Department of Commerce, *Business Statistics, 1971; Survey of Current Business,* various issues; *Social Security Bulletin,* Annual Supplement 1986.

uct development. The resultant poorer industrial performance often leads, in turn, to calls for another round of government involvement in the private sector generally and for the implementation of new industrial policies specifically.

If we overlook the adverse long-term effects of government on the structure and performance of business, we see only pleas for bailouts, subsidies, and other special assistance. But the willingness of government to bail out a Lockheed or a Chrysler is, on reflection, not surprising. It is the price that Congress pays to avoid dealing with the more fundamental problems that arise from the existing pattern of governmental involvement in the economy.

In this context, we also need to recognize that most current aid to industry is designed primarily to carry out other purposes. For instance, loans to airlines are not intended to help the aviation industry but are part of an export strategy. Interest-free working capital provided to aerospace and electronics companies is part of an effort to minimize the cost of defense production (the Pentagon can get the money from the Treasury without paying any interest at all). But those precedents are hardly cogent reasons for doing more along those lines.

The business system would be much better off if all of those government subsidies to private producers were eliminated, and so would the entire economy. The absence of business bailouts would mean lower budget deficits and hence more private investment funds available to business firms—and at lower interest rates. Much of that aid takes the form of political goodies, not good investments, and is distributed very arbitrarily. For example, in 1984, users of the Postal Service paid, on the average, 97 percent of the cost of providing the service, while users of Coast Guard services paid only 58 percent; users of the inland waterways, 9 percent; and the beneficiaries of deep-draft ports and harbors, absolutely nothing.[8] It is hard to find any objective basis for those sharp differences.

As we have seen, the great bulk of federal credit extended to the private sector is also heavily subsidized. The loans to a chosen few are made at interest rates far below those paid by the great majority of companies that rely on their own borrowing ability at banks and other private financial institutions. Moreover, the results of the federal largess are disappointing. For example, despite the more than $10 billion that the Treasury has poured into the merchant marine since 1936, that industry remains on the critical list.[9] More different types of subsidies have gone to that industry than to any other, including tax, spending, credit, and regulatory assistance. Despite—or maybe because of—all that federal interference, nobody buys an American-built ship without receiving generous subsidies. The shipbuilding industry is still sliding downhill.

The recipients of federally provided credit continue to clamor for more. Yet, you do not need to possess the personality of a Scrooge to oppose those requests. It is merely necessary to note the many silent losers in the federal credit game. First, there are the potential borrowers who do not get federal assistance. The slighted groups include many local governments, small and medium-size businesses, home owners, and consumers—all of whom pay more for credit, if it is available to them at all. The competition for funds by federal programs also increases the cost to taxpayers by raising market interest rates and hence the rate at which the Treasury borrows its own funds.

Moreover, if the borrowers default on direct loans or government-guaranteed loans, the Treasury ultimately winds up bearing the total cost of the loan. In such cases, government credit programs become a form of backdoor spending whereby federal expenditures are incurred in the absence of direct appropriations for the purpose. In some other cases, the liabilities are incurred before the congressional appropriations, and the legislature is virtually forced to enact appropriations to cover those commitments. The many billions of dollars recently voted for the Farm Credit System and the Federal Savings and Loan Insurance Corporation are striking examples of this situation.

These federal credit programs are a classic example of robbing Peter to pay—or lend to—Paul. They do nothing to increase the pool of private saving but reduce the amount available in the private market for use by more-competitive firms. But an observation of George Bernard Shaw's explains the political attractiveness of all forms of government subsidy: "A government that robs Peter to pay Paul can always depend on the support of Paul."

4. *Past government bailouts have worked.* That argument is pure myth. As we have seen, that darling of the economic planners—the RFC—was a bust. Almost all of its loans went to companies that subsequently failed. Widespread favoritism and scandals led to the agency's demise. It is not surprising that arbitrary power was used arbitrarily.

But what about Chrysler? The Treasury's generous loan guarantee supposedly was an exception to the theory that such federal intervention is undesirable and ineffective. Promoted by the hard-hitting bestseller written by the company's flamboyant chief executive, the federal bailout of Chrysler is widely acclaimed as a great success—having allegedly produced only winners and no losers.

Once again, the economist has to provide the figurative wet blanket. It is true that the company did not have to file any formal bankruptcy papers, but the specific actions it took closely resemble those of a company going through Chapter 11 bankruptcy. To the numerous creditors who received only thirty cents on the dollar, the pain was at least as great as if the company had formally gone broke. It takes a lot of digging into the fine print of the Chrysler Corporation Loan Guarantee Act of 1979 to learn that the Treasury guarantee of Chrysler borrowing was part of a package that, among other provisions, required the creditors to "make concessions." This permitted the company to pay off more than $600 million in indebtedness by remitting only 30 percent of what it owed.[10] Almost any other company in such circumstances would have been forced to declare bankruptcy.

There are other unpublicized aspects of the Chrysler bailout that deserve attention. In addition to the federal government's generous loan guarantee, the government of Canada provided $170 million in similar loan guarantees. The state of Michigan lent the company $150 million, the state of Indiana $32 million, and Delaware $5 million. Moreover, Chrysler's banks forgave the company $181 million in interest that it owed.[11]

None of these subsidies is mentioned when Chrysler gleefully tells everyone that it paid off all of the loans guaranteed by the U.S. Treasury. It apparently is also too embarrassed to remind the public that, even after it had regained profitability, Chrysler requested an additional bailout from the Treasury—in the form of not having to honor the stock warrants given to the Treasury as part of the original deal. However, that effort to rattle the tin cup was unsuccessful. The federal government sold those warrants over Chrysler's objections, and the proceeds went into the U.S. Treasury. Nevertheless, the Chrysler case is universally, and uncritically, cited as the example of a worthy federal bailout!

5. *Look at foreign experience, especially the Japanese.* A careful examination of overseas experience with government assistance to private industry yields a few surprises. Japan's Ministry of International Trade and Industry (MITI) is frequently heralded as a fine example of the positive contribution of government leadership to business growth. But it is too easy to draw a simple analogy between the rise of MITI's influence and the expansion of its nation's economy. It turns out that the much vaunted successes of Japan's auto industry occurred despite MITI's negative contributions. The friends of MITI conveniently forget that the agency tried to keep Mazda and Honda out of the automobile business, because it badly underestimated the growth of Japan's export market.

And then there was MITI's textile fiasco. Between 1956 and 1974, MITI bought and scrapped 180,000 looms to enforce a textile cartel that it had set up. But, at the same time, about 160,000 illegal looms came into production. In fact, more textile companies were operating in Japan after MITI's efforts than before. What really works well is MITI's public relations apparatus.[12]

Japan's more recent industrial experience provides a refreshing contrast. In response to the rapidly rising yen in world currency markets in 1987, Japanese companies took quick and tough actions to restore their competitiveness. Within weeks or months of the change in the external financial environment, companies adopted vigorous campaigns to improve productivity. Executives reduced their own salaries. Great efforts to upgrade quality were made. Some manufacturing operations were quickly moved to lower-cost locations. All these successful moves were private-sector responses,[13] devoid of government subsidy or direction.

Britain's experiences with government intervention are even sadder than Japan's. The British government, acting through its Industrial Reorganization Corporation, encouraged the Alfred Herbert Company, then the largest British machine tool firm, to take over smaller firms "to eliminate wasteful duplication and permit economies of scale in production, marketing and research." The Herbert Company grew from 6,000 employees in the late 1950s to a peak of 15,000 employees, becoming the largest machine tool organization in the world.

The expansion was financed through almost £50 million sterling of equity investment and loans that the British government provided to the firm over the course of a decade. The results were disappointing, to put it mildly. In 1975, to avoid liquidation, the Herbert Company was nationalized. Its net worth by then was only £1.2 million and its work force was down to 6,700. Despite the additional infusion of almost £40 million over the next five years, sales and employment continued to fall. In 1980, the firm ceased operation. So much for the ability of government to choose between winners and losers.

6. *Forget the theory; look at all the factories that are closing down.* This attitude leads to all sorts of legislative proposals to stop economic change, especially to control "runaway plants." Several states have enacted legislation to make it difficult for a company to move or close down a factory. They require advance notice and various benefits to affected employees.

In Wisconsin, firms closing facilities must give at least a sixty-day notice. Maine requires a similar sixty-day notice plus severance benefits to laid-off workers equal to their average weekly pay times their years of service. Michigan's plant closing law is in the form of a "voluntary social compact." If companies do not inform their employees at least thirty days before a plant is closed, they lose their right to issue industrial revenue bonds and other state financing incentives.[14]

This "King Canute" approach is very shortsighted. Those restrictions discourage companies from making new investments in the affected region. A plant-closing law tells management in effect that, if a project does not work out, it will be difficult to cut the losses. By reducing the pain of unemployment, these statutes also discourage employees from making the concessions necessary to keep their employers competitive and the factories operating. A national plant-closing statute would propel a greater flow of investment to overseas locations not burdened with similar requirements. "Runaway plant" laws are really taxes on unsuccessful businesses, a most unusual form of government intervention in the economy.[15]

Of course, a factory closing is painful to the employees, families, and community involved. But an economy with very few plant closings also probably lacks many openings of new plants. A contrast of recent experience in the United States with that in Western Europe underscores this point. Those who cite foreign precedents to support plant-closing statutes ignore the stagnation of employment in the major West European nations since 1980.

By its very nature, a dynamic economy constantly creates the need to shift capital and labor out of older, declining industries and into newer, more productive ones. That process is painful for some. It is only natural that those who have been employed in the older lines of business will resist the change. But consumer desires change, and business must adapt to that. In this light, "disinvestment" out of stagnant industries is as important as investment in those that are growing. When political forces get involved, it is usually to hinder this process. Lester Thurow has stated the problem succinctly: "Disinvestment is what our economy does worst. Instead of adopting public policies to speed up the process of disinvestment, we act to slow it down with protection and subsidies for the inefficient. . . . [T]hese actions are designed to provide economic security for someone, yet each of them imprisons us in a low productivity area."[16]

The society at large should be helpful to those hurt in the transition—and it is. That is the function of both private philanthropy and the generous array of unemployment compensation and other social programs now available. But to prevent change because it will "hurt" some community is a recipe for national stagnation.

## The Fundamental Case against Bailouts

The most fundamental reason for opposing bailouts is found in the nature of a free competitive economy. It is a world where people sometimes win—and sometimes lose—in their economic pursuits. A private-enterprise system teaches individuals how to avoid failure and pursue success. Those lessons are provided in a hard but objective manner. In a market-oriented economy, individual entrepreneurs and companies that are efficient in meeting consumer needs are profitable. Those that fail to meet those needs, or that do so at too high a cost, sustain losses. Such healthy economies are rough-and-tumble affairs where companies come and go.[17] Thus, it is erroneous to refer to a "profit" system. The American economy is a "profit-and-loss" system. The opportunity to earn a profit is only as available as the possibility of bearing a loss.

Government institutions, on the other hand, are not subject to any such discipline. No federal agency has ever been forced to declare bankruptcy. The typical response of a federal department living beyond its budget is to urge the Congress to appropriate more. Government programs often continue long beyond their original justification and develop lives of their own. There is no shortage of critics who comment about the shortcomings of the "invisible hand" in the market economy. But we have learned painfully and often in recent years that the "fickle finger"—or, rather, the hard fist—of government usually generates far greater problems when it intervenes in economic decision making.

Reliance on the private sector requires acknowledging two key implications. First of all, profits received in the marketplace are not *excessive* or *windfall* or *obscene,* to use words that politicians and journalists have frequently succumbed to. Profits are earned; they are a return on the stockholders' investment. They are a reward for taking risks. Moreover, after-tax earnings are the major source of the saving in this economy. And saving generates the funds to invest in the modernized plant and equipment that enhance this nation's competitiveness in world markets—and make possible future economic growth and rising living standards here at home.

But there is another side to this coin, one that business executives do not always recognize. If profits are not the occasion for government involvement in the economy, neither are the losses that occur in that marketplace a reason for such intervention. Low profitability is no justification for easy credit or high tariffs or other assistance at the expense of consumers and taxpayers. The economic contest is not a matter of business's saying to the consumer, "Heads I win, tails you lose."

The opposition to bailouts is part and parcel of a broader strategy of public policy. Adhering to the principles of economic freedom requires at times specific actions and at other times forbearance. Promoting the concept of free enterprise means giving no favored treatment to any interest group or industry. It means restraining the tendency to reallocate resources from those who are entitled to them by virtue of their own ability to those who receive them by political fiat. That objective is not accomplished simply by trade associations' adopting resolutions opposing social welfare programs. It is even more important to avoid giving the proponents of extravagant social programs the justification that the federal budget is chock full of examples of "welfare for the rich."

The last half century provides an almost endless array of experiences with well-intentioned government interventions in the private economy that did not work out. These examples of government failure range from the scandal-ridden Reconstruction Finance Corporation of the 1930s and 1940s to the waste-laden Office of Economic Opportunity in the 1960s and 1970s and to the counterproductive farm subsidies of the Commodity Credit Corporation, which have survived down to the present.

Perhaps the high—or low—point in the distribution of federal largess occurred in 1982, when a private company advertised its *Government Giveaway Guide* with the promise "How to Collect Free Money from Uncle Sam . . . Whether You Need It or Not!" Two excerpts from the advertisement illustrate the point:

- "Uncle Sam has giveaway programs for everyone. . . ."
- *"Classified Reports* guarantees that this exclusive undercover report will get you at least $500 in free cash from the U.S. Government or your money will be refunded."[18]

Of course, the motivating force of a private-enterprise system is self-interest, but enlightened self-interest. Unlike their counterparts in an environment characterized by government handouts, individuals or businesses prospering in a market economy have to provide something of use to someone else who is willing and able to pay for it. Paul Samuelson has warned that "the divorce of income from effort, and from success in producing goods for which the market will pay money, does gradually take a toll from productivity growth and even from the level of productivity."[19]

Self-interest rather than altruism motivates the economic activities of people and organizations. A private-enterprise system takes advantage of that fact. As Adam Smith put it, "It is not from the benevolence of the butcher, the brewer, or the baker that we expect our dinner, but from their regard to their own interest."[20]

The role of government in this context must be carefully defined. It does not mean being single-mindedly probusiness. That approach normally translates into a cozy partnership between government and business—subsidies and protection for failing industries, "incomes" and industrial policies, government planning, and other interventionist techniques invariably justified on an "exceptions" basis.

It also turns out that the government intervention usually does little to make business more productive. If anything, it provides business an opportunity to avoid facing the reality of the marketplace. Michael Porter of the Harvard Business School notes, on the basis of his research, that the government's role in promoting competitiveness is smaller than the conventional wisdom assumes. He concludes, "When you get away from the few highly visible industries that are studied over and over, such as cars and semiconductors, the role of government is frequently almost nonexistent."[21]

It is ironic that, just when the promoters of "new ideas" for economic policy are soft-pedaling the benefits of reliance on free markets, writers in the Soviet Union are blaming that nation's poor economic performance on the centralization of the Soviet state. Here are some of the "outdated . . . peculiarities of the system of state economic management" that Soviet economists bemoan:

- "a very high degree of centralization in economic decision-making"
- "the inhibition of market forces"
- "a centralized system of allocation of materials and supplies to all enterprises"
- "the centralized regulation of all forms of material incentives for workers"
- "overlapping authority and resulting confusion among ministries and agencies"
- "the limited economic authority and, as a result, the limited economic liability of enterprises for the results of their economic performance"
- "restrictions on all forms of unregulated economic activity in the sphere of production, service and distribution."

It is intriguing to read the Soviets' own description of how individuals attempt to adjust to this "most rigid regimentation of economic behavior":

The population always enjoys a certain amount of freedom to respond to the limitations imposed by the state. . . . When . . . rules and regulation . . . affect the vital interests of certain categories of people, they look for ways to circumvent the constraints and satisfy their requirements. Then the state introduces still harsher measures to block undesirable forms of activity, in response to which the population comes up with more refined methods that make it possible to meet their interests under the new conditions.[22]

## An Economic Policy to Strengthen the Private-Enterprise System

This book is not a plea in behalf of neanderthals or nihilists. There are many important tasks that only government can perform, ranging from ensuring the national security to collecting taxes and providing justice. But one thing that democratic political systems cannot do well at all is to make critical choices between particular firms, industries, regions, or municipalities. The political process is neither effective nor fair in determining which enterprises shall prosper and which shall not. Assigning such decisions to government is most likely to turn any policy of competitiveness into another political pork barrel.

There is an economic policy that can improve the performance of the private economy. It learns from the past and avoids close targeting of government assistance. A positive approach to promote the functioning of the private-enterprise system should focus on creating the underlying conditions favorable to business expansion and job creation. The ingredients are well known:

- Lowering budget deficits, which would directly increase the availability of funds for business expansion—and indirectly reduce the pressure on interest rates.
- Permitting the tax system to be stable for a while, to promote more certainty in investment planning. When the time comes to cut taxes, special consideration should be given to the encouragement of saving and investment.
- Shifting the composition of the federal budget to investment outlays (such as education and R & D) and away from current consumption by means of transfer payments.
- Reforming regulation to cut away the thicket of permits, restrictions, and other regulatory obstacles that any new undertaking faces—be it the building of a factory or the exporting of a new item.
- Stabilizing the growth in the money supply, to encourage a predictable flow of credit and to help spur economic performance.

One warning should be given. These five steps are not a guaranteed cure. There is no assurance that any one region, industry, or company will benefit from less obtrusive government. But the economy as a whole and citizens in general are likely to be better off. The positive approach puts the onus on labor and management in each company to deal with the competitive problems that face them, which is where the responsibility properly belongs.

# PART D

Facing Social
Concerns—
Economically

# 10

# Government and the Poor

Although many people believe that the poor have suffered in the 1980s from budget cutting, the facts do not support that belief. Since the administration of President Franklin Roosevelt in the 1930s, the federal government has made a great effort—especially as measured by dollars spent—to eliminate poverty in the United States. That effort has continued through every subsequent presidential administration, and Ronald Reagan's is no exception.

Over the last fifty years, in spite of ever more ambitious, and expensive, attempts to eliminate poverty, the problem remains as intractable as ever. Spending money on programs for the poor may ease the consciences of many people, but money alone has not generated a solution. The experience of the past half century seems to underscore the eternal verity of the biblical saying "For ye have the poor with you always . . ." (Mark 14:7).

Public policy has been motivated by a more optimistic outlook. There has been no shortage of effort by the federal government to eliminate the need for welfare. In 1935, President Roosevelt declared, "I can now see the end of public assistance in America."[1] FDR's forecast did not come true, despite the expenditure of what were then unparalleled amounts of federal funds for a variety of programs to benefit the poor. The administrations of Harry Truman and John Kennedy experienced the same frustration.

# FACING SOCIAL CONCERNS—ECONOMICALLY

In 1964, President Lyndon Johnson announced, "The days of the dole in our country are numbered."[2] Both the number of Americans in poverty and the size of the antipoverty efforts expanded under the four administrations that followed. Federal spending designed to achieve the Roosevelt-Johnson goal has totaled hundreds of billions of dollars during this period (over $400 billion just during 1981–85). In relative terms, payments to the poor rose from 0.7 percent of the GNP in 1960 to 4.3 percent in 1985. Over the past twenty-five years, federal spending for income support to individuals multiplied five and a half times in constant dollars. Any way it is measured, the outlay of public funds to relieve poverty has been expanding faster than inflation and population combined.

These efforts, while producing some gains, did not bring about the anticipated results. In 1985, the Census Bureau reported that 33 million Americans, 14 percent of the national population, were living below the poverty line, compared with 17 percent in 1965.[3] Clearly, only minor progress was made in the two decades. Nor did the vast outlay of money help satisfy the demands for spending more. But it is wrong for Americans to castigate themselves as a heartless society. In the most recent administrations—those of Jimmy Carter and Ronald Reagan—a far larger share of the nation's resources was devoted to social welfare programs than in Franklin Roosevelt's or Lyndon Johnson's.

Despite all the heated rhetoric about the horrendous cuts in welfare during the Reagan years, the benefit levels of most programs aimed at the poor have remained largely intact. In part, this was due to the unwillingness of Congress to cut as much as the President proposed. It is ironic that, in the case of public assistance, real benefit levels declined more slowly during the first half of the 1980s than during the latter 1970s—largely because of the drop in inflation in the more recent period.[4]

True, significant cuts were made in some means-tested social programs. Nevertheless, the "safety net" of federal support programs is still largely intact for the nonworking poor. According to the Urban Institute, the people removed from the welfare rolls are by and large continuing to work. In 1983, about 3.1 percent of all personal income came from public assistance, food stamps, and other programs for low-income people. Statistically, that is not significantly different from—and certainly no lower than—the 3.0 percent reported a decade earlier, in 1973.

## The Basic Causes of Poverty

The efforts to eliminate poverty may not have been effective, but it was not for lack of trying. This has led some analysts to conclude that traditional social programs are not effective in combating poverty and to direct more attention to the sociological and personal elements of the poor and less to the economics of poverty.[5]

This shift in perspective is a result of the perceived failure of the social programs inherited from the Johnson administration's Great Society. LBJ's war against poverty contained three key points. First, stimulate the economy to create more new jobs. Second, enact civil rights legislation to ensure that all people enjoy equal opportunity for employment. Third, provide income transfers and social programs for those who do not benefit from the growing availability of jobs.

Central to this approach was the notion that poverty is primarily an economic phenomenon caused by income shortfalls in a less than full employment economy. Current research continues to underscore the importance of general economic conditions. William Julius Wilson points out, for example, that poverty lessens when the economy picks up and grows worse when unemployment rises.[6] In such analyses, social issues entered on the fringe when, for instance, discrimination limited the ability of some people to get jobs.

Policymakers during this era overlooked the fact that the Great Society programs also modified the behavior of the poor. While increasing living standards, these programs set in motion forces that act to perpetuate poverty. Recent research suggests that much poverty is caused by the social and personal characteristics of the people classified as poor. The continued availability of income and services to the nonworking poor has made many dependent on society for support. A large part of today's poverty problem is blamed on life-styles, personal habits and attitudes, and even preferences and goals held by the chronically poor.

Members of this school of thought also note that an exponential increase in government expenditures for social welfare over the past quarter of a century has been accompanied by a simultaneous sharp rise in all forms of crime, neglect of basic obligations and responsibilities, widespread adoption of ruinous life-styles, and breakup of families. The total number of serious crimes rose more than sixfold between 1960 and 1980. Since then, the modest attempts to control the growth of social welfare spending have been accompanied by a slight decline in the number of crimes.[7]

Both the rise in crime rates and the expanding welfare outlays may reflect the influence of a third factor—the hard economic conditions of the 1970s. Surely, unintended behavioral effects of welfare policy were also an important contributing factor. According to the newer view on poverty, it is fruitless to expand or even to maintain the failed social programs. The following quotation sums up this negative attitude: "The lessons of history . . . show conclusively . . . that continued dependence upon relief [welfare] induces a spiritual and moral disintegration fundamentally destructive to the national fiber. To dole out relief is to administer a narcotic, a subtle destroyer of the human spirit."[8] That quotation does not come from President Reagan's campaign speeches. It is an excerpt from the State of the Union message delivered by President Roosevelt in 1935.

There is virtually universal agreement in the United States that those who are physically or mentally unable to support themselves should be helped by society with a minimum of hassle. Of course, there is far less agreement on what constitutes an adequate amount of aid. But, over the years, a subtle yet profound broadening has occurred in what it takes to qualify for such aid. Low or no income has become the only qualification necessary for the receipt of welfare, food stamps, and many other entitlements. It is significant that the type of governmental fiscal payments that the public had earlier referred to as "handouts" or "charity" or the "dole" have become transformed in the current budget debate into "entitlements."

As Roger Freeman of the Hoover Institution notes, when low income alone opens the door to public benefits, persons with low drive and few skills—and therefore low earning capacity—may prefer to depend on government welfare rather than to do menial work day after day. "Why should they sweat at cumbersome jobs for not much more money than they can get from the government as their entitlement?" he asks.[9] Certainly, not all the poor share this point of view. Nevertheless, policymakers must face the unpleasant fact that current welfare programs generate unanticipated side effects that may offset the benefits of the direct financial outlays.

During the past decade, the number of children in poverty in states with low welfare benefits has fallen, while the number of poor children in high benefit states has increased significantly.[10] As Charles Murray has written, "We tried to provide more for the poor and produced more poor instead."[11] This is reminiscent of a comment made by Garrett Hardin with regard to famine relief: "There's nothing more dangerous than a shallow-thinking compassionate person. . . . [H]e can cause a lot of trouble."[12]

The sad fact is that researchers investigating the effectiveness of entitlements have found that they reduce the willingness of people to work. In economic jargon, the researchers report "significant net negative impacts . . . on labor supply."[13] As would be expected, different researchers report different numerical results, but welfare's overall negative impact on work effort is clear. These researchers also note that welfare recipients are less likely to find jobs and more likely to quit them than other people.[14]

In comparison with contemporary standards of governmental policy, Freeman comes up with a harsh conclusion: a claim to live off the sweat of other people's brows should be subject to critical and painstaking scrutiny.[15] Yet, this view may be closer to that held by large numbers of the working population than is implicit in current social legislation. A Sindlinger and Company poll in July 1985 reported that 94 percent of all Americans believe that welfare recipients should be required to work.[16]

It is ironic that modern sophisticated research largely corroborates the instinctive notions that underlay one of the very first codifications of social welfare policy, the poor law of 1601 in England. In Elizabethan times, those incapable of work—the aged, the sick, and small children— were helped with public funds. Those able and willing to work were provided with jobs. Those capable of work, but unwilling, were not helped at all.[17]

The realization is growing that many long-term welfare "clients" are families or individuals beset by a multiplicity of personal and social problems that are deeply rooted and do not yield to simple economic approaches like the payment of cash. According to the experts, many poor people do not keep the jobs they find, simply because they cannot get to work on time, will not work a full work schedule, and will not pay attention on the job. Thus, negative attitudes rather than insufficient work opportunities often keep people unemployed. One expert panel does not mince words. It quotes approvingly from the work of Richard Freeman, who reported that, when out of work, the typical inner-city youngster is more likely to spend his time "hanging out or watching TV" than engaging in activities likely to help him get a job.[18] A study at the National Bureau of Economic Research found that children from welfare families do far worse in the job market than children from nonwelfare homes with the same social characteristics and income levels.[19]

The data marshaled by the panel also destroy some widely held myths. Poverty is primarily a children's, not a senior citizens', problem. Three and a half million of the elderly are poor, and thirteen million children are. About 75 percent of the elderly own their own homes, nearly all of which are paid for. Of the elderly officially classified as poor, about one-quarter have home equity of $50,000 or more.[20] As is shown in table 10-1, the older the head of the family, the wealthier the family is likely to be—through age seventy-four. The average family headed by someone sixty-five to seventy-four years of age holds more than twice the dollar assets than the typical family headed by a person thirty-five to forty-four years old. In sharp contrast, the largest and fastest-growing segment of the poor is made up of women who are divorced, separated, or single—and their children.

It is especially fascinating to note the views that many people in poverty hold about their responsibility. A *Los Angeles Times* poll in 1985 reported that 70 percent of all poor women say it is "almost always" or "often" true that "poor young women have babies so they can collect welfare." Also, 66 percent said that welfare "almost always" or "often" encourages husbands to avoid family responsibilities.[21] Only 9 percent of the mothers on welfare worked, while 40 percent of the nonpoor mothers with children under eight worked full-time in 1984.[22]

As we noted earlier, a key factor causing poverty is almost universally neglected in public discussions of the subject: the fathers who

TABLE 10-1

*Family Net Worth, 1983*

| Age of Family Head | Average Net Worth |
|---|---|
| 17–24 | $4,531 |
| 25–34 | 16,651 |
| 35–44 | 40,710 |
| 45–54 | 56,320 |
| 55–64 | 82,115 |
| 65–74 | 84,499 |
| 75 and over | 48,749 |

SOURCE: John Weicher and Susan Wachter, "The Distribution of Wealth among Families" (Paper presented to the Working Seminar on the Family and American Welfare Policy, 1987).

abandon young mothers and let society pay for raising their children. On the other hand, very few men (black or white) who are heads of households are even near poverty—if they have just a high school education. In 1986, less than 5 percent of all black males and less than 10 percent of all black females who met these simple requirements were in poverty. Of the adult black males who were high school graduates in 1986, some 86 percent had family incomes more than twice the poverty level.

It is clear that welfare (technically, Aid to Families with Dependent Children) is no longer a program mainly to help widows or divorced women make the difficult transition to a new status. In 1937–38, the father had died or was incapacitated in 71 percent of the welfare cases. Since then, public assistance has in large measure become a program that finances out-of-wedlock births. In the words of Kevin Hopkins of the Hudson Institute, "By far, the most common means of entry into long-term dependency is through the birth of a child to an unmarried woman."[23] In 1983, about 46 percent of the children receiving welfare benefits were born out of wedlock. Regardless of the race or the age of the mother, children born out of wedlock are more likely to drop out of school and to have illegitimate children.

You do not have to be a right-wing zealot to conclude that there is a powerful connection between the health of the family as an institution and the depth and pervasiveness of the poverty problem. Here are several dramatic examples of that relation:[24]

1. Not one in every ten married-couple families is poor.
2. Men with family responsibilities are less likely to quit jobs until they have secured other employment. If they lose their jobs, they are more likely to be out pounding the streets the next morning.
3. Men living alone consistently have unemployment rates more than double those of family men.
4. Nine out of every ten families on welfare are headed by women. The "feminization of poverty" is real.
5. Never-married women are much poorer than their divorced counterparts. The average family income of a never-married mother with children under eighteen is less than half the average income of divorced women with children. Unmarried mothers stay on welfare much longer (nine years) than divorced mothers (less than five years).
6. A young married couple, both of whom work, may barely earn enough income to be above the poverty level and thus not be included in government statistics on the poor. However, if they live together unmarried, each separately may have a low enough income to be included in the federal tally of the poor.

7. If a married couple gets a divorce and thus splits up the family unit, one or both can be pushed below the poverty line—even though their combined incomes and expenses remain the same.

8. If unmarried persons leave their families to set up their own residences, that simple act can shift those individuals to reported income levels below the poverty line. On occasion, the loss of income can also move the family below the poverty line.

9. Growing up in a female-headed family increases the likelihood significantly that a woman will form a female-headed family of her own. If her childhood family received welfare, the probability is raised that her own family will be on welfare.

10. Nearly 75 percent of the children on welfare are on the rolls because their parents do not support them, frequently because the father has never taken the responsibility for the child or because he has left the home.

Without judging the moral bases of alternative life-styles, one readily sees that there can be very substantial economic consequences of such actions as having a child out of wedlock, getting divorced, or living together without getting married. Most relevant from the viewpoint of public policy is the fact that so much of the cost of such actions is not borne by the individuals making those decisions. The cost is paid in large measure by society as a whole.

In 1984, fewer than one-half of the 8.7 million women with children whose father was not in the household received any money from the fathers of those children. The payments that were made averaged only $1,430 a year.[25] This is not a recent or passing situation. Two decades ago, Senator Daniel Patrick Moynihan commented on this same situation in a rather colorful manner:

> [In olden times] a man who deserted his children, pretty much assured that they would starve, or near to it, if he was not brought back, and that he would be horsewhipped if he were. . . .
>
> The poor in the United States today enjoy a quite unprecedented de facto freedom to abandon their children in the certain knowledge that society will care for them and, what is more, in a state such as New York, to care for them by quite decent standards.[26]

A persuasive case can be made that, in many areas of human conduct, individuals no longer bear the major consequences of their own actions. Of far greater economic and budgetary importance is the tendency for nontraditional living arrangements to become more pervasive (see table 10-2). According to a recent study by the Rand Corporation, if current trends continue, more than half of the first marriages of the women who

# Government and the Poor

TABLE 10-2

## Selected U.S. Population Trends, 1975–1985

| Category | Percentage Increase |
|---|---|
| Married-couple family households | +7 |
| Female-headed households | +42 |
| Households of unrelated individuals | +57 |
| Total U.S. population | +11 |

SOURCE: *1986 Statistical Abstract of the United States; Economic Report of the President, January 1987.*

were thirty-five to thirty-nine years of age in 1985 will eventually end in divorce. Similarly, of that year's six-year-old children, as many as two out of three white children and nineteen out of twenty black children will, by the time they reach eighteen, have lived in a one-parent family at some point. An even greater departure from old norms is the rising phenomenon of out-of-wedlock children, especially among teenagers. Approximately 21 percent of all children born in the United States in 1984 were born out of wedlock. That is a 74 percent increase over the 1960 rate, and the percentage is rising.[27]

During this same period, Supreme Court decisions swept aside a variety of efforts to limit welfare benefits to the family:[28]

- In *King v. Smith* (1968), the Court struck down an Alabama law denying welfare to households that include "substitute fathers"—that is, adult males unrelated to the mother by blood or marriage. That decision in effect made cohabitation more profitable than marriage in most states.
- In *Weber v. Aetna Casualty and Surety Company* (1972), the Court ruled that workers' compensation benefits cannot be limited to legitimate children. That ruling set the stage for barring the government preference for legitimacy.
- In *New Jersey Welfare Rights Organization v. Cahill* (1973), the Court forbade state government preference for marriage over cohabitation in welfare programs.
- In *USDA v. Moreno* (1973), the Court invalidated a provision of the food stamp program basing household eligibility on ties of blood, marriage, or adoption (the traditional definition of a family).

## What Can Be Done?

A key step in dealing with the problem of poverty in the United States is to recognize that it is not primarily a matter of how much money the government should spend on poor people. Nor is it a question of callousness or stinginess, although under current circumstances large sums of money are needed to prevent real hardship in many cases. The basic issue is how to deal with the causes of poverty.

To begin with, we must recognize that economic growth is a necessary but by no means sufficient condition for eliminating poverty. To turn an old phrase, a rising tide does not lift all boats; vessels stuck in the bottom of the river may simply be swamped. Expansion of the national economy does create new employment opportunities for the work force as a whole. Moreover, it makes policy choices easier and politically feasible. Working families will agree more readily to share the national income with those less fortunate when the economic pie is growing. But economic growth cannot alone cure the problem of chronic poverty. If anything, the rising cost of living associated with more rapid economic growth may only make life more difficult for those with little income. Many of the long-term poor have developed attitudes and behavioral traits that make it difficult for them to escape poverty under very favorable economic conditions.

Focusing on a positive approach, a distinguished panel of both liberal and conservative analysts concluded in 1987, "An indispensable resource in the war against poverty is a sense of personal responsibility."[29] The panel went on to point out that climbing out of poverty is no mystery. At its heart, the elimination of poverty is not something that government can do for an individual. Rather, it is something that the individual must undertake, albeit with some help from society.

More often than not, all it takes for a person to move out of poverty is three things: (1) completing high school, (2) getting and staying married (even if not on the first try), and (3) staying employed, though at modest wages like the statutory minimum wage. In this light, it seems counterproductive to advise people on welfare to hold out for "good" jobs rather than to leave welfare status for a "dead-end" job. Work experience itself is a vital part of solving the poverty problem.[30]

Some analysts of the poverty problem are thus led to propose solutions far tougher than the status quo. Martin Anderson urges modern welfare policy to return to the traditional approach of giving aid only to "those who cannot help themselves"[31]—which approximates the Elizabethan poor law. Anderson advocates abandoning the idea of relying on financial incentives to induce people to leave the welfare rolls. He would simply give able-bodied people some advance notice and then stop sending them welfare benefits. Moreover, he would make neither college students nor strikers eligible for welfare.[32]

Since so much of the welfare problem involves unmarried women and their children, several specific ways have been suggested to reinforce parents' responsibility for the support of their children. They range from tough law enforcement to voluntary education. Examples include the following:

- Allowing lawyers to accept child support cases on a contingency fee basis
- Instituting mandatory paternity findings to identify fathers of out-of-wedlock children receiving welfare
- Holding all fathers accountable for meeting child support obligations and making strong efforts to collect from them
- Requiring young mothers on welfare to complete high school and then seek work
- Not paying welfare benefits to mothers under eighteen who are living in "independent households"[33]

The last recommendation would exclude from welfare benefits the many young teenagers who maintain separate households because they depend on welfare money. Under the proposed change, these children (and that is what they are) would have to stay with their parent(s)—or go to work.

Central to the new consensus on dealing with poverty is the conclusion that it has been a mistake to offer welfare benefits without imposing on the recipients the same obligations assumed by other citizens—to try to become self-sufficient through education, work, and responsible family behavior.

It is growing apparent that much of what used to be the conventional wisdom about a sound public assistance program is no longer widely endorsed, especially with reference to the desirability of keeping able-bodied people on welfare rolls for long periods of time. Hopkins describes very candidly what many consider to be the prevailing attitude toward welfare: it is a means by which many women can bear a child outside of marriage without great fear of financial risk and many males can avoid the financial obligations of fatherhood.[34]

The emerging consensus is in favor of encouraging welfare recipients, even those with young children, to get steady work. Serious researchers in the field conclude that trying to increase government transfer payments to the poor sufficiently to eliminate poverty would place in jeopardy the willingness of many other workers to take a host of low-paid and moderately paid jobs. In addition, there is solid evidence to support the widely held belief that welfare recipients migrate to states where they receive the best package of benefits. Furthermore, controlled experimental studies show that required job search or training is far more effective if the option not to work is prevented through a permanent-work requirement.[35]

The Working Seminar on the Family and American Welfare Policy concludes that it is *essential* that all able recipients of welfare be working or enrolled—and, it stressed, for just a limited time—in education and training programs. The seminar members urged that "the overriding emphasis" be placed on personal responsibility for finding jobs in the private sector—rather than on government projects.[36] Work is seen as more than just a way to cut welfare costs and promote self-sufficiency. It confers emotional and psychological benefits on the recipients and brings an opportunity to join the nation's mainstream.[37]

The coming decade may be unusually favorable for moving large numbers of people from welfare to work. Job opportunities for members of minority groups, especially, are expected to expand substantially in the coming decade. The labor force as a whole will grow more slowly as the relatively fewer offspring of the "baby bust" generation succeed the more numerous progeny of the "baby boom" generation. The Hudson Institute estimates that blacks, Hispanics, and other minorities will supply 29 percent of the net addition to the work force between 1985 and 2000, compared with only 18 percent between 1970 and 1985.

The "window of opportunity" may not be as wide open as the numbers suggest. The U.S. Department of Labor forecasts that the coming decade will see a much more rapid increase in high-skill jobs (23 percent) than in low-skill jobs (12 percent). Hence, on average, it will take more ability in mathematics and English to qualify for future employment than is now required. According to recent projections, by the year 2000, people with less than a high school education will be able to fill only 14 percent of all jobs, compared with 18 percent in 1987.[38]

The uneven experience with work requirements and other efforts to reform welfare suggests that major changes should not be introduced on a massive scale or designed for swift results. They should be made in the spirit of experimenting, based on the knowledge that nobody can be certain about what public policy can do to assure the reduction of poverty in America.

An example of the experimental approach is the state of Illinois's Project Chance. The state government claims that this blend of counseling, education, training, and related services helped more than 37,000 welfare recipients find jobs during 1987. The project leaders state that their approach is based on the recognition that individuals are responsible for their own economic well-being. The statements of a few of the successful graduates of Project Chance are heartening:

> I want to depend on myself to support my family. I like to work. . . . It makes me feel good about myself.
>
> It's important to take care of yourself, to pay your own bills, to earn a paycheck. Being on public aid is no free ride—you pay for it in pride.[39]

Most states have not given work requirements a high priority. Saying you tried to get a job by registering with the employment service is usually sufficient to meet the formal regulatory requirements. In West Virginia, however, workfare is seen as a way of providing public services that the state government cannot otherwise afford. Surveys of work site supervision indicate that people taking part in the workfare program were, on the average, about as productive as regular employees.[40]

Some scholars have criticized the workfare approach as a new form of "mass peonage," contending that forcing millions of "impoverished" Americans into an already overcrowded, underpaid labor force will not cure their poverty. Their answer is to raise welfare benefits "at least to the poverty level." Ignoring the concerns of working people who resent supporting able-bodied persons who stay on welfare, Frances Fox Piven and Barbara Ehrenreich phrase the problem in terms of how "to improve the morale of welfare recipients."[41] They take the position that women receiving welfare for raising children should not also be working. This position ignores the fact that, in 1986, some 53 percent of the mothers with children under six were in the labor force—as were 61 percent of all mothers. Barbara Bergmann estimated in late 1987 that more than half of the mothers with children under a year old are employed.[42]

The huge sums annually voted for programs to benefit the poor surely underscore the compassion of the U.S. electorate. Moreover, when a woman on welfare takes on a full-time job, the odds are overwhelming that she is lifting herself out of poverty.

In every state, a mother holding a full-time job at the minimum wage—plus the remaining welfare benefits that she is still eligible for—provide enough income to raise the average welfare family (one mother and two children) above the poverty level. Few women working steadily earn only the minimum wage. In 1984, the median annual earnings of full-time female workers without a high school degree was $10,436, and the minimum wage came to $6,968.

It may be helpful to summarize the key points that emerge from our review of the most current research on the causes and cures of poverty. At the risk of oversimplification, we can present our knowledge in the form of eight blunt statements:

1. Illegitimacy begets poverty.
2. Divorce induces poverty.
3. Dropping out of high school generates poverty.
4. Waiting for the dream job before starting to work assures poverty.
5. Marriage and family prevent poverty.
6. Schooling prevents poverty.
7. Working at almost any job prevents poverty.
8. Individual actions—rather than government or society—can prevent poverty.[43]

It is intriguing that a rather realistic view of the complexity of the poverty problem is presented by the socialist Michael Harrington. He candidly writes that two images have done more to set back the struggle against poverty than "all the efforts of reactionary politicians":

1. "a young black mugger knocking down an aging white woman as he steals her purse"
2. "a welfare mother with a large family, pregnant once again"[44]

It is unlikely that wholesale changes in life-styles, attitudes, and other characteristics of large numbers of low-income individuals can be achieved quickly. It is far more probable that the financial burden of maintaining large social welfare programs will continue to dominate the federal budget. Each month, about 3.7 million families receive benefits through the program of Aid to Families with Dependent Children. That is now the major source of government cash assistance to low-income children and their families and is likely to continue to be for some time. Any improvements will probably occur at the margins, but they are surely worth undertaking.

This review of the results and shortcomings of federal antipoverty

efforts in the United States supports the view that this nation has devoted extremely generous sums to supporting the poor without solving
the fundamental problem of poverty. The compassion underlying much
of current policy overlooks the fundamental—and increasingly relevant—conclusion reached by the philosopher Maimonides almost a millennium ago: the highest form of charity is to put people in the position
where they no longer need charity. Such a tack is likely to lead to more
cost-effective approaches during a period of budget stringency.

# 11

# Protecting the Environment

Although economists and environmentalists often find themselves on opposite sides of specific issues, they occupy some common ground. A healthful environment is essential for the effective conduct of economic and other human activities; even the most theoretical economist breathes the same air and drinks the same water as members of the Sierra Club—in fact, he or she may be a dues-paying member of that organization.

Likewise, a strong economy provides the resources for human activity, including dealing with ecological problems. It also generates the rising living standard that enables citizens to focus on serious concerns beyond the immediacy of paying for everyday necessities. Balancing economic and ecological concerns is hardly an either/or matter.

Any doubt on that score can be resolved by examining the plight of many East European nations. Their weak economies have been unable to support the environmental cleanup taking place in Western societies. The result has been "an ecological disaster zone," where even the snow is black. Fines levied on polluters are ineffective in their socialized economies because the government, as owner of all property, ends up paying the penalties.[1]

The situation is very different in the United States. Rather than subordinating environmental concerns to economic goals, we tend to ignore economic considerations in fashioning public policy on ecological issues. Let us see how these two important aspects of human endeavor can be reconciled.

## Protecting the Environment

Every poll of citizen sentiment shows overwhelming support for doing more to clean up the environment. A public opinion survey by the *New York Times* and CBS News reported in 1983 that 58 percent of the sample agreed with the following strong statement: "Protecting the environment is so important that requirements and standards cannot be too high and continuing environmental improvements must be made regardless of cost."[2]

Nevertheless, despite the continuation of such an overwhelming public mandate and a plethora of new laws and directives by the Environmental Protection Agency (EPA) plus tens of billions of dollars of compliance costs by private industry, the public remains unhappy with the results.

Unfortunately, environmental action is another and extremely important example of the failure of Americans to make tough choices. Those same citizens who want environmental improvements "regardless of cost" vociferously and adamantly oppose the location of any hazardous-waste facility in their own neighborhood. Nor are they keen on paying for the cleanup. Of course, they strongly favor cleaning up the environment, but each of them prefers to have the dump site located in someone else's backyard and to have the other fellow pay for it.

An example of this situation is the reaction of the enlightened citizens of Minnesota to a $3.7 million grant from the EPA to build and operate a state-of-the-art chemical landfill that could handle hazardous wastes with a high assurance of safety. In each of the sixteen locations that the state proposed, the local residents raised such a fuss and howl that the state government backed off. Ultimately, the unspent grant was returned to the EPA.

The Minnesota experience is not exceptional. The EPA was also forced to stop a project to test whether the sludge from a municipal waste treatment plant could be used as a low-cost fertilizer. The public opposition was fierce, even though the EPA was going to use federally owned land and the sludge was expected to increase crop yields by 30 percent.[3]

Since 1980, not a single major new disposal facility has been sited anywhere in the United States. According to a state-by-state review, the outlook for the future is "even more bleak," in large part because of a worsening of the emotional atmosphere surrounding any effort to locate a new dump site.[4] As Professor Peter Sandman of Rutgers University has pointed out, the public perceives environmental matters not only emotionally but also morally. "Our society," he has written, "has reached near-consensus that pollution is morally wrong—not just harmful or dangerous . . . but wrong."[5] Yet, the individuals that make up that same public are reluctant personally to assume the burdens associated with that strongly held view.

This ambivalent attitude toward the environment is not new. In the early 1970s, the National Wildlife Federation commissioned a national survey to ascertain how much people were willing to pay for a cleaner environment. At a time of peak enthusiasm for environmental regulation, the public was asked, "To stop the pollution destroying our plant life and wildlife, would you be willing to pay an increase in your monthly electric bill of $1?" The "no" vote won hands down, 62 percent to 28 percent (with 10 percent "not sure").[6] That study, we should recall, was taken before the big runup in utility bills. Perhaps not too surprisingly, the survey showed strong support for taxing business to finance environmental cleanup.

In other words, most of us Americans very much want a cleaner environment but are neither willing to pay for it nor seriously to inconvenience ourselves. We try to take the easy way out, by imposing the burden on "someone else," preferably a large, impersonal institution. Most of us remain oblivious to the key role that we as consumers play in this process when we continually demand rising amounts of goods and services whose production and distribution generate the great bulk of pollution. Let us try to see how the nation got into this policy box and then examine some opportunities for a solution.

## Trying to Do Everything at Once

Some perspective is provided by a look at whom people trust to recommend regulatory changes. In the case of the Clean Air Act, "environmental groups" receive a positive 74 percent, and "business and industry" is last with 39 percent.[7]

With such a strong mandate to follow the pleas of ecology activists, Congress has, not surprisingly, responded with a vast array of environmental statutes. On New Year's Day 1970, President Nixon signed into law the National Environmental Policy Act, opening a decade of intensive legislative activity aimed at protecting the environment. In the same year, Congress authorized the EPA to set national air quality standards and review state compliance plans. Since then, in an almost nonstop fashion, Congress has given the EPA added responsibilities— for water pollution control, pesticides regulation, safe drinking water, controlling toxic substances, disposing of hazardous wastes, cleaning up hazardous dump sites, eliminating asbestos in schools, regulating ocean dumping, and setting noise standards for railroads and trucks (for examples, see table 11-1).

It is much easier for Congress to express a desire for cleaner air or purer water than for an agency like the EPA to clean the air or purify the water. To be sure, vast sums of money have been spent for these purposes in recent years. From 1970 to 1986, Congress appropriated over $55 billion for the operation of the EPA. The head count of EPA employment rose from a few hundred in 1970 to over nine thousand in 1988. These numbers are dwarfed by the costs incurred in the private sector

TABLE 11-1

*The Multitude of Federal Laws Regulating Hazardous
and Toxic Wastes or Substances*

| Statute | Section of U.S. Code |
| --- | --- |
| Comprehensive Environmental Response, Compensation, and Liability Act | 42 U.S.C. 9601 |
| Resource Conservation and Recovery Act | 42 U.S.C. 6901 |
| Toxic Substances Control Act | 15 U.S.C. 2601 |
| Clean Water Act | 33 U.S.C. 1251 |
| Clean Air Act | 42 U.S.C. 7401 |
| Safe Drinking Water Act | 42 U.S.C. 300(f) |
| Federal Insecticide, Fungicide, and Rodenticide Act | 7 U.S.C. 136 |
| Consumer Product Safety Act | 15 U.S.C. 2051 |
| Occupational Safety and Health Act | 29 U.S.C. 651 |
| Hazardous Materials Transportation Act | 49 U.S.C. 1801 |
| Federal Hazardous Substances Act | 15 U.S.C. 1261 |
| Uranium Mill Tailings Radiation Control Act | 42 U.S.C. 7901 |
| Federal Food, Drug, and Cosmetic Act | 21 U.S.C. 301 |
| Poison Prevention Packaging Act | 15 U.S.C. 1471 |
| Lead-Based Paint Poisoning Prevention Act | 42 U.S.C. 4801 |
| Federal Disaster Relief Act | 42 U.S.C. 5121 |
| Marine Protection, Research and Sanctuaries Act* | 33 U.S.C. 1401 |
| Deepwater Ports Act* | 33 U.S.C. 1501 |
| Outer Continental Shelf Lands Act* | 43 U.S.C. 1801 |
| Intervention on the High Seas Act* | 33 U.S.C. 1471 |
| Trans-Alaska Pipeline Act* | 43 U.S.C. 1651 |
| Ports and Waterways Safety Act* | 33 U.S.C. 1221 |

*These statutes relate primarily to oil as a hazardous substance.
SOURCE: Center for the Study of American Business, Washington University.

to comply with the government's rules on environmental cleanup. The U.S. Council on Environmental Quality estimated the total at over $100 billion for 1988 and over $750 billion for the preceding decade (in dollars of 1986 purchasing power).[8]

These staggering outlays have not prevented the critics from instituting an almost endless array of lawsuits whose main purpose is to get the EPA to act faster and to do more. Typical of the assaults on the EPA is this statement by Congressman James J. Florio of New Jersey: "They are not in charge. They do not have the resources by their own actions to get the work done, and they are more interested in cosmetics than anything."[9]

The plaintive response of the EPA administrator Lee M. Thomas is that "EPA's plate is very full right now."[10] That plate is being heaped higher, too, as regulation of genetically engineered pesticides is added to the agency's responsibilities. Moreover, rapid scientific improvements permit the detection and, perhaps, regulation of ever more minute quantities of pollutants. Meanwhile, John Q. Public (and Jane Q. Public) are making the problem worse. In 1965, the average American disposed of three pounds of garbage a day. By 1985, that figure was up to four pounds each day and rising—in addition to wastes from agriculture, mining, industry, construction and demolition, sewage, and junked autos.[11]

To be sure, the EPA can claim important accomplishments. Between 1970 and 1985, air pollution from vehicles was reduced by 46 percent for hydrocarbons, 34 percent for carbon monoxide, and 75 percent for lead. Oil spills, common in the 1960s and early 1970s, are now rare events. Rivers from coast to coast that were nearly devoid of life teem with fish once again. Lake Erie, so laden with pollutants in 1969 that a river feeding into it caught fire, has been revived.[12]

Despite these successes, the EPA frequently falls short in meeting congressionally mandated goals for pollution cleanup; the number of dangerous dump sites filled with overflowing hazardous wastes continues to mount. A cynic might react to the mountain of environmental impact statements and regulatory issuances that are prepared each year with the plea "Let us mourn for all the trees that are needlessly cut down to meet the paperwork requirements of environmental statutes."

It is too easy for environmental groups to respond to serious ecological problems by blaming them all on neanderthals in the business community who do not care about the air we breathe, the water we drink, or the land we live on—and on the EPA for knuckling under to their pressures. Nor is public policy helped by the mirror image of that activity—business executives accusing both the EPA and environmental groups of not caring a whit about such practical matters as jobs or the economy.

The hard fact is that the status quo in environmental policy is not working. Congress continues to pass high-sounding legislation with unrealistic timetables and inflexible deadlines, while the EPA gets ever greater responsibility and private industry spends billions more on environmental compliance. Meanwhile, serious ecological problems worsen. In the words of the EPA's former administrator William Ruckelshaus, "EPA's statutory framework is less a coherent attack on a complex and integrated societal problem than it is a series of petrified postures."[13] Let us see if there are sensible ways out of this policy quandary.

Any solution to environmental problems is complicated by the simultaneous efforts of state and, often, local agencies to show their concern. Many states have enacted new "right-to-know" statutes. In Missouri, the law requires businesses to send to the local fire department information on toxic substances they use or produce. The reaction to this invitation to flood local government with paperwork was readily predictable by anyone with a knowledge of the problems of complying with existing environmental regulations. The following comment by the chief of the Fire Protection District of Valley Park, Missouri, is typical: "Some companies have already sent us boxes and boxes full of this stuff. We don't have any facility to store it. If there was an emergency at a plant, by the time we went through all the information, it'd be over with."[14]

## Some Economic Solutions

Turning to specific environmental problems, we can start with the controversy over the disposal of hazardous wastes. Instances of toxic-waste contamination at Love Canal, in New York State, and at Times Beach, Missouri, have brought a sense of urgency to the problem. The public mood on the subject of hazardous waste leaves little room for patience—but much opportunity for emotional response.

Emotionally charged responses are encouraged by the fact that even scientists know little about the effects on human health of many toxic substances, such as the various forms of dioxin. Levels of some sub-stances can now be measured by the EPA in terms of parts per billion and occasionally per quadrillion, but even the experts still debate the significance of exposure at those rates. In effect, the scare headlines about chemical health hazards deal with exposures that are akin to the proverbial needle in the haystack. Actually, the needle-haystack com-parison is much too modest. One part per billion is the equivalent of one inch in 16,000 miles, a penny in $10 million, four drops of water in an Olympic-size pool, or a second in thirty-two years.

The most severe reaction to dioxin reported so far by humans is a bad case of chloracne, a severe acne-like rash. The bulk of the available information on dioxin and other hazards is based on extrapolating from data on animal experiments, which is very tricky. Most tests on animals are conducted at extremely high concentrations of the suspected ele-ment, which do not reflect real-world conditions in which the animals (or humans) live. Scientists note that the massive doses that are fed the animals overwhelm their entire bodies. Moreover, a level of exposure that is harmful to one type of animal may not be injurious to another. For example, the lethal dose of the most toxic dioxin (2,3,7,8 TCDD) for hamsters is 5,000 times higher than that for guinea pigs.[15] Extrapolating the results to humans is even more conjectural.

However, our hearts must go out to the people in Times Beach, Mis-souri, and in Love Canal, New York, who have suffered severe psycho-logical and financial damage from the emotional responses to the scare stories they have seen and heard so frequently.

In trying to avoid a repetition of these situations, the EPA has promul-gated detailed regulations on how polluters must keep track of hazard-ous wastes and how they should dispose of them. Because of growing public concern over leaky and dangerous dump sites, Congress in late 1986 extended and expanded Superfund, the program designed to clean up hazardous-waste sites. The law requires companies and, ultimately, consumers to pay in $9 billion by 1991.[16] Yet, despite all this effort and attention, the problem of how to dump hazardous wastes is scarcely less serious than it was in 1980, before Congress passed the original Super-fund law.

As it stands, the law provides for a large fund raised largely through taxes on producers of chemical and petroleum products. The EPA uses this money to identify and clean up hazardous wastes and waste sites. But little progress is made because, as we noted earlier, there is a severe shortage of dump sites.

## Protecting the Environment

A more clearheaded view of waste disposal problems is needed in the United States. Because definitions vary among levels of government, estimates of the amount of hazardous waste disposed of each year in the United States range from 30 million to 264 million metric tons. Most of this waste is buried in landfills because incineration, the safest and most effective means of disposal, is nearly ten times as costly. Even so, government and industry spend over $5 billion each year to manage toxic wastes. The annual price by 1990 is projected to reach $12 billion.[17]

Many experts believe that using landfills is inherently unsafe, if for no other reason than that they are only storage sites. Moreover, there are not enough of them. The EPA estimates that 22,000 waste sites now exist in the United States, and fully 10 percent of them are believed to be dangerous and leaking.

The result: not enough reliable, environmentally safe places to dump toxic substances. Although the EPA wants to clean up as many landfills as possible, it has very little choice as to where to put the material it removes under the Superfund mandate. Taxpayers may wind up paying for the costly removal of waste from one site across the country, only to find later on that they have to pay again for removing it from yet another dangerous site. Meanwhile, legal fees mushroom. The litigation costs involving cleanup at the various Superfund sites are estimated to run somewhere between $3.5 billion and $6.4 billion.[18]

### INCENTIVES FOR LOCATING TOXIC DUMPS

Eventually, society will have to face the main reason for the scarcity of hazardous-waste sites—the "not in my backyard" syndrome. Sites for the disposal of toxic substances have joined prisons and mental hospitals as things the public wants, but not too close by.

The hazardous-waste-disposal problem is not going to disappear unless Americans change to less polluting methods of production and consumption. Until then, greater understanding is needed on the part of the public and a willingness to come to grips with the difficult problems arising from the production and use of hazardous substances. As we found in other areas, dealing with important and continuing national problems inevitably involves making hard choices. Of course, it will cost large amounts of money (probably in the tens of billions of private and public expenditures in the next decade) to meet society's environmental expectations. But spending money may be the easiest part of the problem. Getting people to accept dump sites in their neighborhoods is much more difficult.

The answer is surely an appeal not merely to good citizenship but also to common sense and self-interest. In a totalitarian society, people who do not want to do something the government desires are simply forced to do so, with the threat of physical violence ever present. In a free society with a market economy, in striking contrast, we offer to pay people to do something they otherwise would not do. The clearest example in modern times is the successful elimination of the military draft coupled with very substantial increases in pay and fringe benefits for those who voluntarily serve in the armed forces.

Individual citizens have much to gain by opposing hazardous-waste facilities to be located near them, and there is a basic logic to their position. It is not fair for society as a whole to benefit from a new disposal site, while imposing most of the costs (ranging from danger of leakage to depressed property values) on the people in the locality. But local resistance to dealing with hazardous wastes does impose large costs on society as a whole. Those costs are in the form both of inhibiting economic progress and of having to ship waste from one temporary site to another.

There is a way of reconciling individual interests and community concerns. It is by the use of economic incentives. The idea is to look upon environmental pollution not as a sinful act but as an activity costly to society and susceptible to reduction by means of proper incentives. After all, the prospect of jobs and income encourages many communities to offer tax holidays and other enticements to companies considering the location of a new factory—even though it may not exactly improve the physical environment of the region. Under present arrangements, however, there is no incentive for the citizens of an area to accept a site for hazardous wastes in their vicinity, no matter how safe it is.

But perhaps some areas would accept such a facility if the state government (financed by all the citizens benefiting from the disposal facility) would pay for something the people in that locality want but cannot afford—such as a new school building, firehouse, or library or simply lower property taxes.[19] Unlike an industrial factory, a hazardous-waste facility provides few offsetting benefits to the local residents in the form of jobs or tax revenues.[20]

An episode in 1985 shows the promise of the incentive approach. In the town of Lisbon, Connecticut, an entrepreneur proposed to locate a modern incinerator that would generate both energy from waste and $1 million in tax revenues. Despite the financial incentive and assurance that the incinerator would be equipped with the latest antipollution devices, he was rebuffed. Then the businessman tried another tactic. Instead of saying that the new facility would bring the town $1 million a year income in additional taxes, he promised to pay the property taxes of every landowner in the town for the next twenty-five years. Actually, the total cost would be about the same. But individual citizens could appreciate the direct benefits of the second approach.

Local opposition to the undertaking quickly diminished. A town referendum on the incinerator yielded a vote of 680 in favor and 540 opposed. But that vote was only advisory. Later on, the town planning and zoning commission voted 5 to 4 against the project. The incentive approach, in the case of Lisbon, can be described as producing a near miss. Yet, the incident does show the latent support for making difficult trade-offs when citizens are provided with some reasonable—and, in this case, imaginative—alternatives.

A more direct example of using economic incentives to locate inherently undesirable storage facilities occurred in 1987. A proposed dump site for medical supplies contaminated by low-level radiation was estimated to provide about forty new jobs. Three poor communities in the Mojave Desert region in southern California vied spiritedly for the project, overcoming their concerns over possible environmental impact.[21]

Also in 1987, Senators J. Bennett Johnston, Jr. (Democrat of Louisiana), and James McClure (Republican of Idaho) proposed that a state agreeing to the location of a nuclear disposal site within its borders would receive large incentive payments from the Department of Energy. Over the thirty- to forty-year life of the repository project, these payments would run to several billion dollars. The governor of Nevada, a likely location, denounced the notion as "bribery" and "nuclear blackmail." Yet, in 1978, a state blue-ribbon panel recommended radioactive-waste disposal as a prime alternative use of the Nevada Test Site in the event of a ban on nuclear testing. It does seem that economic incentives can play a role in hazardous-waste disposal, but a good deal of time, patience, and effort may be required.[22]

There is much that government can do to improve environmental policy in other ways. The EPA could reduce the entire hazardous-waste problem by distinguishing between truly lethal wastes—which clearly should be disposed of with great care—and wastes that contain only trace or minute amounts of undesirable materials. To the extent that changes in legislation would be required, the agency should urge Congress to make them.

The experience of a company in Oregon provides insights into why Congress needs to legislate common sense into the antipollution laws. The firm has been dumping heavy-metal sludges on its property for over twenty years. Company officials told the General Accounting Office that they automatically classify the material as hazardous. Why? Because it would be too costly and time-consuming to try to prove that it was not. The GAO learned from several industry associations that other companies, similarly uncertain and wanting to avoid expensive testing costs, simply declare their wastes to be hazardous, whether they really are dangerous or not.[23] That is not the only example in which those complying with environmental regulations lose sight of the fundamental objectives to be met.

A 1987 EPA report concluded that the agency's priorities "do not correspond well" with its rankings by risk of the various ecological problems that it is dealing with. Thus, the agency's own study found areas of high risk but little regulatory effort. A key example is runoff of polluted water from farms and city streets.

Conversely, the study showed that areas of "high EPA effort but relatively low risks" included management of hazardous wastes, cleanup of chemical waste dumps, regulation of underground storage tanks containing petroleum or other hazardous substances, and municipal solid waste.[24] The reason for this mismatch between needs and resources is obvious. The EPA's priorities are set by Congress and reflect public pressure more than scientific knowledge. Driven by the forces of environmental politics, the nation has repeatedly committed itself to goals and programs that are unrealistic. This has meant deploying regulatory manpower unwisely and diverting limited resources to concerns of marginal importance.

The results of this mismatch are substantial. Not all hazards are created equal. Some disposal sites are being filled with innocuous material while truly dangerous substances are or will be, for lack of space, dumped illegally or stored "temporarily." What would help is more widespread application of the legal concept known as *de minimis non curat lex*—the law does not concern itself with trifles.

Back in 1979, a federal circuit court supported the view that there is a *de minimis* level of risk too small to affect human health adversely. It cited that doctrine in turning down the claim that some "migration" of substances occurred from the packaging into the food product. In 1985, the FDA concluded that using methylene chloride to extract caffeine from coffee presented a *de minimis* risk. Hence, the substance is safe for its intended use. In 1987, the National Research Council recommended that the EPA apply a "negligible risk" standard across the board in determining how much of which pesticides may be permitted to show up in food.[25]

## A BIRTH CONTROL APPROACH TO POLLUTION

Over 99 percent of the environmental spending by government is devoted to controlling pollution after waste is generated. Less than 1 percent is spent to reduce the generation of waste.[26] For fiscal 1988, the EPA budgeted only $398,000—or .03 percent of its funds—for "waste minimization." That is an umbrella term that includes recycling and waste reduction.[27]

The most desirable approach is to reduce the generation of hazardous wastes in the first place. Economists have an approach that is useful— providing incentives to manufacturers to change their production processes to reduce the amount of wastes created or to recycle them in a safe and productive manner.

As we noted earlier, the government taxes producers rather than polluters. By doing that, the country misses a real opportunity to curb the actual dumping of dangerous waste. The federal Superfund law is financed with a combination of taxes levied on producers of chemical "feedstocks" and petroleum plus a surtax on the profits of large manufacturing companies and contributions from the federal Treasury. Thousands of companies outside of the oil and chemical industries wind up paying very little, whether they are large polluters or not. Contrary to widely held views, a great deal of pollution occurs in sectors of the economy other than oil and chemicals. The manufacture of a single TV set generates about one hundred pounds of toxic wastes.[28]

Switching to a waste-end fee levied on the amount of hazardous wastes that a company actually generates and disposes of would be far more economically sound than the status quo. That would require a basic correction in that major piece of environmental legislation called the Comprehensive Environmental Response, Compensation, and Liability Act (or "Superfund").

If the government were to levy a fee on the amount of hazardous materials discharged, that would provide an incentive to reduce the actual generation of such waste. Some companies would find it cheaper to change their production processes than to pay the tax. Recycling and reuse systems would be encouraged. Moreover, such a tax or fee would cover imports that are now disposed of in our country tax free. In short, rewriting the Superfund law so that it is more fair would also help protect the environment—and would probably save money at the same time.

Already, some companies are recycling as they become aware of the economic benefits.[29] For example, one chemical firm burns 165,000 tons of coal a year at one of its textile fibers factories, generating 35,000 tons of waste in the form of fly ash. The company recently found a local cement block company that was testing fly ash as a replacement for limestone in making lightweight cement blocks. The chemical company now sells the fly ash to the cement block manufacturer. What used to be an undesirable waste by-product has been turned into a commercially useful material. Simultaneously, the companies are conserving the supply of limestone.

A timber company through its research developed a new use for tree bark, the last massive waste product of the wood products industry. The firm designed a bark processor that made it the first domestic producer of vegetable wax, an important ingredient in cosmetics and polishes. A factory in Illinois had been creating a veritable sea of calcium fluoride sludge (at the rate of 1,000 cubic yards a month) as a by-product of its manufacture of fluorine-based chemicals. The company found that the sludge could be mixed with another waste product to produce synthetic fluorspar, which it had been buying from other sources. Recycling the two waste products now saves the firm about $1 million a year.

Incentives to do more along these lines could be provided in several ways. The producers could be subsidized to follow the desired approach. In this period of large budget deficits, that would, of course, increase the amount of money the Treasury must borrow.

A different alternative is to tax the generation and disposal of hazardous wastes. The object would be not to punish the polluters but to get them to change their ways. If something becomes more expensive, business firms have a natural desire to use less of the item. In this case, the production of pollution (specifically, hazardous wastes) would become more expensive. Every sensible firm would try to reduce the amount of pollution tax it pays by curbing its hazardous wastes. Adjusting to new taxes on pollution would be a matter not of patriotism but of minimizing cost and maximizing profit. The pollution tax approach appeals to self-interest in order to promote the public interest.

Charging polluters for the pollution they cause gives companies an incentive to find innovative ways to cut down on their discharges.[30] These fees would raise costs and hence prices for products whose production generates a lot of pollution. It is wrong to view that as a way of shifting the burden to the public. The relevant factor is that consumer purchasing is not static. Consumer demand would shift to products that pollute less, because they would cost less. To stay competitive, high-polluting producers would have to economize on pollution, just as they do with other costs of production. Since pollution imposes burdens on the environment, it is only fair that the costs of cleaning up that pollution should be reflected in the price of a product whose production generates this burden.

Nine countries in Western Europe have adopted the "polluter pays" principle. In these nations, pollution control is paid for directly by the polluting firm or from the money collected from effluent taxes. The West German effluent-fee system, the oldest in operation, began before World War I. It has succeeded in halting the decline in water quality throughout the Ruhr Valley, the center of West Germany's iron and steel production. It is also serving as a model for a more recent French effort.[31]

Practical problems make changes in pollution policy difficult in the United States. Both the regulators and the regulated have an interest in maintaining the current approach. Pollution taxes have little appeal in the political system, particularly in the Congress. Many reject a pollution tax on philosophical grounds, considering pollution charges a "license to pollute." They believe that putting a price on the act of polluting amounts to an attitude of moral indifference toward polluters. That gets us back to the point made earlier, that many people look at ecological matters as moral issues—which makes it especially difficult to adopt a more rational and workable approach.

THE PUBLIC SECTOR DRAGS ITS FEET

A word of caution: many people fall into a common trap—that of associating polluters exclusively with business. Many companies do generate lots of toxic waste, and not all of them handle it properly. But the same can be said about government agencies, hospitals, schools, and colleges. Moreover, the EPA lacks the enforcement power over the public sector that it possesses over the private sector. Reports of plant closings because of the high cost of meeting environmental standards are common. In contrast, there is no record of a single government facility closing down because it was not meeting ecological requirements.

It is not surprising that the General Accounting Office (GAO) says that the performance of federal agencies in carrying out the requirements of hazardous-waste disposal "has not been exemplary." A GAO report issued in 1986 says that, of 72 federal facilities inspected, 33 were in violation of EPA requirements; and 22 had been cited for Class 1 (serious) violations. Sixteen of the 33 facilities remained out of compliance for six months or more. Three had not been in compliance for more than three years.[32] A follow-up report by the GAO in 1987 showed little further progress. Only 4 of 11 federal agencies had completed the identification of hazardous-waste sites and none had finished assessing the environmental problems they had uncovered. Of 511 federal sites failing to meet EPA standards, only 78 had been cleaned up.[33]

A major offender is the Department of Defense, which now generates over 500,000 tons of hazardous waste a year. That is more than is produced by the five largest chemical companies combined.[34] The lax situation uncovered by the GAO at Tinker Air Force Base, in Oklahoma, is typical of the way in which many federal agencies respond to the EPA's directives: "Although DOD [Department of Defense] policy calls for the military services to . . . implement EPA's hazardous waste management regulations, we found that Tinker has been selling . . . waste oil, fuels, and solvents rather than . . . recycling. . . ."[35]

The GAO reported that two of the five commercial waste sites receiving the base's wastes had major compliance problems. Also, personnel at Tinker Air Force Base were dumping hazardous wastes in landfills that themselves were in violation of EPA requirements. In one case, the EPA had been urging the Oklahoma Department of Health for several years not to renew its permit. In another instance, the State Water Resources Board was seeking a court order to close the site. Civilian agencies, including those in state and local governments, continue to be reluctant to follow the same environmental standards that they impose on the private sector.[36]

To put it mildly, the federal government does not set a good example in complying with its own environmental directives. It expects the private sector to take environmental concerns far more seriously than it does itself. The point is not to let anyone off the hook. The solution is quite obvious: what is sauce for the private-sector goose should also be sauce for the public-sector gander.

Also, federal policy arbitrarily excludes one of the largest single sources of pollution from the EPA's effective jurisdiction: the runoff of pesticides and fertilizers from farms.[37] The EPA reports that, in six of the agency's ten regions, pollution from farms and urban streets is the principal cause of water quality problems. But pollution from these sources remains unregulated.

## Protecting the Environment

Large quantities of agricultural pollution can be controlled fairly easily at low cost by using limited-till plowing techniques. In striking contrast, industrial pollution control has often been pushed to the limits of economic feasibility. Nevertheless, Congress follows a double standard: for urban and industrial pollution it requires the imposition of tough and detailed standards to qualify for permits to discharge wastes. For rural and farm pollution, the EPA is merely given money to study the problem.

Again, we see the failure to make tough decisions. Like the rest of us, Congress wants a cleaner environment. But so far it has not mustered the will required to impose the most modest pollution controls on a politically powerful group of constituents. To be sure, farm families want a cleaner environment—but it is always nice to get someone else to pay for your desires.

## Regulation Is a Broader Issue

Although economists are often accused of being patsies for the business community, environmental economics makes for strange alliances. So far, business interests have opposed the suggestions of economists for such sweeping changes in the basic structure of government regulation as using taxes on pollution. Despite the shortcomings of the present system of government regulation, many firms have paid the price of complying with existing rules. They have learned to adjust to regulatory requirements and to integrate existing regulatory procedures into their long-term planning.

As any serious student of business-government relations will quickly report, the debate over regulation is miscast when it is described as black-hatted business versus white-hatted public-interest groups. Almost every regulatory action creates winners and losers in the business system and often among other interest groups. Clean-air legislation, focusing on ensuring that new facilities fully meet standards, is invariably supported by existing firms that are "grandfathered" approval without having to conform to the same high standards as new firms. Regulation thus protects the "ins" from the "outs."

There are many other examples of regulatory bias against change and especially against new products, new processes, and new buildings. Tough emissions standards are set for new automobiles but not for older ones. Testing and licensing procedures for new drugs and new chemicals are more rigorous and more thoroughly enforced than for existing substances. Safety standards are established for new cars, not for existing vehicles.

Other nonenvironmental motives come into play in the political arena for which government policy is set. Unions and unionized employers favor tough enforcement of job safety and health rules because such unionized companies already meet those standards or come close. Many nonunionized firms, in contrast, may be operating far below these standards. Hence, regulation in such circumstances helps reduce any competitive gap between high-cost firms with tough safety standards and those low-cost companies with easier standards.

This ability to profit from the differential impacts of regulation helps explain why business shows little enthusiasm for the use of economic incentives and prefers current regulatory techniques. But the reform of regulation is truly a consumer issue. The consumer receives the benefits from regulation and bears the burden of the costs of compliance in the form of higher prices and less product variety. Thus, the consumer has the key stake in improving the current regulatory morass.

The problems of regulatory choice are not limited to environmental policy. Most social legislation is written in absolutes. Regulatory statutes declare that workers will be protected, that energy will be conserved, and that consumer products will be safe. But when conflicts among these—and other—worthy goals develop, as they inevitably must, there is no way of deciding which goal is to have priority or what trade-offs are to be made among them. Given the nation's reluctance to make hard choices, this increasing gridlock in regulatory programs is not surprising. The following chapter presents approaches for overhauling the entire regulatory apparatus.

## A NECESSARY DIGRESSION ON CANCER

One approach to eliminating that gridlock in regulatory policy is to focus on the underlying public concern that is driving the pressures for more sweeping environmental and other social regulation. That concern is the worry about cancer. The regulatory waters have become badly muddied by the public's misconception of the causes of cancer. A widely held notion is that the environment is primarily responsible. There is, of course, a germ of truth to that belief.

It turns out that several years ago a distinguished scientist—John Higginson, director of the World Health Organization's International Agency for Research on Cancer—assigned the primary blame for cancer to what he labeled "environmental" causes. His highly publicized finding that two-thirds of all cancer was caused by environmental factors provided ammunition for every ecological group to push for tougher restrictions on all sorts of environmental pollution.

However, upon a more careful reading, it is clear that the eminent scientist was referring not to the physical environment but to the age-old debate of "environment" versus "heredity" as the main influence on human beings. In the case of cancer, he was identifying voluntary behavior—such as personal life-styles and the kinds of food people eat —as the main culprit responsible for cancer. Dr. Higginson specifically pointed out, "But when I used the term environment in those days, I was considering the total environment, cultural as well as chemical . . . air you breathe, the culture you live in, the agricultural habits of your community, the social cultural habits, the social pressures, the physical chemicals with which you come in contact, the diet, and so on."[38] But that explanation has not slowed down the highly vocal ecology groups that latched on to a "catchy" albeit confused theme—the extremely carcinogenic environment in which Americans supposedly live.

More recently, one university scientist tried to add some objectivity to the cancer debate by quantifying the issue. Professor Harry Demopoulos of the New York Medical Center examined why approximately 1,000 people die of cancer each day in the United States. About 450 of the deaths, or 45 percent, are attributable to diet. Citing the work of Dr. Arthur Upton of the National Cancer Institute, Demopoulos noted that eating more fresh fruits and vegetables and curtailing fat consumption would be most helpful.[39] Clearly, obesity is not the type of environmental pollution that justifies the EPA's increasingly onerous standards.

The second major cause of cancer deaths, according to Demopoulos, is the consumption of excessive quantities of distilled liquor and the smoking of high-tar cigarettes. These voluntary actions resulted in 350, or 35 percent, of the cancer deaths. Again, this is not the environmental pollution that motivates most ecology activists.

A distant third in the tabulation of leading causes of cancer are occupational hazards, which account for 5 percent of the total. Demopoulos believes that this category may have leveled off and be on the way down. He reasons that many of the occupationally induced cancers are due to exposures two or more decades ago, when scientists did not know that many chemicals were capable of causing cancer.

A fourth category, accounting for 3 percent, is caused by exposure to normal background radiation. The fifth and last category of causes of cancer (accounting for 2 percent) is preexisting medical disorders. These include chronic ulcerative colitis, chronic gastritis, and the like. The remaining 10 percent of the cancer deaths in the United States are due to all other causes; it is noteworthy that air and water pollution and all the other toxic hazards that are the primary cause of public worry are in this miscellaneous 10 percent, not in the 90 percent. Government policy is unbalanced when the great bulk of the effort deals with a category of risk that is only some fraction of one-tenth of the problem.

Hard data can dissipate much of the fear and fog generated by the many cancer-scare stories that the public has been subjected to in recent years. Overall, cancer death rates are staying steady or coming down. The major exception is smoking-related cancer. For the decade 1974–83, stomach cancer was down 20 percent, cancer of the cervix-uterus was down 30 percent, and cancer of the ovary was down 8 percent.

Life expectancy is steadily increasing in the United States (to an all-time high of seventy-five, for those born in 1985)[40] and in most other industrialized nations, except the Soviet Union. This has led the cancer expert Professor Bruce Ames of the University of California to conclude, "We are the healthiest we have been in human history."[41] That is no justification for resting on laurels. Rather, Ames's point should merely help lower the decibel level of debates on environmental issues and enable analysis to dominate emotion in setting public policy in this vital area.

# 12

# *Regulation as a Consumer Issue*

In the preceding chapter, we saw that there is a reciprocal relation between environmental regulation and economic performance. That point can be generalized. All types of government regulation of business can affect the health of the economy. Thus, any comprehensive effort to achieve a stronger and more competitive economy must include an agenda for regulatory reform.

## Government Regulation and the Consumer

At first glance, the government imposition of socially desirable requirements on business appears to be an inexpensive way of achieving national objectives. It seems to cost the government little (aside from the expenses of the regulatory agencies themselves, usually overlooked) and therefore is not recognized as much of a burden on the taxpayer.

But the public does not escape paying the full cost. Every time an agency, in its attempt to safeguard occupational safety and health, imposes on business a more expensive method of production, the cost of the resultant product will necessarily rise. Whenever a commission supervising the safety of products imposes a standard that is more costly to attain, some products will increase in price. The same holds true for the activities of agencies protecting the environment, monitoring the food and drug industries, and so forth.

Although the costs of compliance with the directives of government agencies are buried in corporate cost accounts, such costs amount to a substantial hidden tax on the consumer. If consumers knew how much they were paying for regulation, they would probably be very upset. The high cost generated by rule making results in large part because government agencies do not feel great pressure to worry about it. Compliance costs show up not in their budgets but in those of the private sector.

At issue is not the desirability of the objectives of regulatory agencies; that subject will be examined a little later. Rather, the point is that the public does not get a "free lunch" by imposing government requirements on private industry. Although the costs of complying with regulation are not borne by taxpayers directly, they show up in higher prices of the goods and services that consumers buy and, often, in reduced product variety.

Perhaps more important than the amount of money involved is the increasing intervention by government in the daily lives of its citizens. Decisions by one or more government agencies alter, influence, or even determine what we can buy, how we may use the goods and services we own, and how we earn our daily living. Government decisions increasingly affect what we wear, what we eat, and how we play.[1] Few items of business or consumer expenditures escape regulation by one or more national, state, or local government agencies. Table 12-1 gives a representative sample limited primarily to the federal level.

## Regulation and the Business Firm

The pervasive expansion in the regulation of business that has been occurring in the United States in recent years is also altering fundamentally the relation between business and government. The concept of a regulated industry has become archaic. We now live in an economy in which every company feels the power of government in its day-to-day operations.

If we could accurately measure the pervasiveness of government

TABLE 12-1

## The Broad Scope of Government Regulation

| Category | Regulatory Agency |
|---|---|
| Air travel | Federal Aviation Administration |
| Automobiles | National Highway Traffic Safety Administration |
| Bank deposits | Federal Deposit Insurance Corporation and Comptroller of the Currency |
| Boats | Coast Guard |
| Bus travel | Interstate Commerce Commission |
| Cigarettes | Public Health Service |
| Consumer credit | Federal Reserve System |
| Consumer products generally | Consumer Product Safety Commission |
| Consumer products containing chemicals | Environmental Protection Agency |
| Cosmetics | Food and Drug Administration |
| Credit union deposits | National Credit Union Administration |
| Drinking water | Environmental Protection Agency |
| Drugs (prescription and over-the-counter) | Food and Drug Administration |
| Eggs | Department of Agriculture |
| Election campaigns | Federal Election Commission |
| Electricity and gas | Federal Energy Regulatory Commission and state public service commissions |
| Exports | Departments of Commerce and Treasury |
| Firearms | Bureau of Alcohol, Tobacco, and Firearms |
| Flood insurance | Federal Insurance Administration |
| Food | Food and Drug Administration and Department of Agriculture |
| Housing | Federal Housing Administration and local building codes |
| Imports | International Trade Commission and Department of Treasury |
| Land | Office of Interstate Land Sales Registration and local agencies |
| Livestock and processed meat | Packers and Stockyards Administration |
| Meat and poultry | Animal and Plant Health Inspection Service |
| Milk | Federal and state departments of agriculture |
| Narcotics | Drug Enforcement Administration |
| Newspaper and magazine advertising | Federal Trade Commission |
| Pensions | Internal Revenue Service and Department of Labor |
| Petroleum and natural gas | Department of Energy |
| Potatoes | State Agricultural Agencies |
| Medical fees | Professional Standards Review Organizations |
| Radio and television | Federal Communications Commission |
| Railroad and bus travel | Interstate Commerce Commission |
| Savings and loan deposits | Federal Home Loan Bank Board |
| Stocks and bonds | Securities and Exchange Commission |
| Telephone service | Federal Communications Commission and state public service commissions |

intervention, we would not find the economists' favorites—electric utilities and railroads—at the top of the list. More likely, it would be such giants of the manufacturing sector as automobile, aerospace, and chemical companies, with the oil industry and health services not too far behind.

It is hard to overestimate the rapid expansion and the great variety of the American government's involvement in business. The major growth of government regulation is not in the traditional independent regulatory agencies, such as the Federal Communications Commission. (As will be discussed later, significant "deregulation" is occurring in the old-line regulatory commissions.) Rather, federal power over business is expanding by use of the operating bureaus of government—in the Departments of Agriculture, Commerce, Energy, Health and Human Services, Interior, Justice, Labor, Transportation, and Treasury—and by means of separate executive branch units, such as the Environmental Protection Agency. Approximately 85 percent of the budgets for federal regulation is assigned to social regulation and only 15 percent to the older forms of economic regulation.[2]

No business today, large or small, can operate without obeying a myriad of government restrictions and regulations. Entrepreneurial decisions fundamental to the business enterprise have become subject to government influence, review, or control—such decisions as what lines of business to go into, what products and services to produce, which investments to finance, how to produce goods and services, where to make them, how to market them, what prices to charge, and what profit to keep.

Virtually every major department of the American corporation has one or more counterparts in a government agency that controls or strongly influences its internal decision making. There is almost a "shadow" organization chart of public officials matching the formal structure of each private company. The scientists in corporate research laboratories now do much of their work to ensure that the products they develop are not rejected by lawyers in regulatory agencies. The engineers in manufacturing departments must make sure the equipment they specify meets the standards promulgated by Labor Department authorities. Marketing staffs must follow procedures established by government administrators in product safety agencies. The location of business facilities must conform with a variety of environmental statutes. The activities of personnel staffs are geared in large measure to meeting the standards of the various agencies concerned with employment conditions. Finance departments bear the brunt of the rising paperwork burden imposed on business by government agencies.

Few aspects of business escape government review or influence. As a result, important internal adjustments have been taking place in the structure and operation of the typical corporation. Each major business function has undergone an important transformation. These changes have increased the overhead costs of doing business and often deflected management and employee attention from the conventional tasks of designing, developing, producing, and distributing new and better or cheaper goods and services. The cost of complying with domestic regulation can be a significant handicap in competing against foreign firms that produce under less burdensome regulatory regimes.

Numerous chief executives report that one-third or more of their time is now devoted to governmental and public policy matters—dealing with the many federal, state, and local regulations that affect the company, meeting with a wide variety of civic and special-interest groups that make demands on the organization's resources, and increasingly participating in the public policy arena. Donald Rumsfeld, former chief executive of a major pharmaceuticals company, has described very personally the pervasiveness of government involvement in business:

> When I get up in the morning as a businessman, I think a lot more about government than I do about our competition, because government is that much involved—whether it's HEW, IRS, SEC, FTC, FDA. I always understood the problem intellectually, but the specific inefficiencies that result from the government, injecting itself into practically every aspect of our business— that is something one can feel only by being here.[3]

The impetus for most of the expansion in government power over business does not come from the industries being regulated; generally, they have shown a minimum of enthusiasm for EPA, OSHA, EEOC, ERISA, and the rest of the government's alphabet soup. If anything, companies claim that their "benefits" from these regulations are negative. The pressures for the new style of regulation come, rather, from a variety of citizen groups concerned primarily with noneconomic aspects of national life—environmentalists, consumer groups, labor unions, and civil rights organizations.

To say or write that the regulated industry is "capturing" its regulators is, to put it kindly, a quaint way of viewing the fundamental shift in business decision making taking place, the shift of power from private managers to public officials. Yet, the core of the economist's version of the "capture" theory still holds—public policy tends to be dominated by the organized and compact pressure groups that attain their benefits at the expense of the more diffused and larger body of consumers.

But the nature of those interest groups has changed in recent years. Rather than the railroad baron (a relatively easy target for attack), the villain of the piece has often become a self-styled representative of the public interest who has succeeded in identifying his or her personal prejudices with the national well-being. It is fascinating—and perhaps ironic—how much business firms, in performing the traditional middleman function, serve the unappreciated and involuntary role of proxy for the overall consumer interest. That is most apparent in the case of retailers opposing restrictions on imports that would raise the prices of the goods they buy—and sell.

## Examining the Benefits of Regulation

The benefits of regulation should not be overlooked. To the extent that government rules result in healthier workplaces, safer products, and so forth, these benefits are very real. These words have been chosen very carefully. The mere presence of a government agency does not automatically guarantee that its worthy objectives will be achieved, nor are we justified in jumping to the opposite conclusion that no government agencies can achieve any good. The difficult and double-barreled question that needs to be answered is, How much benefit does the regulation produce and is it worth the cost? Society's bottom line is not the impact of regulatory actions on government or on business but the effect on consumers and on citizens generally.

The relevant issue is therefore not a broadly philosophical one: Are you for or against government intervention? Rather, it involves a very practical question: Does this specific type of government activity work? The sad reality is that it often does not or that it works against the interest of the consumer. This reality has been recognized in some areas. As is pointed out later in this chapter, deregulation of the airlines has reduced the costs of traveling substantially. Cutting back the regulation of railroads and trucking has likewise benefited consumers, albeit indirectly, by permitting competition to hold down the cost of shipping commodities.

## Regulation as a Consumer Issue

Consider drug regulation by the Food and Drug Administration (FDA). A look at the mortality data—rather than at the rhetoric—shows that, for decades, the leading causes of death in this country have been heart attacks and strokes. There exists a series of new drugs for these illnesses called beta blockers, which were in widespread use in the United Kingdom and other developed nations for many years before they could be purchased in the United States.

This nation, however, lagged in the introduction of these drugs because of the antiquated procedures of the FDA. According to the research performed at the University of Rochester Medical School by Dr. William Wardell, one of these beta blockers, practolol, can save ten thousand lives a year in the United States.[4] That is a real measure of the cost of the delayed introduction as a result of the slow pace of FDA approval of new pharmaceuticals.

Beta blockers are not the only drugs whose use has been delayed by the FDA. Dr. Wardell examined the list of drugs actually approved as safe and effective. In case after case, the United States was one of the last countries to permit their introduction. It was the twenty-second country in the case of the anti-inflammatory drug fenoprofen, the thirty-ninth country for the oral cephalosporin cephalexin, and the fortieth country for the antitubercular antibiotic capreomycin.[5]

These delays are not surprising, given the cardinal rule for bureaucratic survival: Do not stick your neck out. If you were an FDA reviewer and had approved practolol quickly, you would have been taking a risk. If anybody suffered an adverse reaction, you might have borne the responsibility. On the other hand, if you delay approving the drug, the potential users are unlikely to complain, since they do not know about it and quickly pass from the scene. As a result, the cautious regulator asks for more studies—and more delay.

Consider the results of this bureaucratic process of decision making: if sixteen people are harmed by the side effects of a drug in use, that becomes front-page news. If ten thousand people die prematurely because approval of a new drug has been delayed, the public is unaware. This is one example from among many where the real costs of regulation are expressed in terms not of dollars but of lives—and where tougher choices on the part of government officials would enhance consumer welfare.

## Deregulation Is Working

Progress has been made during the last decade in cutting back some of the older forms of economic regulation, where competition in the marketplace can do a better job of protecting the consumer than the imposition of bureaucratic judgments on private enterprise. A brief review of how this came to pass is instructive.

The partial deregulation of American transportation, telecommunications, energy, and financial markets over the past ten years has been a triumph of ideas over entrenched political interests. For ninety years, from the establishment of the Interstate Commerce Commission (ICC) in 1886 to the passage of the Toxic Substances Control Act in 1976, government regulation of American economic activity continually expanded, and it created in its wake powerful constituencies who benefited from the regulation.

Yet, this trend in government rule making has changed dramatically and perhaps irrevocably during the past decade, resulting in remarkable benefits for the American economy. Deregulation has lowered the cost of producing goods and services. It has offered most American consumers a wider array of choices. And it has substantially bolstered the international competitiveness of the economy.

What caused the shift toward deregulation was not a realignment of political forces. The most significant developments were supported by a bipartisan coalition in both the legislative and the executive branches of the federal government. Consumer activists offered support at vital points, as did leaders of both political parties. But the most important role was played by a very unusual set of actors in the public policy arena: economists, political scientists, legal scholars, and similar purveyors of ideas.

### THE INTELLECTUAL SUPPORT FOR DEREGULATION

Three streams of research dealing with different aspects of regulation reached a confluence in the early 1970s.[6] The first focused on the heavy and widely distributed burdens that economic regulation imposed on the economy, especially in the field of transportation, and the smaller and far more concentrated distribution of any benefits that resulted. The second research effort dealt with the fundamental nature of the regulatory process, especially the relations between regulators and those regulated. The third area of research focused on the cost of regulation, especially to the consumer.

## Regulation as a Consumer Issue

It was in the airline industry that the research results were most widely accepted. The clearest example of the heavy cost of regulation was demonstrated by the price differences for trips on regulated and nonregulated airlines. Interstate travel was under the jurisdiction of the Civil Aeronautics Board (CAB); intrastate travel was beyond the CAB's jurisdiction. Because of regulation, someone flying 300 miles from Portland, Oregon, to Seattle, Washington, was paying more than a traveler flying 500 miles in California, going from San Diego to San Francisco.[7]

Most American economists writing in this field also concluded during the 1970s that Interstate Commerce Commission (ICC) regulation was protecting the carriers (railroads, truckers, and their unions) while increasing costs to shippers by billions of dollars a year.[8]

A consensus gradually emerged. Transportation regulation in the United States did not protect its purported beneficiaries—consumers—but instead benefited the employees, executives, and shareholders of the companies being regulated. Government rule making shielded entrenched firms from potential new competitors, and that kept a high-price umbrella over the regulated industry.

A second, and related, stream of research focused on the notion that regulation resulted primarily from the efforts of key interest groups and ultimately benefited those regulated (the now widely held "capture" theory of regulation). In this view, as the only political force in the regulatory agency's environment with any stability, the industry eventually forced the agency to accommodate to its needs.[9] In developing and refining that notion, Professor George Stigler and his colleagues at the University of Chicago contended that regulatory policy reflects the interests and the power of the concerned groups, not necessarily the consumers.[10] In 1982, Stigler was awarded the Nobel Prize in economic science for his pioneering work in this field.

By the mid-1970s, the connection was complete. On both theoretical and empirical grounds, the fundamental justification for much of the existing body of regulation, especially of the economic type, was demolished. Particularly in the case of transportation, it was demonstrated that the rule-making process succeeded primarily in protecting entrenched companies from new competition. Rather than being helped, consumers suffered the higher prices reflecting the "dead weight" losses resulting from regulation. Although specific estimates of the economic cost of airline regulation varied widely, it became clear that the burden on the traveling public was substantial.[11]

The third line of research, focusing on costs to consumers, saw the topic move from the academic journals and the business pages to the front pages and the nightly news. That occurred in the mid-1970s with the publication of widely distributed research on the high cost of regulation.[12] The issue hit a responsive chord with the media, influential policy groups, and, finally, the Congress.[13] A few simple concepts made it attractive. First, in a period of escalating inflation, a strategy of deregulation presented policymakers with an opportunity to deal with that critical issue in a way that did not involve a trade-off with jobs. Indeed, reduced regulation would cut both costs and barriers to production and employment.

Second, the burdens of regulation were summed up as a hidden tax on the consumer ($63 billion in 1976 for a sample of federal regulatory programs).[14] This cost increase was buried in the form of higher prices, but it was very real and often regressive. Third, the notion of benefit-cost analysis, which had been used to screen out clearly uneconomical expenditure projects for decades, also proved to be useful when applied to regulation. Although the implementation required dealing with many difficult conceptual and statistical problems, the general notion of weighing costs against benefits generated a positive reaction.

Finally, a variety of carefully researched examples of regulatory silliness and nonsense reached the public consciousness. Perhaps the first was the dead haul—the requirement that resulted in trucks returning empty, despite ample opportunity to fill them with cargo. The public needed no great expertise to resent the waste that resulted.

This unusual form of applied research focused increasingly on the Occupational Safety and Health Administration. OSHA jokes (based on that research) became a staple of business conversation. Did you hear the one about the OSHA rule that spittoons have to be cleaned daily? Is it true that OSHA made one little company build separate "his" and "her" toilets even though the only two employees of the firm were married to each other? Did OSHA really issue a bulletin to farmers telling them to be careful around cows and not to step into the manure pits?[15]

Clearly, by the late 1970s, support for regulatory reform had become widespread. It included business executives who found themselves pestered with a flood of rules to follow and reports to file, lawyers and political scientists who thought that the regulatory agencies often were captured by the industries being regulated, and economists who believed that regulation reduced competition and increased costs. Some congressional hearings on the subject yielded support for less regulation from such disparate groups—and surprising allies—as the American Conservative Union and the Consumer Federation of America.

PROGRESS ON DEREGULATION

Actual progress on deregulation was slow until dramatic momentum developed in the middle and late 1970s (see table 12-2). In 1968, an obscure Supreme Court decision permitted non-AT&T equipment to be hooked into the Bell telephone system. In the following year, the Federal Communications Commission (FCC) allowed a non-Bell company to connect its long-distance network with local phone systems. Although

TABLE 12-2

*Landmarks in Deregulation*

| | |
|---|---|
| 1968 | Supreme Court permits non-AT&T equipment to be hooked up to Bell System. |
| 1969 | MCI is allowed to connect its long-distance network with local phone systems. |
| 1970 | Interest rates on deposits of $100,000 and over are deregulated. |
| 1972 | FCC sets domestic satellite open-skies policy. |
| 1975 | SEC ends fixed brokerage fees for stock market transactions. |
| 1975 | Rate bureaus for trucking firms and railroads are prohibited from protesting independent rate filings. |
| 1977 | Air cargo is deregulated; airlines are given more freedom in pricing and easier access to new rates. |
| 1978 | Congress partially decontrols natural gas. |
| 1978 | OSHA revokes 928 "nitpicking" rules. |
| 1978 | CAB is phased out, ending its control over airline entry and prices. |
| 1978 | EPA begins emissions trading policy. |
| 1980 | FCC eliminates most federal regulation of cable TV and of consumer premises equipment. |
| 1980 | Motor Carrier Act removes barriers for new entries and lets operators establish fares and routes with little ICC interference. |
| 1980 | Depository Institutions law phases out interest rate ceilings and permits S&Ls to offer interest-bearing checking accounts. |
| 1980 | Staggers Rail Act enables railroads to adjust rates without government approval and to enter into contracts with shippers. |
| 1981 | President Reagan decontrols crude-oil prices and petroleum allocations. |
| 1981 | FCC eliminates much radio regulation. |
| 1982 | New bus regulatory statute allows intercity bus companies to change routes and fares. |
| 1982 | Garn–St. Germain Act allows S&Ls to make more commercial and consumer loans and removes interest rate differentials between banks and S&Ls. |
| 1984 | AT&T agrees to divest local operating companies as part of antitrust settlement. |
| 1984 | Individual ocean shipping companies are allowed to offer lower rates and better service than shipping conference. |

these two actions attracted little attention at the time, they triggered the forces that ultimately led to the breakup of the Bell system.

In 1970, interest rates on deposits of $100,000 and over were deregulated. Again, one move toward deregulation ultimately led to another. As securities firms took advantage of that "loophole," banks responded. Thus, a process was set in motion that has resulted in the lifting of interest rate ceilings, the payment of interest on consumer demand deposits, and enhanced competition among financial institutions.

Two important regulatory changes took place in 1975. The Securities and Exchange Commission (SEC) ordered an end to the practice of fixed brokerage fees for stock market transactions, and the ICC prohibited rate bureaus for trucking firms and railroads from protesting independent rate filings by members. Clearly, the regulatory ice was breaking.

In 1977, the Civil Aeronautics Board (CAB), under the chairmanship of the economist Alfred Kahn and with the support of the economist member Elizabeth Bailey, instituted several changes that ultimately led to deregulation. The CAB gave airlines increased freedom in pricing and easier access to routes they had not previously served. The results were spectacular. Fares for tourists fell drastically, planes filled up, and airline profits soared. The CAB experience provided a striking example of how regulation had been hurting the consumer (the traveling public) and how any gains to the regulated industry had long since been dissipated. In 1978, a bipartisan coalition in Congress passed legislation phasing out the CAB and its authority to control entry and prices.

The year 1980 was an extremely eventful one for economic deregulation. In that year, the FCC eliminated most federal regulation of cable television. The economist Darius Gaskins became chairman of the ICC, and the economist Marcus Alexis was appointed a member of the commission. That, in turn, encouraged (or scared) the trucking industry into supporting congressional assumption of leadership in the reform of regulation in this field, in the expectation that the results would be less drastic than desired by the ICC. Later in the year, a new trucking law provided much more freedom to individual truckers in pricing, made entry much easier, and eliminated many costly ICC restrictions—but the ICC presence was retained. Also passed in 1980, the Staggers Rail Act provided the railroads with new pricing freedom.

In 1981, the executive branch took the leadership on regulatory reform. Building on the groundwork of the Ford and Carter administrations, President Reagan issued a new executive order directing the regulatory agencies under his jurisdiction to perform cost-benefit analyses prior to issuing new rules.[16] A formal review process was placed under the auspices of the Office of Management and Budget.

As a result of these efforts, the rapid rate of regulatory expansion in the 1970s was followed by a substantial deceleration in the 1980s. No new regulatory agencies have been created since 1981.[17] Staffing for regulatory agencies is down, as are their expenditures in real terms.[18] Progress toward deregulation was made in a few areas. President Reagan decontrolled crude-oil prices and petroleum allocations and quietly terminated the Council on Wage and Price Stability. The FCC eliminated much regulation of the radio industry.

Although the Reagan administration virtually stopped the growth in the issuance of new rules, it did not make any significant cutbacks in the structure of regulation. For the most part, it left laws unchanged. A backlash in the environmental area (fueled in part by the controversial personalities of some of the administration's appointees, such as James Watt and Anne Burford) put the regulatory-reform movement on the defensive after the initial burst of change in early 1981. The initial effort to rewrite environmental protection statutes, for example, was abandoned in the face of strong congressional opposition. If the political environment shifts again to favor more regulation, the various federal agencies are in a position to adapt to that reversal quite readily.

Although regulatory reform was one of the four original pillars of "Reaganomics" (along with tax reduction, budget cutting, and anti-inflationary monetary restraint), it never received as high a priority as the other three. Nevertheless, some modest progress has continued to be made. Banking legislation enacted in 1982 allowed savings and loan associations to make more commercial and consumer loans. Also, the interest rate differentials between banks and thrift institutions were removed.

The Bus Regulatory Reform Act of 1982 allowed bus companies to change routes and fares. In 1984, the Shipping Act permitted individual ocean shipping companies to offer lower rates and better service than did shipping "conferences." Also in that year, AT&T agreed to divest local operating companies as part of its historic antitrust settlement with the Justice Department.

In one key area, the regulation of foreign trade, substantial backsliding has occurred. Since 1981, the Reagan administration has renewed or extended restrictions on the import of automobiles, meat, motorcycles, sugar, steel, textiles, and many other products. Simultaneously, control over exports, often justified on foreign policy or national-security grounds, has been tightened.

In environmental and safety rule making, wholesale deregulation has not been the reformers' goal in either the Carter or the Reagan administration. The emphasis here has been on relating the costs of regulation to their benefits and thus reducing the economic burdens of the regulatory process. Responding to the critics of its regulatory approach, the Occupational Safety and Health Administration (OSHA) eliminated or modified 928 of its "nitpicking" rules. The Environmental Protection Agency (EPA) experimented with "bubble" or "offset" policies designed to give companies more flexibility in complying with environmental standards.

The courts have often been barriers to the adoption of more economically efficient regulations. For example, in 1981 a federal court ruled out cost-benefit tests performed for a proposed cotton dust standard, because it held that the law did not provide for basing OSHA rulings on economic criteria. Nevertheless, the increasing support for reviewing the costliness and desirability of proposed new regulations—an approach started by President Ford, continued under President Carter, and expanded under President Reagan—has clearly slowed down the pace of federal rule making.

CONSUMER PROTECTION THROUGH DEREGULATION

The general impact of deregulation on the American economy has been positive. The lessened government intervention has expanded the role of competition and market forces. Virtually every study of the changes has concluded that they have resulted in lower costs, thus raising demand and creating new opportunities for both producers and consumers of the previously regulated activities.[19]

Competition among airlines has been especially vigorous; twenty-six new carriers entered between 1978 and 1985, and nineteen have left. This has exerted great downward pressure on labor and overhead costs. Airline productivity has risen, average air fares have declined greatly, and volume has gone up sharply. The number of city pairs served by more than one airline increased by 55 percent from 1979 to 1984. While some passengers no longer have direct flights, the proportion of passengers changing planes actually decreased from 27 percent in 1978 to 25 percent in 1984.[20]

Moreover, despite several highly publicized air crashes and "near-misses," the overall safety record of air travel has improved since

# Regulation as a Consumer Issue

### TABLE 12-3

### Improved Airline Safety since Deregulation

| | 1972–1978 | 1979–1986 | Percentage Change |
|---|---|---|---|
| *All Commercial Aviation* | | | |
| Total accidents | 1,574 | 1,423 | −9.6 |
| Fatal accidents | 349 | 311 | −10.9 |
| Fatalities | 2,776 | 1,923 | −30.7 |
| Accident rate[a] | 2.35 | 1.73 | −26.4 |
| Fatal-accident rate | 0.52 | 0.38 | −26.9 |
| *Major Scheduled Airlines*[b] | | | |
| Total accidents | 214 | 132 | −38.3 |
| Fatal accidents | 34 | 20 | −41.2 |
| Fatalities | 1,265 | 804 | −36.4 |
| Accident rate | 0.54 | 0.27 | −50.0 |
| Fatal-accident rate | 0.09 | 0.04 | −55.6 |
| *Charter Airlines*[b] | | | |
| Total accidents | 24 | 27 | +12.5 |
| Fatal accidents | 5 | 6 | +20.0 |
| Fatalities | 589 | 334 | −43.3 |
| Accident rate | 1.55 | 1.44 | −7.1 |
| Fatal-accident rate | 0.32 | 0.32 | 0.0 |
| *Air Taxis and Commuters*[c] | | | |
| Total accidents | 1,336 | 1,264 | −5.4 |
| Fatal accidents | 310 | 285 | −8.1 |
| Fatalities | 922 | 785 | −14.9 |
| Accident rate | 5.20 | 3.95 | −24.0 |
| Fatal-accident rate | 1.25 | 1.04 | −16.8 |

[a]Accident rates are calculated in terms of accidents per 100,000 flight hours.
[b]Those airlines with aircraft with more than thirty seats or freight carriers with payload capacity of more than 7,500 pounds.
[c]Carriers operating aircraft with thirty seats or fewer, or payload capacity of 7,500 pounds or less. Prior to 1975, commuter and air taxi statistics were not recorded separately.
SOURCE: Data provided by the Department of Transportation.

deregulation (see table 12-3).[21] The accident rate declined 26 percent, from the average of 2.35 accidents per 100,000 flight hours during 1972–78 to 1.73 per 100,000 hours during 1979–86.

A recent Brookings Institution study shows that airline deregulation has saved consumers $6 billion a year through lower fares and better service. At the same time, the airline industry has generated an additional $2.5 billion in annual profits.[22] Not expected by many proponents of deregulation, however, was the tendency for consolidation of airlines. Initially, the number of carriers in the United States rose, from thirty-six in 1978 to ninety-eight in 1983, but subsequently declined, to seventy-four in 1986.[23]

As of late 1987, a handful of major trunk lines were coming to dominate passenger air traffic, and passenger complaints about flight delays and lost luggage were rising. In specific central hubs, the dominant carrier's market share was quite high: Northwest had an 87 percent share of the Memphis departures, US Air 83 percent in Pittsburgh, TWA 82 percent in St. Louis, and Continental 72 percent in Houston.[24]

The structure of the industry is still evolving, and the long-term effects of the merger movement on price and service have yet to be determined by the newly unleashed competitive forces. In any event, new potential for competition does now exist in the industry. Moreover, airlines remain subject to the scrutiny of the federal government's antitrust authorities and to the possibility of renewed regulatory legislation on the part of the Congress.

For the railroads, revenue per ton-miles (a good measure of unit cost) has been declining in recent years while volume (total revenue ton-miles)—and operating income—have been on an upward trend line. For trucking, comprehensive data are harder to come by; 65 percent of a large sample of shippers recently reported lower trucking rates and improved services. The number of new firms entering the industry has far exceeded the loss of older companies. The number of ICC-authorized carriers increased from 18,000 in 1980 to 33,000 in 1984.[25]

Reduced regulation, ranging from outright deregulation to the simplification and streamlining of rule making, has enabled the competitive process to work better. Depositors in financial institutions have been receiving higher interest rates on their money than they would otherwise have gotten as a greater variety of companies compete for their business. Long-distance telephone users find that greater competition has resulted in lower rates. Simultaneously, the traditional subsidies to local service have been eliminated. Moreover, the deregulated industries experienced far-above-average rapid increases in productivity. Compared with a little more than 3 percent yearly growth in manufacturing productivity—and less than that in the service sector generally—airlines, railroads, and telecommunications averaged productivity increases of 5–10 percent a year during 1980–86.[26]

Inevitably, the wrenching changes brought about by deregulation have generated counterpressures by the interest groups that have lost the benefit of government protection.[27] The managements of many deregulated firms have seen their pay and perquisites decline to the competitive norm. Some companies have not been able to survive in the new competitive environment and have gone bankrupt or have been acquired by stronger firms.

Overall, the cost of producing goods and services in the United States is lower today than it would be if deregulation had not occurred. Opportunities have been created for new enterprises and for their employees. The position of American industry in an increasingly competitive global economy has been strengthened, and, most fundamentally, the welfare of the consumer has been enhanced. These positive accomplishments outweigh the transitional costs incurred in moving from a more regulated to a more competitive environment. In any event, a decade of active reduction of economic regulation seems to have drawn to a close. The deregulatory momentum developed during the 1970s has been lost in the 1980s.

Some observers anticipate a flood of new social regulation beginning in 1989 that will swamp that of the early 1970s. The environmental economist Lester Lave of Carnegie-Mellon University believes that the accumulating pressure of inaction on this front during the Reagan years "is about to explode." This is not a development that he welcomes.[28]

Lave notes that the scientific basis of the social-regulatory decisions of the 1970s was slim and often reflected outmoded or even incorrect science. Billions of dollars were wasted on sewage treatment plants that were never operated, tall stacks that merely diffused air pollution over larger areas, and jerry-built auto-emission controls. "In the haste to be responsive to public demands," Lave has written, "Congress and the regulators guessed rather than wait for facts and analysis to guide multi-billion dollar decisions."

How do we avoid repeating the errors of the 1970s and 1980s? Doing so will not be easy. For one thing, the Reagan administration's term *regulatory relief* should be promptly abandoned. The sensible goal is not to reduce the burden on business by easing the enforcement of existing regulation but to ensure that the regulations that are enforced benefit the consumer. Nor is it desirable to impose regulatory burdens on the economy merely because such actions enable elected officials to show they are "responsive." Rather, the objective should be to determine which regulations make economic sense, which should be modified, and which lack sufficient justification in an economy in which efficiency and equity are both dominant concerns. Let us try to develop such a useful approach.

## Another Wave of Regulatory Reform

*The First Step Toward Regulatory Reform is Educational.* The public must come to understand that it is paying very substantially for the supposedly good things that government regulators are doing.

Economists are prone to take measurements of economic phenomena. The numbers, of course, are not an end in themselves but an input to decision makers. The measurement of the costs and benefits that flow from government regulation is not merely a technical matter. This information can be used to show the public and the government the large amounts of resources being devoted to meeting federal mandates. Such analysis also helps shift the public dialogue onto higher ground. The pertinent policy questions are no longer absolutes: Are you for or against clean air or safe products? Increasingly, the public discussions are in terms of less emotional and long-neglected questions: How well is the regulatory process working? and Are there better ways of achieving the public's desires?

Congress needs to curtail its traditional response of creating a new bureau whenever it confronts a difficult problem. The symbolism involved may be good politics, at least in the short run, but such empty gestures undermine citizen confidence in government—and also contribute to the budget problem. It would be helpful if the Congress endorsed the kind of common sense embodied in the federal appeals court decision that stopped OSHA from issuing new benzene regulations. The court's language is instructive: "Although the agency does not have to conduct an elaborate cost/benefit analysis . . . it does have to determine whether the benefits expected from the standards bear a reasonable relationship to the costs imposed by the standard."[29]

*The Second Step is to Recognize that Merely Creating a Government Bureau and Giving it Large Amounts of Money and Power Does Not Necessarily Mean That the Air Will be Any Cleaner or the Water Any Purer.* The results may be the opposite. The environmental label has been used to justify subsidies to politically powerful regions of the country, notably producers of soft ("dirty") coal. As we noted earlier, in a misguided effort to keep off the market medicines that may generate any adverse side effects, the regulatory authorities often deprive patients of newer, more effective products.

In fact, regulatory activity can generate unexpected negative effects, such as the stifling of innovation. The engineer-lawyer Peter Huber questions whether Henry Ford's original Model T could have survived today's environmental challenges: "Darn thing was dangerous; why you could break your arm cranking it."[30]

*The Third Step is to Sort Out Regulatory Programs That are Worth the Costs they Impose from Those That Fail a Benefit-cost Test.* The regulation of entry and pricing in the airline market by the now defunct Civil Aeronautics Board (CAB) was an example of regulatory activities not worthwhile. The elimination of the CAB has lowered the real cost of air travel and increased the travel choices available to most passengers. Simultaneously, however, the resultant greater volume of air travel has increased congestion, airline delays, lost baggage, and so on.

On the other hand, despite their many shortcomings, social regulatory agencies such as OSHA and the FDA conduct a variety of activities that contribute to the public welfare. That does not necessarily mean that every OSHA or FDA rule and requirement is optimally conceived or even necessary.

Environmental protection, product safety, and other regulatory efforts should be related to costs to the consumer, availability of new products, and employment. A parallel can be drawn to macroeconomic matters, where important and conflicting objectives are recognized and attempts to trade off are made (for example, as between rapid growth and inflation). This reconciliation of regulatory and broader goals can be made at the initial stages of the government process, when the President proposes and the Congress enacts new regulatory programs. In structuring regulatory programs, emphasis should be placed on the development of basic principles to guide the companies subject to regulation (such as economic incentives). This approach contrasts sharply with the traditional case-by-case adjudication so beloved by generations of attorneys.

A formal requirement for all regulatory agencies to perform benefit-cost analysis of proposed regulations is a useful check on expansions of government activity that would not help the average citizen.

Benefit/cost analysis has been used for decades in examining government spending programs. Its application to regulation has been attacked by both ends of the political spectrum—by the far left, because not every proposal for government intervention passes a benefit/cost test, and by the far right, because benefit/cost analysis can be used to justify some types of government intervention. No analytical approach is totally value free, but benefit/cost analysis has less ideological baggage than other alternatives do. To an economist, *overregulation* is not an emotional term; it is merely shorthand for regulation for which the costs to the public are greater than the benefits.

Critics who are offended by the notion of subjecting regulation to a benefit/cost test unwittingly expose the weakness of their position. They must fear that their pet rules would flunk the test. After all, showing that a regulatory activity generates an excess of benefits is a strong justification for continuing it. Benefit/cost analysis is a neutral concept, giving equal weight to a dollar of benefits and a dollar of costs. The painful knowledge that resources available to safeguard human lives are limited causes economists to become concerned when they see wasteful use of those resources because of regulation.

Fundamentally, the task is not to perform statistical tests on proposed rules, helpful though that may be. More basically, the public—and its legislative representatives—must come to a better understanding of the limits to the effective use of governmental power over private decision-making.

Regulatory reform is not really based on a concern with technical measurements or administrative procedures. Government decision makers need to view the regulatory mechanism differently than they do now. Rather than relying on regulation to control every facet of private behavior, the regulatory device needs to be seen as a powerful tool to be used with great care and discretion. Basically, it is attitudes that need to be changed. Experience with the job safety program provides a cogent example. Although the government's safety rules have resulted in billions of dollars in public and private outlays, the goal of a substantially safer work environment has not been achieved.

A more satisfying way of improving the effectiveness of government regulation of private activities will require a major change in the approach to regulation, and one not limited to the job safety program. Indeed, I cite that program merely as an illustration. If the objective of public policy is to reduce accidents, then public policy should focus directly on the reduction of accidents. Excessively detailed regulations are often merely a substitute—the normal bureaucratic substitute—for hard policy decisions.

Rather than placing emphasis on issuing citations to employers who fail to fill forms out correctly or who do not post the required notices, stress should be placed on the regulation of those employers with high or rising accident rates. Fines could be levied on those establishments with the worst safety records. When the accident rates decline toward some sensible standard, the fines could be reduced or eliminated. But the government should not be overly concerned with the way a specific organization achieves a safer working environment. Some companies may find it more efficient to change work rules, others to buy equipment, and still others to retrain workers. Making this choice is precisely the kind of operational business decision making that government should avoid but that now dominates regulatory programs.

*The Fourth Step in Reforming Federal Regulation is to Change or Repeal the Basic Statutes.* For starters, here is a modest agenda for revising the basic statutes that authorize and govern the regulation of business in the United States:

1. *Environmental law should make much more use of market-based approaches.* The legislation on water pollution control should be overhauled. Rather than specifying effluent standards based on a presumed degree of technology that may not be achievable in the future, government authorities should be authorized to charge per unit of effluent. This approach uses the price system to provide an incentive for reducing pollution. Increases in prices of high-polluting products would provide a spur to innovation in techniques to reduce the amounts of wastes discharged; those antipollution efforts would stem not from idealism but rather from a straightforward desire to maintain competitive positions. This would be more cost-effective than the present reliance on standards, which are almost invariably postponed because of court battles or lack of sufficient technology.

Economic approaches to pollution can produce substantial savings for taxpayers and consumers. A study of the Delaware Estuary showed that effluent fees could achieve the desired degree of water purity at half the cost of conventional regulatory methods.

2. *Progress on deregulation of transportation should be accelerated.* The agencies that still regulate prices and the entry and exit of firms in the transportation industry—the Interstate Commerce Commission and the Federal Maritime Commission—should be eliminated. Their interment would end the CAB's monopoly of the federal graveyard for regulatory commissions. Reliance on the competitive forces of the marketplace will ensure more efficient and less costly transport for business and personal travelers. Similarly, cabotage laws (such as the Jones Act, which limits shipping between American ports to U.S. flag-ships) should be repealed.

3. *Regulation of financial institutions should be reduced.* Statutes that unduly restrict competition in the banking system should be re-

pealed, especially the McFadden Act, which limits the geographic expansion of commercial banks, and the Glass-Steagall Act, which inhibits their entry into other types of financial services.

4. *Remaining vestiges of energy price regulation should be repealed.* Recent history is instructive. In spite of the howls of outrage at the time, the elimination by President Reagan in 1981 of price and allocation controls over gasoline and petroleum products was followed, with the inevitable lag, by lower prices. The deregulation of natural gas is likely to have similarly beneficial results.

5. *The regulation of exports should be cut back drastically.* While export controls on highly classified military equipment are likely to remain—and they should—such restrictions should not be imposed merely as an effort to achieve foreign or domestic policy objectives. The embargoes on grain exports were exercises in futility. The restriction of exports of items readily obtainable in world markets does not hurt the foreign buyer as much as it punishes domestic producers and their employees.

6. *The regulation of imports through quotas should be terminated.* Study after study demonstrates that quotas and other quantitative restrictions on imports hurt the total domestic economy more than they benefit the specific industrial sector they are designed to protect—and they do so even more than tariffs. At least tariffs work through the price system and, unlike quotas, allow some of the benefits to accrue to the U.S. Treasury and ultimately to American taxpayers.

Under all forms of trade restriction, consumers wind up paying higher prices. Those other domestic industries that purchase the now higher-priced products become less competitive, and they often then join the chorus for government intervention. Moreover, the incentive of the "protected" companies to become more efficient is reduced in the process.

7. *A fundamental rewriting of the statutory framework for social regulation should be undertaken.* Unrealistic goals and objectives, such as "zero discharge," should be modified or, better yet, eliminated. Their continued presence undermines confidence in the overall effectiveness of government activities. The strongest proponents of government intervention in the marketplace conclude that such tasks are simply not possible.

Likewise, in giving the EPA the task of overseeing the cleansing of the nation's water, the Congress established the goal of "zero discharge" of untreated waste by 1984. In retrospect, the task was impossible, and there is considerable evidence that Congress realized this at the time.[31]

## Regulation as a Consumer Issue

Reforming the regulatory process is an uphill battle. An insight into the difficulty involved is provided by the results of a nationwide Gallup poll that shows how poorly informed the American public is on these matters. Half of those interviewed could not name even one federal regulation that affected them or their family. Only 17 percent knew that the executive branch is responsible for issuing regulations; 47 percent thought Congress was. More than half could not name any difference between laws and regulations. Among those who did name a difference, the most popular response was that laws were mandatory, while regulations were optional.

The most fundamental need is to help the public understand the limits of government rule making. Even if the EPA were staffed entirely with Newtons and Einsteins, it could not meet the present statutory expectations of cleaning all of the water, air, and land surfaces in and around the United States, nor could the Consumer Product Safety Commission effectively regulate the two million companies producing the ten thousand products within its jurisdiction. The need is not for greater compassion, commitment, or technological expertise—those we have in abundance. What we require now is the willingness and the courage to make difficult choices among the many alternative demands for government regulation of private activity.

# PART E

## An Agenda for Post-Reagan America

# PART II

## An agenda for

## Post-Keynesianism

# 13

# *The American Future: How to Make Difficult Choices*

In this chapter and the one that follows, I will try to show how we can develop a public policy agenda for the period after the presidency of Ronald Reagan. It is more than a matter of an author's attempting to impose his preferences on a willing reader. Setting national priorities is not a simple task, and we will have to cover quite a bit of ground. However, the patient reader will be rewarded with a specific set of policy priorities for the United States in the coming decade.

## Economic Forecasting in Perspective

You may wonder why credence should be given to the views of any economist, including the well-intentioned author of this volume. Let me offer some explanation of why economists continue to make forecasts and, more particularly, why the public should pay attention to them. Although highly publicized forecasts of the next month or quarter of the year have been off the mark frequently, economists have done much better with annual prognostications. Over a period of a year, many specific economic crosscurrents offset one other. That is why humorists in the economics profession (and there are some) contend that St. Offset is the patron saint of economic forecasting. Indeed, the record of professional forecasters at projecting a calendar year ahead is far better than the public realizes. Looking back at the record of the last several years, we see that annual forecasts of the GNP have, on balance, been useful for business and government decision makers.

In late 1982, for example, most professional forecasters projected a substantial increase in the economy's growth rate—typically, a dramatic shift from a decline of 2 percent in 1982 to a positive expansion in the neighborhood of 3 percent in 1983.[1] The actual growth in 1983 of 3.7 percent was not fundamentally off the mark. Thus, economic forecasters in late 1982 were essentially right in saying that 1983 would be a turnaround year, a period of reasonable growth, compared with the negative trend of 1982. Those who relied on that economic assumption were not misled.

Likewise, the prevailing projection in the fall of 1983 was reasonably helpful. Forecasters generally anticipated a substantial acceleration in the growth rate of the American economy, from 3.7 percent in 1983 to 5 percent or more in 1984. The expansion for the year reached well over 6 percent. Similarly, in the fall of 1984, virtually every forecaster saw a major slowdown in economic growth in 1985, at one-half or less of the preceding year's rate—and we surely delivered. The actual figure was 3.0 percent. Again, in the fall of 1985, the prevailing forecast for 1986 was a growth rate similar to that of 1985—correctly projected at 2.9 percent. In the fall of 1986, once again, the standard prognostication was a growth rate for 1987 similar to 1986's—and that, too, prevailed.

Those who anticipate pinpoint accuracy in economic extrapolations will be disappointed. But the standard economic projection has been helpful in indicating general directions and trends for the year ahead. Indeed, over the past ten years, the prevailing annual forecasts of economic growth and inflation were within 1.2 percentage points of the actual result.[2] Not bad, but admittedly these prognostications are not candidates for the *Guinness Book of World Records*.

As we look to the decade ahead, we cannot be certain of the external environment facing policymakers. A useful start can be made by considering three alternative scenarios that citizens and policymakers in the United States might encounter in the next presidential administration.[3]

# The American Future: How to Make Difficult Choices

We must be chastened by the knowledge that in making forecasts, we still face the fundamental limitation, as expressed in ancient times by Pliny the Elder, "The only certainty is that nothing is certain."[4]

## A DOOM-AND-GLOOM SCENARIO

First we conjure up a scenario far different from recent experience. The Reagan presidency is succeeded by an administration dedicated to reversing many of the changes made in the first half of the 1980s. Renewed emphasis on the welfare state leads to substantial tax increases for middle- and upper-bracket taxpayers to help finance expansion of services for and benefits to those in the bottom part of the income pyramid. Adoption of capital budgeting obscures for a while the rise in the budget deficit.

A new wave of social regulation, covering tightened rule making in product and job safety and environmental purity, imposes additional obstacles to the formation of enterprises and to the construction of factories, stores, and office buildings. Antibusiness rhetoric fills congressional hearings and becomes front-page news. Companies respond by cutting back; employment slips, and imports rise.

Financial markets react adversely to these new developments. Interest rates turn up sharply. The inflow of foreign investment slows down and soon halts. Inflation accelerates, but the Federal Reserve System is slow in responding, trying to avoid precipitating a recession. The return to double-digit inflation scares foreign investors, who begin a modest flight of their capital out of the United States. Another rise in interest rates results in downturns in business capital spending and in housing construction.

Social unrest becomes more visible, in urban centers and rural areas alike, as people in distress expect little benefit from the status quo. Waves of nationwide strikes halt the growth of the economy. Inflation erodes the real value of worker earnings, but tough foreign competition keeps managements in most industries from agreeing to more-generous labor settlements. Union-management relations sour, and productivity in manufacturing suffers, encouraging further inroads by foreign producers in U.S. domestic markets. Meanwhile, business profits deteriorate. A wage-price spiral gets under way, further heating up inflationary pressures. Double-digit inflation returns to the American economy.

With the annual budget deficit in excess of $200 billion at the outset of the downturn, Congress is reluctant to stimulate the economy by cutting taxes or voting for new spending programs. To compound the problem, the Federal Reserve belatedly shifts to an anti-inflationary policy of tight money. Once again, it does too much too late. The massive reduction in the availability of credit precipitates a deep recession.

The overseas reaction is severe. More foreign capital is pulled out of the United States. The combination of rising budget deficits and the domestic refunding of maturing debt (previously held overseas) puts further upward pressure on U.S. interest rates. The combination of reduced earnings and higher interest rates forces many highly leveraged firms to the wall. Banks bear the brunt of the rising bankruptcies of American companies that they financed. Some of the weaker financial institutions go under. Confidence of investors, both at home and abroad, is eroded very substantially. The prices of gold, silver, and other precious metals shoot up rapidly, as American investors join the exodus of capital from the United States. Panic selling forces stock exchanges to halt trading. The President calls the Congress into emergency session.

At this point, readers may anticipate the alarm clock ringing, awakening us all from this economic nightmare. To be sure, I do not attach the same degree of likelihood to this doom-and-gloom scenario as to the other outcomes I will be presenting. But the point needs to be made that, with some bad luck and stupid policy-making (a combination that cannot be ruled out), the underlying problems facing the United States could become quite severe and even get out of control.

AN UPBEAT SCENARIO

On the other hand, we can think of a time when Americans take a more positive attitude toward the problems facing the nation. The new administration in Washington in 1989 sets a different policy emphasis for the federal government. It focuses on ways of improving economic performance by strengthening the competitive position of the United States in world markets. Regulatory burdens are reduced. The Congress votes down new compulsory fringe benefits. A sustained period of economic growth gets under way. The rise in tax collections—and concomitant reductions in unemployment compensation and other transfer payments—yields a steady decline in the budget deficit.

In this scenario, the United States finally makes many of the tough choices that have been postponed during the 1970s and 1980s. The composition of federal spending is shifted substantially from politically attractive consumption-oriented expenditures (welfare, farm subsidies, retirement, and other handouts) to economically important investment-oriented outlays, such as education, research and development, and new roads and airports (infrastructure). A secondary shift occurs, within the broad category of aid to producers, away from farm price supports and other subsidies that reduce output and to incentives for new investment and hence rising output.

In this picture, the pace of economic growth in the United States quickens, to an average of more than 3 percent a year. Rising productivity holds down inflationary pressures. Unemployment declines to about 5 percent. Strike activity remains close to the current all-time low. Wage and benefit increases, on the average, match the rate of inflation.

As is shown in table 13-1, the numbers describing such a decade of growth are very impressive.[5] The gross national product more than doubles in the course of ten years, from $3.8 trillion in 1986 to $8.0 trillion in 1996. Even after the effects of inflation have been boiled out, the real GNP shows a rapid rise over the decade, from $3.7 trillion to $5.2 trillion.

A good indicator of the underlying health of the economy is the expectation that total saving rises from $536 billion in 1986 to $800 billion in 1996. This money finances new factories and other productive facilities. The number of civilian jobs expands steadily, from 110 million in 1986 to 130 million ten years later. These and the other statistics contained in the table portray a healthy, dynamic economy. Abroad, confidence in American leadership is strengthened.

Nevertheless, Pollyanna does not rule the land. Serious problems continue to bubble below the tranquil surface. Further polarization occurs between upper- and lower-income groups, with continued bitterness on the part of those whom prosperity passes by. Trouble spots include portions of the farm belt, the oil country, some central-city ghettos, and rust bucket towns. Nevertheless, a growing number of areas participate in the expanding economy, and hope keeps a lid on potential social disruption.

The possibility of unpredictable crises always has to be considered.

TABLE 13-1

*Projected Growth of the U.S. Economy*

|  | 1986 | 1996 |
|---|---|---|
| Industrial production (1977＝100) | 129 | 188 |
| GNP (dollars in trillions) | $3.7 | $8.2 |
| Real GNP (1986 dollars in trillions) | $3.7 | $5.2 |
| Gross saving (1986 dollars in billions) | $536 | $800 |
| Civilian employment (millions) | 110 | 130 |

Terrorists or revolutionaries might knock out the Saudi oil capability. A Bhopal-type explosion might occur in North America. The President of the United States might die in office. The United States might get involved in a shooting war in Central America, on the order of our earlier commitments in South Korea and in Vietnam. But, in the upbeat scenario, concerns over these remote possibilities are assigned merely to contingency planning.

MUDDLING THROUGH

Finally, let us consider a third scenario, which basically extends the status quo. The federal government continues to be bedeviled by the twin deficits of foreign trade and domestic budget. But no significant departure is made from current policy, so little additional progress can be anticipated. In effect, the country follows a "muddle through" approach. Given its tremendous resource base, in both material wealth and educated people, the United States is likely to succeed in muddling through. Some close calls, however, may well occur in this third scenario.

Real growth in the economy as a whole peters out, and more talk is heard about recession. Inflation starts to rise more rapidly, while unemployment stops declining. The term *stagflation* is used once again to describe the combination of rising inflation and sluggish economic growth.

Trouble spots in society are allowed to fester. The national attitude sounds like "Do not do anything today that can be postponed until tomorrow—or the day after." Fortunately, the national luck holds out. The characteristic sign of the times is the one proclaiming, tongue in cheek, "The end of the world has been postponed." This muddling-through attitude currently pervades a large portion of business thinking. A 1987 survey of the chief executives of America's largest companies typifies this outlook (see table 13-2 for highlights of the Conference Board survey).[6]

The heads of major companies anticipate a crosscurrent of forces to be operating over the coming decade: increasing taxation and government regulation at home and erosion of the U.S. share of world markets overseas; American industry becomes more price competitive but has little chance of winning back the shares of world markets lost in recent years. The education and work experience of the huge post–World War II baby crop has a very positive influence on the U.S. economy. Yet, a continuing negative factor is the slim chance that the budget deficit will be cut to less than $50 billion ten years from now.

# The American Future: How to Make Difficult Choices

TABLE 13-2

## The U.S. Economy over the Coming Decade
### 1987 Survey of Executives of Major Corporations

| POSSIBLE EVENT | LIKELIHOOD |
|---|---|
| *High Probability* (60 percent or more) | |
| U.S. industry will become increasingly price competitive. | 69 |
| Severity of taxation will increase to deal with the deficit. | 68 |
| Low saving rate of U.S. will continue. | 65 |
| The educated baby boomers will have a positive influence on U.S. economy. | 64 |
| U.S. share of world markets will erode. | 64 |
| Environmental regulation will intensify. | 62 |
| Direct foreign investment in U.S. will rise rapidly. | 61 |
| *Medium Probability* (41–59 percent) | |
| Problems of farmers will not have a major adverse impact on the U.S. economy. | 54 |
| Per capita standard of living in U.S. will trend upward. | 52 |
| U.S. import restrictions will increase considerably. | 52 |
| No major depression will occur during coming decade. | 50 |
| U.S. will suffer a major financial crisis. | 49 |
| The decade will be generally deflationary. | 47 |
| High debt will precipitate greatly increased inflation. | 47 |
| Regulation of industry will increase. | 44 |
| U.S. interest rates will be lower than today. | 43 |
| Social problems will slow the growth of the U.S. economy. | 41 |
| *Low Probability* (0–40 percent) | |
| An energy shortage will occur. | 39 |
| The budget deficit will fall below $50 billion a year. | 32 |
| Advancing technology will eliminate jobs. | 29 |
| A major shortage of labor will occur. | 27 |
| U.S. manufacturers will win back most of the market share recently lost to foreign competition. | 26 |

SOURCE: *Conference Board Perspectives*, 1987, no. 6.

In sum, American business executives estimate a fifty-fifty possibility that the United States will avoid a major depression during the coming decade—which is a good statistical approximation of the odds of successfully muddling through. But none of this is foreordained.

It is unlikely that any of the three scenarios will occur in the 1990s exactly as I have described them. A combination or variation is more probable, depending on future decisions to be made in both the public and the private sectors. Some of the tough choices leading to the upbeat scenario will probably be made, but very likely not enough to avoid all of the ugly situations that occur in the doom-and-gloom scenario.

It is useful to emphasize the basic continuity of American institutions. We do not live in a linear world. Trends do not continue unfolding in a straight line indefinitely. Counterpressures arise to arrest or modify or even reverse the most durable trend. In a real sense, the American economy is Newtonian—the more important actions generate counteractions. Talk about megatrend shocks, negative-sum economies, and other melodramatic use of buzzwords needs to be taken with more than the proverbial pinch of salt.

## The Process of Reordering Priorities

Forecasting is not the only difficult part of developing a new set of national priorities. We need to consider the protracted process through which priorities are changed. I refer not to the technical details of legislative deliberations but to the important substantive factors that are often overlooked.

We must begin by acknowledging the basic dilemma that has been noted in virtually every preceding chapter: we Americans are reluctant to make the hard choices that face us in each area of economic decision making. Rather than choosing, we have acted as if we had sufficient wealth, technology, and knowledge to fight a major war *and* to wipe out poverty; to quickly eliminate inflation *and* unemployment; to vote for a totally safe environment *and* still retain all of the benefits of a modern high-tech society; to cut taxes, increase spending, *and* balance the budget; to work and produce less *and* to consume more.

In short, we believe that living in as affluent a society as ours, we have the resources and skills to become a relaxed society, deserving to enjoy the accustomed fruits of labor (not always our own). But the events of recent years are providing an extremely rude awakening to the realities of the modern world. Global competition and unprecedented budget and trade deficits are demonstrating dramatically the limits of this nation's economic capacity. Although people are reluctant to admit it, the United States just does not have the capability to meet all of the demands that have been placed on the national agenda—certainly not to the degree that we would like. As a result, we Americans are in the process of learning that—sooner rather than later—we have to make difficult choices.

## The American Future: How to Make Difficult Choices

These choices do not primarily involve making selections between good and bad undertakings, which is relatively easy to do. Rather, the decisions are between different amounts and types of "good." These are inevitably most difficult to do. As James Madison wrote, "The choice must always be made, if not of the lesser evil, at least of the greater, not the perfect, good. . . ."[7]

A few examples may help bring this point into clearer focus. Many citizens want to see the government encourage economic growth by devoting rising shares of the federal budget to education, training, and other "investments" in people. Others want to improve the status of senior citizens and advocate a liberalizing of payments of health (through Medicare) and retirement (through Social Security). Some want to enhance the competitiveness of the nation's industries by doing more to apply science and technology to the designing of new products and modernizing of production processes. Still others are concerned about the external threats to the United States and want to increase aid to our allies and to shore up weaknesses in our own military establishment, especially in the area of readiness. Cutting across all of these important interest groups are the demands for larger airports, more efficient air navigation systems, safer roads and bridges, and other similar outlays for infrastructure.

To most Americans, none of these alternatives is inherently undesirable. Except for true libertarians, spending more on education and health is a plus. Promoting the national security is also a universally shared objective, except perhaps for a few staunch pacifists. But common sense tells us that we cannot increase the share of the federal budget devoted to each department and agency of government. The constraints of arithmetic are overwhelmingly compelling.

But those constraints are especially pressing at a time of continuing triple-digit budget deficits. Until recently, assigning a popular program a constant share of a steadily growing federal budget meant making available rapidly rising absolute amounts of money. However, at a time when a firm lid is necessary on federal outlays, a substantial absolute increase in spending for one benefit program must inevitably be accompanied by a cutback in another.

The truth is that most of us are hypocritical when it comes to expressing our views on what we want from government. We favor economy in the abstract, while we pressure our congressional representatives to expand federal spending that benefits our industry or region or interest group. If we give the process any thought, we blithely assume that the money will be available because "they"—the rest of society—will acquiesce in the curtailment of their benefits. In my many years of public service, I cannot recall a single instance in which the members of an interest group advocating a new government benefit wanted to pay for it themselves, by cutting back a government service they were already receiving.

CHOOSING AMONG PRIORITIES

Setting priorities involves more than merely identifying or even ranking desirable programs. The hard but necessary nitty-gritty decisions are in terms of "a little more of this" and "a little less of that." That is the essence of changing priorities—taking a billion out of the defense budget and adding a billion to the Department of Education (or vice versa). The problem, however, is that we are much better at saying "more of this" than at saying "less of that." And this is the source of many of our national problems.

We can readily complete the first half of the decision-making process, deciding that we want simultaneously more leisure and a higher standard of living, more security and a higher income, more government services and lower taxes, a bigger national defense and a smaller public sector.

We are not so good, however, at confronting the second set of choices. We need to decide what we want *less* of, be it environmental cleanup or national defense or health care or recreational facilities. Thus, we are faced with a two-part question: How much of a "good" do we want, and how much are we willing to pay for it? This question does not arise only in connection with dealing with the federal budget, nor is its impact limited to the public sector.

For example, a popular fad is to urge Congress to impose social requirements on business, in the form of "mandated benefits." Because that spending is "off budget" and does not have to be paid for by taxes, it seems to be a "neat" idea. But ignoring the impact of such generosity on the productivity and competitiveness of the American business system means failing to take account of important and adverse side effects. In a very real sense, American workers pay for those "free" benefits by the loss of some jobs to lower-cost foreign producers. Few participants in the debate on "mandated benefits" are even aware of the painful trade-off between higher living standards for some workers and unemployment for others. That trade-off between labor benefits and economic productivity may be made deliberately or by default, but it is made.

Other trade-offs with important national repercussions involve such matters as deciding how much equality we want in our society and how productive that society will be. The late Arthur Okun, of the Brookings Institution, explained this most clearly in his "leaky bucket" analogy. He demonstrated that the arbitrary transfer of income from one segment of society to another exacts a cost—the reduction in output that the redistribution process inevitably entails because of its adverse effects on people's incentives to work, save, and invest. Given his relatively liberal value judgments, Okun was willing to sacrifice some of the "income pie" to achieve more equal shares. But he had no illusions about the substantial cost of doing so.[8]

Still other trade-offs involve returning to a simpler society versus obtaining the fruits of technology. We should not delude ourselves about the costs to be incurred—as well as about the benefits that might be achieved. Despite all the scare stories, advances in science and technology have reduced disease, increased life spans, and made possible a growing variety of human experiences—such as improved travel and communication and enhanced leisure time. Thus, stopping the advance of science also means halting economic and social progress.

Finally, the trade-off between security and opportunity is perhaps the most difficult one to make, as it involves decisions at the levels of the individual, the family, private institutions, and public policy. For example, forcing a company to guarantee specific jobs usually also makes it less likely that the firm will expand or that the workers will ever hold better jobs. These are the kinds of painful economic choices that are at the heart of determining our future.

## LIMITING GOVERNMENT ACTION

Any effort to set priorities needs to recognize the limits of political decision making. Putting liberal and conservative labels aside, we must admit that government cannot effectively settle every question facing a free society. Consider the great variety of consumer desires. In a political setting, it is appropriate that the majority usually decides. But to follow that approach universally is foolish.

For example, when the original Henry Ford declared that automobile buyers could choose any color so long as it was black, prospective purchasers with different preferences had recourse to the products of other companies. But if the same Henry Ford had been secretary of a nationalized department of automotive production, the minority desires would have remained unfulfilled. In our daily lives, there is rarely need for unanimity of choice. Here is where the market system automatically meets individual needs far more effectively than the best-intentioned political decision making.

Returning to the example of the automobile, we see that if 1 percent of the population desires a car painted in blushing pink, the market can meet the demand—provided some people are willing to pay the price. There is no need to impose a single, dominant viewpoint on all automobile purchasers or on all citizens generally.

Another way of avoiding the imposition of a single viewpoint in public policy is to recognize the value of a "portfolio" or diversification approach. A parallel can be drawn with investors who are smart enough to see the financial opportunities associated with investments in, say, high-tech industry. They are also usually intelligent enough to know that only by luck will they actually be able to identify the individual companies that will profit most from these opportunities.

Consequently, such investors choose portfolios of investments, some of which will yield high returns and others of which will turn out to be lemons. On the average, however, the financial returns may be high, because the commitment has not been limited to the common stock of a single firm. The investments have been spread out over a portfolio of investment instruments representing a large number of different companies.

In contrast, policymakers at the federal level often identify a real social or regulatory problem but then foolishly commit themselves to a single course of action. That is comparable to investors' limiting their investment to the stock of a single firm.

Such a narrow commitment is unduly presumptuous of government's own ability to pick the right solution the first time. It is also unduly risky and, within a federal system, quite unnecessary. Independent actions by strong state and local governments on complex social issues are a good way to "diversify" the nation's portfolio of policy actions. The actions by some state banking authorities in authorizing variable-interest-rate mortgages was a good example of such state-level policy innovations that later were adopted throughout the nation.

The United States is one of the few nations in the world blessed with a federal system of government in which states have powers independent of the national government. Such a structure automatically provides, in effect, a portfolio that can offer the advantages of diversification if allowed to work—by restraining the federal government from trying to tackle all of the problems facing the country. It is fascinating to note that, in recent years, the federal government has been marked by fiscal distress while the individual states have demonstrated remarkable resiliency.

The intergovernmental expert John Shannon concludes, on the basis of this experience, that our decentralized federal system vindicates the wisdom of the framers of the Constitution—"of not placing all of our policy eggs in Washington's basket."[9]

The patience of the reader is now rewarded. Having disposed of the somewhat tedious, but important, preliminaries, we can get down to the nitty-gritty business to which this book is dedicated. The next and final chapter raises and attempts to answer the specific questions involved in establishing a new set of national priorities for the 1990s.

# 14

# The Choices Facing America

Americans face a series of strategic decisions in the years ahead and especially during the next presidency. Achieving the benefits of the upbeat scenario is feasible, but only if we make a great many hard choices, in the public sector as well as in the private sector and on the part of consumers as well as of producers. Let us proceed to wrestle with those key questions of public policy in order to develop a framework for decision making in the 1990s.

## Developing a Framework for Decision Making

We can identify three basic categories of responses in dealing with public policy issues: conventional conservative, conventional liberal, and new directions. As a general proposition, the approaches I will label "conservative" reduce the role of government—with a few salient exceptions, such as promoting business interests and national defense. The conventional "liberal" approach expands the government's role— except in such matters as defense. The category "new directions" is a euphemism for my personal predilections, especially as developed in earlier chapters. It contains suggestions involving departures from traditional approaches to solving the problems facing the United States.

Let us now apply that framework to nine key areas of national policy: the budget deficits, defense, welfare, education, taxation, ecology, foreign trade, bailouts, and takeovers.

REDUCING THE BUDGET DEFICITS

You do not have to succumb to apocalyptic warnings of impending economic doom to acknowledge that the most pressing area of public-sector decision making is that of bringing down the huge budget deficits. In any event, government spending and taxation are key segments of economic activity directly influenced by public policy.

Despite their universal lip service to the goal of lower deficits, liberals and conservatives—and Democrats and Republicans—are locked in what seems to be a perpetual battle over which part of the federal budget should be cut. In general, Republicans and conservatives favor reducing civilian programs, such as welfare, aid to education, housing, and the like. But a great many of them would sooner see the deficit rise than halt or even slow down the planned growth in military outlays.

The conventional liberal and Democratic approach is the mirror image of the Republican-conservative position. It emphasizes curbing defense expenditures and simultaneously maintaining or accelerating the growth of expenditures for social and other civilian programs. Many would, albeit reluctantly, favor tax increases in order to deal with the continued high levels of red ink reported by the Treasury.

Neither the liberal nor the conservative approach is working, as the seemingly endless progression of triple-digit deficits shows. Both approaches are fundamentally flawed because they start off the budget process by ruling major areas of expenditure off limits to the pruning knife. That approach is a guarantee of failure to control the growth of government. Any veteran of budgeting, whether in business or in government, knows that soft spots exist in every budget submission. Presi-

| Issue | Conventional Conservative | Conventional Liberal | New Directions |
|---|---|---|---|
| BUDGET DEFICITS | Cut social programs. | Cut defense. | Hit every spending item. |
| | Accept deficits before cutting defense. | Raise taxes before cutting social programs. | Change budget process. |
| | | | Reform Congress. |

dent Harry Truman, who had served for many years on the Senate Appropriations Committee, was fond of saying that he never saw a budget that could not be cut.

The task of budget cutting is made more urgent by warnings like that of the OMB's former associate director Kathryn Eickhoff: "The worst may be yet to come."[1] She has in mind potential new demands on the federal purse that range from catastrophic health insurance to the replacement of worn-out bridges and roads and the bailout of sick financial institutions. Clearly, the issue of controlling federal spending merits a conspicuous position on the nation's future policy agenda.

The size and timing of budget reductions involve a careful balancing of many factors. Across-the-board freezes or uniform percentage reductions in appropriations sound simple but are impractical. Some categories—notably, interest on the national debt—are firm legal obligations. Reneging would push financial markets into turmoil. To curtail certain other types of spending, such as financing the completion of a road or airport under construction, would be patently wasteful. Still other activities—collecting taxes is an obvious example—contribute to bringing down the deficit. A more basic shortcoming of the "simple" approach to cutting government outlays is that it hits the wasteful program no harder than the well-administered operation. Across-the-board cuts provide the wrong incentives to government administrators.

Good budgeting entails far more than substituting a scalpel for the meat ax. What is needed is to identify, and eliminate, entire government programs that generate more costs than benefits. That requires carefully examining individual appropriations accounts in each governmental department and agency. However, focusing on such "microeconomic" concerns as the efficiency and effectiveness—and even fairness—of each government undertaking is not enough. Budget cutters must recognize potential "macroeconomic" effects. For example, very large and abrupt shifts in the size of federal purchases can disrupt the economies of major regions of the country. In contrast, on many occasions, curtailing the total flow of government spending would help dampen inflationary pressures.

Thus, it would have been easier for the economy to adjust to slashes in federal spending in 1984, a year of robust growth, than in the more slowly growing economy of 1987. It is now necessary to convince the public—and especially financial markets—that the legislative and the executive branches are both determined to carry through a sustained multiyear effort to trim the deficit substantially and steadily. That is far more desirable than making dramatic one-time cuts or establishing un-realistic targets whose attainment is continually postponed.

Unfortunately, the way in which the Congress now conducts its business is not conducive to making tough decisions on budget matters. Although reorganizations are notoriously upsetting to the people affected, departures from the status quo on Capitol Hill are desirable. As a start, several changes in the budget process could help in controlling federal spending. Consolidating the overlapping and competing powers of the Budget and Appropriations committees surely would be a positive move. It would reduce the opportunity for buck-passing and increase the power of those members of Congress charged with budgetary oversight. Shifting to a two-year budget cycle would cut the time devoted to routine reviews of agency operations and enable the key congressional committees to focus on the major items and issues of expenditure. The "game" of authorizing continuing programs just a year at a time (and thus giving the authorization committees a role in the annual budget process) should be eliminated. But such constructive changes are no panacea.

More fundamentally, only an altering of the basic structure of the Congress will curb the pressures for more spending. The proliferation of subcommittees within Senate and House committees has led to the establishment of a multitude of little congressional "empires." The chairman of each subcommittee, usually aided by the highest-ranking minority member, takes some aspect of federal operations under his or her wing—and shields it from effective control by the White House or even the responsible cabinet secretary.

The incentives for expanding the federal programs within each subcommittee's sphere of influence are both obvious and powerful.[2] Just holding hearings on some "hot" issue generates much television, radio, newspaper, and magazine coverage. Public hearings are an effective way to create instant celebrities among otherwise anonymous members of the Congress.

When a subcommittee responds to the "problem" by proposing some new expenditure program, that inevitably generates a political plus. The direct beneficiaries become strong supporters of the subcommittee—and often generous contributors to the political action committees of its members. The desired change is obvious: reduce substantially the number of congressional subcommittees. The real challenge is to get voters to convince their congressional representatives that such a shift is politically popular and, conversely, that maintaining the status quo will be viewed adversely by an electorate increasingly impatient with the unwillingness of the Congress to vote lower appropriations.

The most effective way to control federal spending is for the voters to put the onus on the Congress to cut spending—to ridicule Congress for being "the gal who cain't say no" to organized pressure groups. That means that changing the structure of government, however helpful, will not suffice. The people in those institutions will still have to make difficult decisions, and they will do so only if forced to by voters. The first time a member of Congress gets reelected for crowing over the number of pork barrel projects in his (or her) own district that got canceled will be the time we will know we are making progress on the budget. And when a Senator gets defeated because he boasted too much (rather than too little) about the many "goodies" that he obtained for his state, then we will be sure we are on the way.

As was pointed out at the start of this discussion on budget deficits, changing the budget process and reforming the structure of Congress will help. But there is no substitute for a careful review of the individual items in the budget. Unfortunately, not only is the budget unbalanced but so is the current public dialogue on the budget. In the various public forums—be they congressional hearings, presidential press conferences, or professional publications—attention is focused on proposals for new taxes and changes in existing taxes. Very little consideration is given to the specifics of reducing government spending.

Just compare how much time the tax committees devote to examining suggestions to raise revenues and how little time the appropriations committees assign to considering proposals to reduce the official budget requests. It is understatement that 99 percent of the time spent at appropriations hearings is devoted to listening to agency representatives justify higher budgets. It would be a sharp break with tradition—but surely worth a try—for Congress to devote one day of open hearings for each department of government to provide ample opportunity for the proponents of budget cuts to testify. That would help educate the public.

As a starter, I suggest considering the ten examples of wasteful government programs presented in chapter 3. Those suggestions typify the opportunities as well as the obstacles. None of the ten spending programs merits inclusion in an austerity budget. But all of the ten—and many others like them[3]—are supported by one or more powerful interest groups that have learned how to flex their muscles and thus scare off any effort at economizing. The heart of the budget problem is to change the attitude of people rather than the structure of government.

## The Choices Facing America

Let us proceed from the general to the specific and tackle the two largest items of federal spending—defense and entitlements. The reader will note that I have not raised the subject of tax increases. I do not mean to be inflexible on that matter. It is from a sense of priorities that I focus on the opportunities for spending cuts first and defer tax changes to a later section.

### GETTING MORE BANG FOR THE MILITARY BUCK

The annual debate on the military budget has become as contentious as it is predictable. Conservatives advocate larger outlays and liberals smaller budgets. But neither approach—"Bigger is better" or "Small is beautiful"—is a sensible way of making decisions on national-security matters. Reforming the entire military procurement process, as was proposed in chapter 4, would provide more bang per buck. So would the introduction of economic incentives in the setting of military pay scales. But beyond that there is the basic need for choosing among individual weapon systems and cutting back or even canceling those that add the least to our military capability.

During his long service as secretary of defense, Caspar Weinberger hardly ever encountered a weapon system that he did not like. No weapon system approved by the Carter administration was canceled during the escalation of defense budgets in the first term of the Reagan administration. It is hard to avoid the conclusion that Ronald Reagan (or perhaps Cap Weinberger) considered Jimmy Carter a military genius. After all, the Reagan administration merely superimposed its own priorities on those of the preceding administration. It is hard to recall any other new administration that treated its predecessor's programs with such respect.

We must recognize that the day of lavish military budgeting is over, at least for the time being. The annual military budgets approved by the Congress rose by 50 percent in real terms (above inflation) between the fiscal years 1980 and 1985. But a sharp reversal has occurred since then. The annual level of defense appropriations, in real terms, actually declined in fiscal 1986, 1987, and 1988. Tough actions are now necessary

| Issue | Conventional Conservative | Conventional Liberal | New Directions |
|-------|---------------------------|----------------------|----------------|
| DEFENSE | Bigger is better. | Small is beautiful. | Cancel weapon systems. Change Pentagon buying. Use pay incentives. |

to close the very wide gap between the reduced level of defense appropriations enacted by the Congress in recent years and the still ambitious spending programs of the Department of Defense. The fact is that the long-term plans of each of the military services include far more weapon systems than future budgets will be able to finance.[4]

Rather than facing up to the difficult strategic choices that have to be made—a clear example of the need to establish priorities—the Pentagon has been keeping current levels of spending low by postponing outlays to future years. The Department of Defense has been juggling payment dates for personnel and equipment between fiscal years, stretching out the production rates on many aircraft and missile programs and reducing current purchases of spare parts and support equipment. This approach does not save the taxpayer any money. Rather, it guarantees that serious budget problems will arise in future years.

To delay writing a government check from September 30 (the last day of one fiscal year) to October 1 (the first day of the next fiscal year) is not to make any genuine economy. Also, uneconomically low production rates, as was noted in chapter 4, are inherently wasteful. The Department of Defense does not get the benefits of lower costs that result from mass production. Arbitrary stretch-outs discourage the private investment in manufacturing facilities that would lower the cost of military production. Moreover, such "economies" as reducing spare and support appropriations from $17.5 billion in fiscal 1986 to $14.1 billion in 1988 ($13 billion in 1986 dollars) diminish the readiness of the armed forces and downgrade their operational capability. It is distressing to learn that, between 1980 and 1987, real budget authority for investment in new weapon systems grew by 82 percent, while the funds to operate the expanding military arsenal rose by only 25 percent.[5]

There is no substitute for making hard decisions to close down the production lines of specific low-priority military programs. Rather than relying on temporary adjustments and stretch-outs, the more marginal military weapon systems (those that add a very modest degree of capability to the equipment they would replace) should be canceled. It is not so much a question of laymen's making those decisions as forcing the people in charge of the Department of Defense to make some choices.

A strong case can be made for cutting back substantially the procurement of the next generation of offensive nuclear weapons carriers. Some of these new weapon systems are redundant. As a means of overcoming Soviet air defense, the Stealth bomber follows B-1 bomber production and two generations of air-launched cruise missiles. Some strategic experts contend that these two new weapons lack a clear strategic rationale. Since the Soviets have been moving toward mobile missiles, the Trident II submarine-launched long-range missile system will be coming on line at about the time when the targets they are designed to hit (such as hardened missile silos) will be declining substantially.

The Strategic Defense Initiative (SDI, or "Star Wars") is an important, and expensive, research program. Unfortunately, some of its more enthusiastic supporters ignore the key lessons of the past: make the decisions on production *after* the completion of full tests of the experimental and developmental effort. Otherwise, the potential for waste—in both time and money—is overwhelming. Enthusiasm is no substitute for careful analysis.

As former Assistant Secretary of Defense Lawrence Korb has pointed out, military planners should understand that it is not possible to do everything at once. He notes that "the alternative is to do everything badly."[6] In the military area, especially, there is no substitute for hard choices—and they have not yet been made.

### TACKLING THE WELFARE PROGRAMS

Soft spots in the budget are by no means limited to military programs. One of the largest civilian areas of federal spending, and one of the more controversial, is welfare and related efforts to alleviate poverty. As was shown in chapter 10, the problem of poverty has not been solved by quadrupling the amount of money spent for the purpose over recent decades. The traditional liberal approach—be compassionate—does not suffice. But neither does the prevailing conservative response—just reduce the budget for welfare. The standard positions, both liberal and conservative, are inadequate.

It is the attitudes and incentives of people that need changing, and that is not a task for which government agencies are well suited. As we have seen, the path out of poverty is well known: education, family, and work. The odds are overwhelming that any youngster who finishes high school, takes a job, and gets married will stay out of poverty. Each of these three actions reinforces the others. A high school diploma improves the

| Issue | Conventional Conservative | Conventional Liberal | New Directions |
|---|---|---|---|
| WELFARE | Cut government spending. | Increase government spending. | Emphasize school, work, family. |

chances that a youngster will be offered a job. With that income, he or she can afford to get married. And having the responsibility of supporting a family makes it more likely that the youngsters will get and keep income-producing work. In contrast, the knowledge that the government will take the financial responsibility for children reduces the incentive to get married or even to finish school and go to work.[7]

The federal government needs to focus its resources and efforts on eliminating the obstacles in the path that leads out of poverty. The existence of high unemployment rates among sixteen- and seventeen-year-old high school dropouts does not mean that a shortage of jobs is the fundamental problem. Rather, those children have not completed the minimum amount of schooling necessary to function in a modern society, and they should be encouraged to do so.

Government should try to avoid well-meaning but counterproductive diversions. Raising the compulsory minimum wage deters young people from getting that necessary initial work experience. No amount of posturing by unions who represent workers with incomes way above the minimum wage will change that fundamental relationship. Raising welfare payments to that minimum, as is often suggested, diminishes the incentive to gain the work experience necessary for advancing out of welfare.

The lessons of the past are clear: welfare experience generates more welfare experience, while work experience generates more work experience. Merely examining the array of jobs listed with any local employment service office is instructive. The number of low-skilled but unfilled positions at the bottom of the employment ladder is substantial.

The next administration might well consider whether the concept of welfare as an entitlement should be abandoned as the unhelpful triumph of the heart over the mind. A fresh start would call for all able-bodied people to learn that the financial responsibility for raising children once again belongs to the parents, not to some unknown taxpayer who has never met them. Kevin Hopkins has put it directly and clearly, "If you need money, get a job."[8]

FIXING THE EDUCATIONAL SYSTEM

"It's a national disgrace." That is how D. Allen Bromley, the Yale physicist and former vice-chairman of the White House Science Council Panel on the Health of U.S. Colleges and Universities, describes the American high school system. "Our pre-college system has essentially collapsed and is not vaguely competitive with that of other countries," he concludes.[9]

## The Choices Facing America

| Issue | Conventional Conservative | Conventional Liberal | New Directions |
|-------|---------------------------|----------------------|----------------|
| EDUCATION | Permit prayer in school. | Busing for integration. | Focus concern on education. |

Bromley's findings may be overstated. Nonetheless, it has become fashionable to lambaste the educational establishment for the shortcomings of our young people, and much of the criticism is deserved. Simultaneously, it is popular to attack President Reagan and the Congress for using the meat ax on the education budget; and large cuts were indeed made early in the administration.

But the fundamental failure must be sought elsewhere. The average teacher is both conscientious and reasonably well trained. Moreover, educational shortages do not reflect real funding shortages; the overall financing trend has been steadily upward. The fault—in the judgment of this educator-parent-citizen—lies with parents as citizens.

If that notion jars conventional thinking, just consider the three features of public school that generate by far the most compelling interest among parents and citizens generally. What truly gets the adrenaline flowing? At the risk of offending many concerned citizens, I must report that those three features are busing to the schools, prayer in the schools, and athletics after school. I can recall no occasion when any organized parental concern with basic educational matters ever began to rival the emotions aroused by the controversies over prayer, busing, and sports. Whatever the merits of those three issues, none of them is central to teaching students the skills and knowledge required for modern society.

Americans need to remind themselves of the obvious: the basic role of the school system is to educate the young people of the nation. From the viewpoint of operating the educational system, the social, religious, and athletic questions are, at best, secondary. In the worst circumstances, the focus on those secondary questions is disruptive and counterproductive to achieving the goal of educating the nation's children. To improve the nation's schools requires a reorientation of citizen thinking away from what an educator must describe as well-intentioned special interests. Schools and parents must put learning first.

### REFORMING TAX REFORM

Over the years, supply-siders have vehemently attacked anyone making too much of a fuss about controlling spending. (I write from lots of

| Issue | Conventional Conservative | Conventional Liberal | New Directions |
|-------|---------------------------|----------------------|----------------|
| TAXATION | Raise taxes on consumption. | Raise taxes on upper incomes. | Tackle the budget first. |

experience on that score.) In their convoluted world, those voicing great concern about government spending and deficits betray a hidden agenda to rescind the tax cuts. But the truth is the reverse: if we do not deal with the deficits by cutting the growth of federal spending, there will be no realistic alternative to a tax increase.

Given the current composition of federal programs, raising tax rates is a confession of failure to control government outlays. If supply-siders truly want to preserve the two rounds of personal tax reductions enacted in the 1980s, then they have to get off the sidelines and enter the battle of the budget with both fists swinging.

Taxation is an area of public policy that separates liberals from conservatives and, typically, Democrats from Republicans. To be sure, no politician wants to increase taxes. It is just that some overcome that reluctance more quickly than others. Liberals and Democrats, in the current environment, frequently wind up taking the lead in proposing various types of federal revenue raisers. They tend to focus on reversing the recent tax cuts enjoyed by upper-income earners or on other ways of adding to the tax burden of "the rich."

It takes longer for conservatives and Republicans to get around to advocating tax increases, especially while Ronald Reagan remains in the Oval Office. Yet, many conservatives-Republicans down deep have a thirst for another round of tax reform. They want to see a fundamental shift in the federal revenue structure away from a primary reliance on income taxation and toward a tax system based mainly on consumption. Perhaps an important subliminal reason for adopting a consumption-oriented tax system is that many of the advocates think that their personal tax burdens will decline. The stated arguments for supporting the change are much more high-minded—reduce the burden on saving and investment, promote efficiency because business expenses would no longer be tax deductible, adopt a tax system more comparable to those of our overseas competitors, and, of course, reduce the budget deficits.

But an important negative accompanies any renewed debate on tax policy: it shifts attention away from the urgent need to control federal spending. Moreover, the 1980s have already witnessed an unusual number of changes in the Internal Revenue Code. The economy—as well as taxpayers, both business and individual—would benefit from an extended period of stability in the tax system. Uncertainty, fueled by speculation about future tax changes, is devastating for new investment. It would be helpful if Congress were to turn its attention to other matters (especially budget cutting) so that citizens could make their personal and business plans on the assumption of continuity in tax policy. Although the 1986 Internal Revenue Code falls far short of perfection, we can live with it. Unfortunately, it is well known that the very threat of new tax legislation accelerates the collections of congressional political action committees.

CLEANING UP THE ECOLOGY LAWS

Environmental policy is another area of public concern likely to receive substantial attention in the next presidential administration. The new White House staff will find that the positions advocated by both business and ecological groups are singularly unhelpful; they are mirror images. Self-interest is obvious on the part of business representatives who favor an easing of environmental rule making. Yet, the reverse attitude on the part of ecological organizations—that more restrictions are always better than fewer—is no improvement.

As was explained in chapter 11, the real need is for public policy to discourage the creation of pollution in the first place; otherwise the EPA will always be in the frustrating position of trying to deal with an ever more rapidly growing mountain of environmental hazards. To anyone who has studied the basic principles of economics, the solution is obvious—make the act of polluting more expensive so that people will go out of their way to avoid generating pollution. The idea is not as radical as it might seem. Pollution fees have been used in Western Europe for years and with reasonable success.

Unfortunately, there is an unspoken, but powerful, alliance between business and environmental groups that is intent on opposing any specific suggestion to reduce the incentive to pollute. Most environmental

| Issue | Conventional Conservative | Conventional Liberal | New Directions |
|-------|---------------------------|----------------------|----------------|
| ECOLOGY | Relax environmental rule making. | Toughen environmental rule making. | Shift to incentive approaches. |

groups are dominated by lawyers, and litigation comes naturally to them. That attitude is encouraged by a variety of statutes that provide generous reimbursement for legal costs to those who challenge environment regulations or the way they are carried out. Often the payment is made whether the "intervener" wins or loses the case.[10] Naturally, all this has required business firms to set up legal staffs in self-defense. The result is better business for attorneys, rather than more rapid progress toward a cleaner environment.

But I am not setting up the reader for a plea to shift the responsibility for environmental policy from lawyers to economists. At its heart, the preventing of pollution and cleaning up of hazardous dump sites is a technical task, best directed by scientists and engineers. Great Britain has achieved approximately the same degree of environmental improvement as the United States, with a substantially lower burden on its economy. The key difference is that there are fewer disputes in British courts and more joint efforts between scientists and engineers in the public and private sectors. In the absence of adversary relations, there is greater opportunity to develop more effective methods of dealing with environmental hazards.

Given the dissatisfaction with the status quo on environmental matters, the basic aim of existing ecological law needs to be revised. The goal should not be to punish people or organizations for the act of polluting or disposing of wastes. Rather, public policy should positively encourage all citizens to make, buy, and use products whose production and use generate less pollution; that is not done by mere pleas to be kinder to the environment. Rather, it requires innovations like stiff taxes on the creation of pollution.

Nobody really wants to pay more for the things he or she buys. But, as we have learned with some pain over the past decade, having to pay more for energy has encouraged the United States to use less energy than it did in the early 1970s. Having to pay more for products that cause much pollution would, similarly, discourage us from making and buying those products. Voluntarily, we would find ourselves shifting to a low-pollution economy.

The needed new direction in public policy requires a sustained effort at public education. That effort could well take for a guiding principle the point made by Dr. J. Richard Crout, when he was director of the FDA's Bureau of Drugs: "In the business of regulation, there are few clear-cut choices between vice and virtue. There are only hard compromises among competing desirable goals."[11]

| Issue | Conventional Conservative | Conventional Liberal | New Directions |
|---|---|---|---|
| FOREIGN TRADE | "Fair trade" to help business. | "Fair trade" to help unions. | Free trade. Improve competitiveness. |

## FAIR VERSUS FREE TRADE

It is fascinating to watch a "debate" on television dealing with foreign trade. In an effort to be fair, a program on textile imports usually includes representatives of both the textile companies and the Textile Workers Union. Invariably, the viewer is surprised by the love affair between the two groups.

However, that format betrays ignorance of the underlying issue, which is not a labor-versus-management question at all. Rather, the real conflict is between a particular group of producers (be they those of steel or autos or textiles) and consumers in general. Of course, the unions and the company managements in a given industry can quickly agree on policy proposals that will help them at the expense of the rest of society. Missing from the TV program, and from most other public discussions on foreign trade, are representatives of the public interest, the consumers who are hurt by the price increases that result from reduced competition.

The typical proposal to deal with the rise in imports requires the government to stem that inflow. Such action tends, at least in the short run, to be helpful to the domestic industry that has been losing its market share. But it does little to enhance the efficiency of the protected industry, and the resultant higher prices reduce the competitiveness of the domestic industries using the "protected" product. Given the high (albeit hidden) cost of protectionist actions, some new directions will need to be explored in the decade ahead.

An alternative to restrictions on international trade is increases in the competitiveness of the industries that have been hard hit by imports. That is no easy task. Because there are many reasons why American companies have been losing their market positions, no single solution will suffice. As has already been explained in detail, the run-up in the value of the dollar in the early 1980s was the equivalent of a substantial increase in the price of American goods competing with foreign products. The most practical method of evening the scales is to restore the dollar to its previous position. Trade restrictions—enacted in the guise of promoting "fair trade"—will not do it. A more effective response is

*277*

to reduce the extraordinary budget deficits whose financing puts so much pressure on the dollar.

Beyond such general fiscal measures, individual industries will benefit from controlling their costs and raising their productivity. But that is not a task for Washington. Rather, it is the responsibility of the management and workers in each company. These alternatives to protection are much harder than simply blaming problems on foreigners, but they are also far more effective.

AVOIDING BAILOUTS

*Bailout* is a pejorative term, and everybody is reluctant to favor the government's providing such a special benefit to anyone. Yet, both liberals and conservatives often support bailouts of specific companies. Conservatives tend to wind up agreeing on an ad hoc basis that the government should come to the aid of a specific "worthy" enterprise, be it Lockheed or Penn Central. Many liberals, in contrast, prefer a more orderly and comprehensive policy, whereby standards are set in advance for selecting the enterprises to be helped. In its most highly developed form, this latter approach is known as "industrial policy."

A third alternative invariably surfaces during the debates on specific bailouts but is usually dismissed as a do-nothing policy—that of opposing all bailouts as undesirable involvement in private business. Selective subsidies put unprotected companies at a disadvantage. After all, it is unfair for the government to subsidize one company (such as Chrysler) and not its competitors. Also, the willingness of Uncle Sam to come to the rescue of individual companies that get into financial difficulty sends the wrong signal to all private enterprises: feel free to take the riskiest long shot, because if it does not work out, the government will come to your rescue. Heads you win, tails they lose. That is what economists call a "moral hazard."

As a practical matter, it is easy to adopt a policy against bailouts when no compelling plea for such help is being made. The test is to follow that course when an "urgent" problem surfaces. In a competitive economy, we can anticipate that one or more large institutions will get into serious difficulty from time to time.

| Issue | Conventional Conservative | Conventional Liberal | New Directions |
|-------|---------------------------|----------------------|----------------|
| BAILOUTS | Oppose bailouts except for a few worthy cases. | Adopt a more fair and uniform bailout policy. | Avoid all bailouts. |

## The Choices Facing America

Refraining from bailing out companies makes it less likely that individual enterprises will get into financial difficulties and need help from the federal government. The resultant lower level of federal spending—and thus a smaller deficit to be financed—means more credit available for the private sector, and at lower interest rates. Say's law (supply creates its own demand) works with a vengeance in this area of public policy: the potential supply of bailouts generates a demand for such aid. The likelihood of the government's coming to the rescue reduces the willingness of operating management to take tough actions to curb costs. It also makes it less likely that organized labor will tailor its demands to the company's limited financial capability. Conversely, a credible nonbailout policy will increase the likelihood that labor and management will make the tough decisions that maintain business competitiveness. The experiences of the 1980s tend to confirm the effectiveness of that laissez-faire policy.

### TAKEOVERS

To an observer of the current American business scene, the response of many companies to the threat of takeovers is discouraging. As a general proposition, company managements sincerely believe in competition. Better than anyone else, they know that the competitive process keeps companies on their toes by forcing them to design new products, develop more economical ways to produce, and keep prices down.

But the gap between theory and practice is wide. To be sure, companies always encourage competition among their suppliers. It is the rivalry with their own competitors that tests the limits of their commitment to the concept of free enterprise. *Price chiselers* seems to be the preferred term to describe those terrible companies that compete against your own firm by selling at lower prices or buying at higher prices.

Takeovers involve a special form of competition: the rivalry among groups of executives for control of a given firm. Human nature being what it is, the existing management rarely welcomes any competition in the market for "corporate control," to use the technical term. Of course, the existing management believes it can do a much better job

| Issue | Conventional Conservative | Conventional Liberal | New Directions |
|-------|--------------------------|----------------------|----------------|
| TAKEOVERS | Strengthen the hand of management. | Protect the communities affected. | Keep government out of corporate battles. |

for the shareholder than can those outsiders who know nothing about the company, and often they are right. Many of them have dedicated the major share of their working lives to the company, and they do not believe it fair for them to be turned out in favor of a group that merely offers their shareholders a "few" dollars above whatever happens to be the going market price for their shares.

Management usually feels so strongly about the matter that it goes to great lengths to make sure that the shareholders are not forced to decide whether they want to keep the old management or go with the new. Competition is all right when you are buying and selling cars or refrigerators, but there need to be limits. At least, so goes the implicit argument for more government regulation of takeovers.

Conservatives, and especially organizations representing the top managements of the larger firms, generally want the government to pass laws that deter unwanted takeovers. Liberals, many of whom are not especially enamored of big business, often support those proposals. However, they cite broader concerns of public policy, such as protecting the employees and the surrounding community from mass layoffs, large pay cuts, and other changes that the new management might make. It is fascinating to see how often conventional liberals and conventional conservatives wind up on the same side when they get down to the wire of public policy decision making.

In pressing for a larger role for government, both groups overlook the responsibility of the boards of directors of companies—especially the outside directors who are not members of the management—to represent the interests of the shareholders. If the governing boards of American corporations are really doing their jobs, new legislation may not be needed. But if the boards are merely rubber stamps for the management, pressures for additional laws will continue to mount.

Such diverse actions as the government's deterring takeovers or restricting imports or bailing out a company are all variations on the same theme: the public sector favoring private interests at the expense of the rest of society. Laissez-faire (government keeping its hands off) may sound like a do-nothing policy. But such forbearance is more even-handed and also the key to a productive and competitive economy.

## AMERICA AND THE REST OF THE WORLD

Any realistic assessment of the prospects of the American economy in the coming decade needs to be based on the realization that an important new factor has entered the economic equation—the various developing nations that have become significant competitors in the international marketplace. The relative positions of the older economies will never be the same. Being "number one" across the spectrum of global competition is simply no longer a realistic objective for any one country. Protectionist restrictions on international commerce may slow down, but cannot prevent, important shifts in the role that each nation will play in the years ahead.

Economic history provides a useful perspective. In the nineteenth century, European investors financed in large measure the construction of the canals, railroads, and heavy industry that enabled the United States to become a global economic power. But when that occurred, the European monopoly over the world economy was eliminated, although their trade continued to rise in absolute terms. A word of warning is in order: American borrowing from abroad in the nineteenth century bore little relation to the rising indebtedness of the 1980s. When foreign investors in the nineteenth century bought stocks or bonds from our companies, the money was generally put to productive use. In many cases, the profits from those enterprises far exceeded the cost of the capital that was provided.

In contrast, in recent years the U.S. Treasury has been borrowing heavily abroad to finance deficits arising from rapid expansions in defense outlays, entitlements, farm subsidies, and interest payments. No matter how worthy or necessary those items of federal expenditure may be, they represent current consumption. These federal expenditures are not investments that generate a future return to repay or even cover the interest on the Treasury securities.

However, a process is now taking place that is analogous to our experience in the preceding century. Investment funds provided by the United States and other developed nations have been helping to create a new set of actors on the world economic stage, mainly in the Asian rim. Once again, the return to the status quo is not in the cards. In the short run, the adjustments are painful to many established sectors of the advanced societies.

On the supply or cost side, the older industrialized nations are finding that the differentials between the wages of their workers and those in the newly industrialized nations are shrinking. On the demand side, the residents of those newly industrialized countries can be expected soon to become consumers on a scale that corresponds to their industrial prowess.[12]

Over the long run, these changes make for a stronger international trading system. In turn, the expanded flow of international trade and investment will result in higher living standards for consumers generally. That was the experience of the nineteenth century, and it is being replicated as we approach the twenty-first century. But the effects are uneven, and there are losers as well as winners. Where the United States will stand in any subsequent international ranking will depend in large measure on our own actions, past, current, and future.

Clearly, we are no longer the overwhelmingly dominant economic force in the world. This nation, which accounted for nearly 50 percent of the GNP of the non-Communist world in 1950, is down to less than 30 percent at present. We are heading for a level of 20 percent or less by the end of the century.[13] In many competitive sectors, this country is no longer first. However, the new wealth of Japan, West Germany, and other West European and Asian nations means that they now possess the capacity to take on more of the burden of providing aid to the poorer, developing nations. That would help reduce our budget deficits—an objective that those countries have been urging vehemently.

In a more fundamental way, the nations of Western Europe and the Asian rim need to realize that the United States is not likely to continue adjusting its policies to ensure a healthy world economy while its major trading partners enjoy the luxury of pursuing policies aimed solely at domestic goals.[14] For their own self-interest—the only reliable justification for a country's actions—those other nations ought to take on larger shares of such important common responsibilities as maintaining the security of the non-Communist world, submerging domestic protectionist pressures, and maintaining monetary and fiscal policies that help generate noninflationary economic growth. By no means would such changes in international relations eliminate this country's extensive role on the world stage. But other nations would be recognizing the new world economic reality and going beyond their current passive roles of supporting players.

## Conclusion

Probably the most difficult problems that will face the American people during the coming decade will be questions that are not now on anyone's agenda. The analyses presented here will, I hope, be helpful to citizens who want to think seriously about new approaches to the issues of the 1990s. If there is any overriding theme that emerges from this

# The Choices Facing America

book, it is that the next President must be a tough manager of the nitty-gritty business of government. The need is not for drama but for performance. Yet, to marshal and maintain the necessary public support, the occupant of the Oval Office must inspire as well as direct.

It seems clear that, after the eight years of Ronald Reagan's administration, the American people expect substantial changes in government policy. President Reagan surely has shifted—and in many ways improved—the nation's policy agenda. The next administration, Republican or Democrat, will start from where he leaves off. But the policy pendulum will probably continue to swing; a return to the position of January 1981 is unlikely.

Many observers anticipate a more activist stance in recognizing and acting on national problems. Some reaction against the current relaxed attitude toward the budget and trade deficits may be in the cards no matter who moves into the Oval Office in January 1989. A visible movement away from what seems to many to be a passive probusiness attitude on regulatory matters may also be inevitable. After a long period of decline, the union movement is trying to revitalize itself, and government can be expected to influence that new trend. Some of these developments may be merely surface adjustments, similar to the modest changes proposed by several Republican presidents following Franklin D. Roosevelt's ambitious New Deal reforms. In any event, a public-sector analogue to product differentiation is natural. The next President will attempt to leave his own mark on American history.

A SAMPLE ECONOMIC AGENDA

Let us try to develop a policy agenda for the coming decade, drawing on key elements of the preceding analysis and adding a few new items. These are questions likely to be facing the next President, although the answers he comes up with may be very different:

I. Deal with the budget deficits by controlling government in its many dimensions.
  A. Reform the governing institutions.
    1. Change the budget process.
      a. Adopt multiyear budgeting.
      b. Combine the budget and appropriations committees.
      c. Eliminate duplication of authorizations and appropriations.
    2. Tighten the congressional committee structure.
      a. Reduce the number of subcommittees.
      b. Extend budget cutting to congressional staffs.

B. Make budget cuts in every department and agency.
1. Start with the military.
   a. Cancel several marginal weapon systems.
   b. Streamline military procurement.
   c. Postpone retired pay for newcomers until age fifty or fifty-five.
   d. Adjust pay scales to reflect labor market conditions.
2. Tackle the entitlements.
   a. Cap automatic increases in Social Security.
   b. Limit eligibility for welfare to people who cannot fend for themselves.
3. Phase out farm subsidies in four years.
4. Require each department head to identify one large low-priority program and eliminate it.
C. Defer tax reform to a future agenda.
1. Initiate careful planning for a possible next round.
2. Do not put the cart of tax reform before the horse of budget cuts.

II. Enhance American competitiveness in the world economy.
A. Elevate education to a higher national priority.
1. Assign 2 percent of all budget cuts to higher spending on the education of the American people.
   a. Avoid expanding the educational bureaucracy.
   b. Ship the money directly to schools and colleges.
2. Focus national attention on the basic task of the schools—to educate the people.
3. Let noneducational concerns take a backseat for a while.
B. Try to make the regulatory apparatus work better.
1. Appoint heads of regulatory agencies with concern for balance and fairness.
   a. Avoid the 1970s experience of using regulation to hit business.
   b. But also avoid the 1980s episodes of favoring business.
   c. Focus on the intended beneficiary—the consumer.
2. Give environmental regulation high priority.
   a. Break the logjam in disposing of hazardous wastes by introducing economic incentives.
   b. Simplify rule making by using effluent charges to clean the water.
3. Overhaul the regulations inhibiting foreign commerce.
   a. Eliminate obstacles to our own exports.
   b. Convert quotas on imports to revenue tariffs.
C. Refrain from adding to the expenses of production.
1. Avoid imposing medical and other personal costs on business payrolls.
2. Do not tax the efficient to bail out the inefficient.
3. Do not tax the working people to support those who can work but choose not to.

III. Instill a sense of priorities by selecting a limited number of key policy areas for action.

There is something special to be gained just from making some of the tough choices contained in the preceding policy agenda. It is to demonstrate to ourselves that we as a people do indeed have the ability to make difficult and unpopular decisions. Lawrence Malkin reminds us of the great—and still relevant—line that Ronald Reagan used when he was sworn in as governor of California in 1967, "The truth is there are simple answers. There are just not easy ones."[15]

We can comfort ourselves with the knowledge that, to the extent that we make those tough decisions, we will be developing the basis for a more productive economy. That, in turn, will generate a higher standard of living for our citizens and, simultaneously, the ability to devote resources to a variety of social and other noneconomic purposes.

If anyone—politician or professor—offers a simple and easy, albeit innovative, solution to the problems besetting the United States, prudence requires that we react with great skepticism. The hard fact is that, as a nation, we have run out of painless answers. The appropriate symbol of public policy for the next four years is a belt being tightened. But it is not just a matter of encouraging a new attitude of frugality in the public sector.

SOME ECONOMIC PERSPECTIVE

The need of these times is to slow down the pace of consumption—by government, private organizations, and individuals—and to encourage the saving that is necessary to finance investment in a brighter future. The reduction of the massive trade deficits to manageable size will require a significant decrease in the growth of domestic spending in the United States and a further decline in the value of the dollar. These adjustments are inevitable; the sooner they occur, the less painful they will be. Large reductions in the budget deficit (eliminating most of the present "structural" deficit in the budget) should be accompanied, at critical times, by a judicious easing of monetary policy—to help keep the nation out of recession or, at least, to minimize any decline in the national economy.[16]

We Americans have to make a closer connection between the macro and micro aspects of economic life. We expect the benefits of economic efficiency in the form of a rising standard of living. But we are reluctant to change our personal work and consumption habits or to suffer the dislocations necessary to bring about change and progress.[17] Too many of us still think that it is a job for the other fellow.

The time to pay the piper is now. No President or Congress can repeal the concept of compound interest. The longer we as a nation wait to pay our personal and national indebtedness, the bigger will be the bill. The party will soon be over. Our favorite four-letter words must become *hard work*. Americans today face a belated rendezvous with reality.

# NOTES

## Chapter 1

1. Former Secretary of Commerce Peter G. Peterson has entitled his warning along these lines "The Morning After," *Atlantic,* October 1987, pp. 43–69.

2. David A. Stockman, *The Triumph of Politics: Why the Reagan Revolution Failed* (New York: Harper & Row, 1986).

3. The White House, *A Program for Economic Recovery* (Washington, D.C.: Government Printing Office, 1981), p. 1.

4. Charles R. Hulten and Isabel V. Sawhill, *The Legacy of Reaganomics* (Washington, D.C.: Urban Institute Press, 1984), pp. 1–2. For a more negative view of the Reagan presidency, see Robert Lekachman, *Visions and Nightmares: America after Reagan* (New York: Macmillan, 1987).

5. Phillip Cagan reaches a similar conclusion: "The results of the Reagan program are mixed. . . . [M]any of the administration's failures ironically stemmed indirectly from its successes." Phillip Cagan, ed., *The Impact of the Reagan Program* (Washington, D.C.: American Enterprise Institute, 1986), pp. 1–4.

6. *Economic Report of the President, January 1987* (Washington, D.C.: Government Printing Office, 1987), p. 278.

7. "Major Work Stoppages: 1986," *U.S. Department of Labor News,* March 6, 1987, p. 1.

8. The Reagan administration also succeeded in targeting social spending more narrowly to the poor. The share of benefits going to eliminate poverty increased. See John C. Weicker, "The Reagan Domestic Budget Cuts: Proposals, Outcomes, and Effects," in Cagan, ed., *Reagan Program,* p. 7.

9. Philip Shabecoff, "After 85 Years, the Era of Big Dams Nears End," *New York Times,* January 24, 1987, p. 6.

10. John Herbers, "Local Government in U.S. Is Reshaped by Federal Moves," *New York Times,* November 30, 1986, p. 1.

11. John Shannon, "The Return to Fend-for-Yourself Federalism: The Reagan Mark," *Intergovernmental Perspective,* Summer–Fall 1987, p. 36.

12. Presidential Task Force on Regulatory Relief, *Reagan Administration Regulatory Achievements* (Washington, D.C.: The White House, August 11, 1983).

13. "Opinion Roundup," *Public Opinion,* November–December 1987, p. 26.

14. A. Gary Shilling, *The World Has Definitely Changed* (New York: Lakeview Press, 1987).

15. *Public Opinion,* February–March 1983, p. 19.

16. William Branson et al., *Expected Fiscal Policy and the Recession of 1982* (Cambridge, Mass.: National Bureau of Economic Research, 1986).

17. Seymour Martin Lipset and William Schneider, "The Confidence Gap during the Reagan Years, 1981–1987," *Political Science Quarterly,* Spring 1987, p. 4.

18. See White House, *Program for Economic Recovery.*

19. "The lesson learned from past data thus appears to be that changing aggregate tax rates does not cause spending to change." George M. Von Furstenberg et al., "Have Taxes Led Government Expenditures? The United States as a Test Case," *Journal of Public Policy* (1987): 321.

20. Paul Craig Roberts, *The Supply-Side Revolution* (Cambridge: Harvard University Press, 1984), chaps. 2 and 3.

21. These views were expressed by a high Treasury official while the Budget Working Group was meeting with department heads defending their budgets against proposed cuts.

22. Martin Feldstein, "Supply-Side Economics: Old Truths and New Claims," *American Economic Review,* May 1986, pp. 27–28.

23. Jean Jacques Servan-Schreiber, *The American Challenge* (New York: Atheneum, 1968).

24. Adam Smith, *An Inquiry into the Nature and Causes of the Wealth of Nations* (New York: Modern Library, 1937), p. 681.

25. "[T]here is an ironic but substantial inverse correlation between the degree of consensus among economists and the degree of public acceptance of their findings." Walter W. Heller, "What's Right with Economics?" *American Economic Review,* March 1975, p. 5.

## Chapter 2

1. William Armstrong, "Wasteful Spending," *Congressional Record,* May 27, 1987, p. S7213.

2. Computed from Office of Management and Budget, *Budget of the United States Government, Fiscal Year 1988* (Washington, D.C.: Government Printing Office, 1987), table 2.

3. Federal investment outlays, however measured, have been a declining share of the federal budget during the 1980s. Charles L. Schultze, "Alternative Measures of Federal Investment Outlays," in Charles R. Hulten and Isabel V. Sawhill, eds., *The Legacy of Reaganomics* (Washington, D.C.: Urban Institute Press, 1984), pp. 175–78.

4. President's Private Sector Survey on Cost Control, *A Report to the President* (Washington, D.C.: Government Printing Office, 1984).

5. Peter G. Peterson, "The Morning After," *Atlantic,* October 1987, p. 44.

6. *Proposals to Deal with the Social Security Notch Problem* (Washington, D.C.: American Enterprise Institute, 1985).

7. Peterson, "Morning After," p. 61.

8. See Michael J. Boskin et al., "Social Security: A Financial Appraisal across and within Generations," *National Tax Journal,* 40 (1987): 19–34.

9. John Makin, "Blame Entitlements for the Deficit," *Washington Post Weekly,* March 9, 1987, p. 29.

10. Quoted in Robert W. DeGrasse, Jr., *Military Expansion, Economic Decline* (Armonk, N.Y.: M. E. Sharpe, 1983), p. 6.

11. "Aspin Accounting Standards," *Wall Street Journal,* July 6, 1987, p. 12.

12. Compare the current situation with that suggested by a 1980 report of the General Accounting Office: "Attrition of first-term enlisted personnel—their separation from service before completion of their tours—has become a serious and costly problem for the All-Volunteer Force, affecting its ability to maintain full strength and combat readiness."

# Notes

Comptroller General, *Attrition in the Military—An Issue Needing Management Attention* (Washington, D.C.: General Accounting Office, 1980), p. 1.

13. Comptroller General, *The Defense Budget: A Look at Budgetary Resources, Accomplishments and Problems* (Washington, D.C.: General Accounting Office, 1983), pp. iii–viii.

14. *U.S. News and World Report,* October 31, 1983, p. 18.

15. Cait Murphy, "Who Is Holding Up Grace Commission Reform?" *Policy Review,* Fall 1986, p. 63.

16. Brooks Jackson, "Moves to Close Bases, Reduce Other Waste in Military Often Fail," *Wall Street Journal,* July 16, 1982, p. 1.

17. Lindsey Gruson, "Military Cites Waste in Law Forcing Coal Use in Europe," *New York Times,* June 8, 1986, p. 14.

18. Office of Management and Budget, *Special Analyses, Budget of the United States Government, Fiscal Year 1988* (Washington, D.C.: Government Printing Office, 1987), p. C-8.

19. *Budget of the United States Government, Fiscal Year 1988,* p. 2–14.

20. Comptroller General, *Federal Price Support for Honey Should Be Phased Out* (Washington, D.C.: General Accounting Office, 1985).

21. *Budget of the United States Government, Fiscal Year 1988,* p. 2–15.

22. See chapter 10 for details.

23. Computed from *Budget of the United States Government, Fiscal Year 1988,* table 10, and *Budget of the United States Government, Fiscal Year 1986* (Washington, D.C.: Government Printing Office, 1985), table 20.

24. *A Proposal to Index Local History Files* (Jefferson City, Mo.: Missouri Committee for the Humanities, 1982).

25. Quoted in Gary Klott, "Your Taxes at Work," *New York Times,* May 26, 1987, p. 8.

26. Ibid.

27. Ibid.

28. "Rules Panel in House to Take Latin Trip," *St. Louis Post-Dispatch,* November 27, 1983.

29. Stephen Moore, "Congress' Dirty Dozen: Budget Process Horror Stories," *Heritage Foundation Backgrounder,* September 10, 1987, p. 2.

30. Senate Committee on Environment and Public Works, *Water Resources Development Act of 1983* (Washington, D.C.: Government Printing Office, 1983).

31. Howell Raines, "Thatcher's Capitalist Revolution," *New York Times Magazine,* May 31, 1987, p. 76.

## Chapter 3

1. For reasons to favor a capital budget for the federal government, see Michael J. Boskin, "Capital Budget Is a Useful Tool," *Wall Street Journal,* December 2, 1986, p. 34.

2. Office of Management and Budget, *Special Analyses, Budget of the United States Government, Fiscal Year 1988* (Washington, D.C.: Government Printing Office, 1987), pp. D1–D30.

3. Ibid.

4. "Opinion Roundup," *Public Opinion,* March–April 1987, p. 25.

5. Barry Goldwater, "And They Call This Government?" *Washington Post Weekly,* October 27, 1986, p. 24.

6. Cited in Jonathan Rauch, "Biennial Budgeting Taking Root," *National Journal,* September 27, 1986, p. 2319.

7. Ibid., pp. 2318–19.

8. *99th Congress Committees, 1985–1986* (Washington, D.C.: Congressional Quarterly, 1985), p. 3.

9. For the case in favor of a constitutional amendment, see Alvin Rabushka, "A Constitutional Cure for Deficits," in Laurence H. Meyer, ed., *The Economic Consequences of Government Deficits* (Boston: Kluwer-Nijhoff Publishing, 1983), pp. 183–99. For other views, see the chapters by Peter Aranson, Roger Noll, and Kenneth Shepsle.

10. Quoted in Louis Rukeyser, *What's Ahead for the Economy* (New York: Simon and Schuster, 1983), p. 92. Also, veterans tend to have higher family incomes than nonveterans. Hence, their ability to share in the costs of medical care is likely to be at least as great as that of nonveterans. See Congressional Budget Office, *Veterans Administration Health Care* (Washington, D.C.: Government Printing Office, 1984), p. 51.

11. David E. Sanger, "NASA's Staggering Bills for Getting Off the Ground," *New York Times,* September 6, 1987, p. 16E.

12. Quoted in William Proxmire, *Uncle Sam—The Last of the Bigtime Spenders* (New York: Simon & Schuster, 1972), pp. 25–26.

13. "[R]epeated postponements of resumed shuttle flights speak against augmenting [with a *Challenger* replacement] such an expensive repair-prone system." Molly K. Macauley, "The Trade-in Value of That Fourth Shuttle," *New York Times,* July 9, 1987, p. 22.

14. Quoted in Wendy L. Wall and Thomas F. O'Boyle, "An End of Subsidies Would Endanger Many Farmers," *Wall Street Journal,* July 7, 1987, p. 12.

15. Rudolph G. Penner, "Kowtowing to the Elderly," *New York Times,* May 23, 1982, p. E–3.

16. Kim R. Holmes, "Strengthening America's Defense: Six Steps," *The Heritage Lectures* (Washington, D.C.: Heritage Foundation, 1987), p. 12.

17. Lawrence J. Korb, "A Blueprint for Defense Spending," *Wall Street Journal,* May 20, 1987, p. 32.

18. Alvin L. Schorr, "Redefining Poverty Levels," *New York Times,* May 9, 1984, p. 27.

## Chapter 4

1. Barry J. Shillito, "How to Implement Our Sound Weapons System Acquisition Policies," *Defense Management Journal,* Fall 1971, p. 26.

2. Ibid.

3. *Recent Developments in Government Profit Policy* (Washington, D.C.: Federal Executives Institute, 1987), p. 1.

4. Department of Defense, General Services Administration, and National Aeronautics and Space Administration, *Federal Acquisition Regulations System* (Washington, D.C.: Government Printing Office, 1987).

5. Department of Defense, *Defense Acquisition Circular, 18 August 1986* (Washington, D.C.: Government Printing Office, 1987).

6. *Federal Government Business Aspects Which Entail Unnecessary Expense* (St. Louis: McDonnell Douglas Corporation, 1975).

7. Cited in J. Ronald Fox, *Arming America* (Boston: Harvard University, Graduate School of Business Administration, 1974), p. 285.

8. See also Marjorie Hunter, "Pentagon's Fruitcake: Quite Rich, of Course," *New York Times,* December 23, 1985, p. 18.

9. Thomas G. Pownall, "Defense Procurement Can Improve," *Financier,* November 1986, pp. 44–48.

10. See Fred Hiatt and Rick Atkinson, "The Defense Boom: Uncle Sam Is a Dream of a Customer," *Washington Post Weekly,* April 29, 1985, p. 19.

# Notes

11. Congressional Budget Office, *A Review of the Department of Defense, December 31, 1983, Selected Acquisition Report* (Washington, D.C.: Government Printing Office, 1984).

12. Comptroller General, *DOD Acquisition Programs, Status of Selected Systems* (Washington, D.C.: General Accounting Office, 1987); Comptroller General, *AMRAAM Cost Growth and Schedule Delays* (Washington, D.C.: Government Printing Office, 1987). See also Thomas L. McNaugher, "Buying Weapons: Bleak Prospects for Real Reform," *Brookings Review,* Summer 1986, pp. 11–15.

13. Comptroller General, *Assessing Production Capabilities and Constraints in the Defense Industrial Base* (Washington, D.C.: General Accounting Office, 1985).

14. Richard A. Stubbing, *The Defense Game* (New York: Harper & Row, 1986), p. 226.

15. Comptroller General, *Impediments to Reducing the Costs of Weapon Systems*, p. 5.

16. Fox, *Arming America*, p. 440.

17. Ibid., p. 442.

18. Gregory A. Fossedal, "More Audits Won't Curb Defense Waste," *Wall Street Journal,* June 30, 1986, p. 20.

19. Bill McAllister, "A Bureaucracy Buster at the Postal Service," *Washington Post Weekly,* October 26, 1987, p. 33.

20. "Admiral Wants Ships to Jettison Paper, Take On Fuel and Ammo," *New York Times,* May 5, 1987, p. 15.

21. Michael Rich and Edmund Dews, *Improving the Military Acquisition Process* (Santa Monica: Rand Corporation, 1986).

22. Cynthia Mitchell and Tim Carrington, "Antique Arsenals," *Wall Street Journal,* October 8, 1987, p. 1; Mark Mehler, "Westinghouse Can Be Sure of Its Place in CIM History, *Electronic Business,* February 1987, p. 18.

23. Cited in Stubbing, *Defense Game,* p. 225.

24. Michael Isikoff, "Two Can Bid More Cheaply than One, the Pentagon Learns," *Washington Post Weekly,* May 4, 1987, p. 31.

25. Comptroller General, *Cost Effectiveness of Dual Sourcing for Production Price Competition Is Uncertain* (Washington, D.C.: General Accounting Office, 1984).

26. "G.M. Chooses Pratt for Military Job," *New York Times,* March 27, 1986, p. 28. The Navy maintains that the original contractor "could best judge which firm was both technically and price competitive to perform second source competition." Letter to the author from Everett Pyatt, Assistant Secretary of the Navy, May 28, 1986.

27. Comptroller General, *Assessment of the Study of Defense Contractor Profitability* (Washington, D.C.: General Accounting Office, 1986), pp. 23, 29.

28. Congressional Budget Office, *A Review of the Department of Defense December 31, 1983, Selected Acquisition Reports* (Washington, D.C.: Government Printing Office, 1984), pp. 22–23.

29. "The Military Retirement System," *Washington News,* April 28, 1985, p. 2.

30. Congressional Budget Office, *Setting Personnel Strength Levels* (Washington, DC: Government Printing Office, 1987), p. 11.

31. Martin Anderson, "The All-Volunteer Force Is Working," *Commonsense,* Fall 1979, p. 12.

32. The Committee for Economic Development concluded in 1958 that the risk that defense spending of up to 15 percent of the GNP, "or if necessary even more, will ruin the American way of life is slight indeed." *The Problem of National Security* (New York: Committee for Economic Development, 1958), p. 27. See also Bernard Udis, ed., *The Economic Consequences of Reduced Military Spending* (Lexington, Mass.: Lexington Books, 1973); Henry W. Briefs and Joseph L. Tryon, "Economic Growth: Issues and Prospects," in David M. Abshire and Richard V. Allen, eds., *National Security* (New York: Frederick A. Praeger, 1963), pp. 833–73; "Statement of Robert F. Hale, Assistant Director, National Security Division, Congressional Budget Office, before the Committee on the Budget, U.S. House of Representatives," September 14, 1987, p. 5.

33. Emile Benoit and Kenneth E. Boulding, *Disarmament and the Economy* (New York: Harper & Row, 1963).

34. The poll's sampling error is plus or minus three percentage points. "Military Outlay Cut Wins Favor in Poll as a Deficit Tactic," *New York Times,* August 13, 1987, p. 9.

35. John U. Nef, *War and Human Progress* (New York: W. W. Norton, 1963), p. 416.

36. C. F. Bastable, *Public Finance* (New York: Macmillan, 1895), pp. 67–68.

## Chapter 5

1. Joint Committee on Taxation, *Estimated Revenue Effects of the Possible Conference Compromise* (Washington, D.C.: unpublished worksheets, August 16, 1986), table 1.

2. For details see *Explanation of the Tax Reform Act of 1986* (Houston: Pannell Kerr Forster, 1986); *Tax Reform Act of 1986* (St. Louis: Rubin, Brown, Gornstein & Co., 1986); *Tax Reform 1986* (Chicago: Arthur Andersen & Co., 1986).

3. Henry J. Aaron, "The Impossible Dream Comes True: The New Tax Reform Act," *Brookings Review,* Winter 1987, p. 6. See also Del Bradshaw and Richard B. McKenzie, *Tax Reform as a Tax Increase in 1987* (St. Louis: Washington University, Center for the Study of American Business, 1987).

4. Internal Revenue Service, *Instructions for Form W-4* (Washington, D.C.: Government Printing Office, 1987).

5. Quoted in Gary Klott, "Tax Forms on Mortgage and I.R.A.'s Are Long," *New York Times,* August 14, 1987, p. 24.

6. Quoted in Gary Klott, "New Forms, New Confusion," *New York Times,* September 1, 1987, p. 26.

7. Ibid.

8. Letter to the author from the chief executive of a company whose board of directors he serves on, dated December 19, 1986.

9. Quoted in Aileen Jacobson, "Proposed Tax Bill Means Business, Preparers Say," *Newsday,* August 15, 1986, p. 41.

10. Joel Prakken, Laurence Meyer, and Chris Varvares, *The Senate Finance Committee Staff Option for Tax Reform* (St. Louis: Washington University, Center for the Study of American Business, 1986). See also *New Tax Law to Cut U.S. Employment Growth by 510,000 Jobs* (Lexington, Mass.: Data Resources, 1986); Steven M. Fazzari, "Tax Reform and Investment," *Monthly Review of the Federal Reserve Bank of St. Louis,* January 1987, pp. 15–27.

11. K. J. Kowalewski, "Home Equity Lines: Characteristics and Consequences," *Federal Reserve Bank of Cleveland Economic Commentary,* June 1, 1987, pp. 1–4.

12. Jeffrey H. Birnbaum, "Business's Schism over Tax Overhaul Reflects the Divide-and-Conquer Strategy of Proponents," *Wall Street Journal,* December 5, 1985, p. 54.

13. See Allen Sinai, *The Tax Reform Act of 1986: Winners and Losers* (New York: Shearson Lehman Brothers, 1986); Gilbert A. Harter, *How Tax Reform Would Affect Companies with Different Growth and Profitability Characteristics* (Midland, Mich.: Dow Chemical Co., 1986).

14. Gary Klott, "Rostenkowski Proposes Tax Rate Rise in Future," *New York Times,* September 5, 1986, p. 1.

15. *Money for Nothing: The Failure of Corporate Tax Incentives, 1981–84* (Washington, D.C.: Citizens for Tax Justice, 1986).

16. Murray L. Weidenbaum, *Do Tax Incentives for Investment Work?* (St. Louis: Washington University, Center for the Study of American Business, 1986).

# Notes

17. Michael J. Boskin, *The Impact of the 1981–82 Investment Incentives on Business Fixed Investment* (Washington, D.C.: National Chamber Foundation, 1985).

18. Henry J. Aaron and Harvey Galper, *Assessing Tax Reform* (Washington, D.C.: Brookings Institution, 1985).

19. See George N. Carlson, *Value-Added Tax* (Washington, D.C.: Department of the Treasury, 1980).

20. Charles E. Walker and Mark A. Bloomfield, eds., *New Directions in Federal Tax Policy for the 1980s* (Cambridge, Mass.: Ballinger, 1983).

21. George L. Perry, "Getting Back on Track: An Economic Overview," *Brookings Review*, Spring 1987, p. 85.

## Chapter 6

1. Department of Commerce, International Trade Administration, *U.S. Industrial Outlook, 1987* (Washington, D.C.: Government Printing Office, 1987), chaps. 21–43.

2. Senate Committee on Finance, *Tax Reform Act of 1986*, pt. 1 (Washington, D.C.: Government Printing Office, 1986).

3. Paul W. McCracken, "Governance and the Gridlock," *Wall Street Journal*, September 2, 1987, p. 18.

4. *U.S. Export Controls* (Washington, D.C.: Department of State, Bureau of Public Affairs, March 1985), p. 1. An informal estimate of the reach of export controls yields a figure of 35 percent of American merchandise exports. Susan F. Rasky, "What Is Good for Security May Be Bad for Business," *New York Times,* October 18, 1987, p. E5.

5. Peter G. Germanis, "Getting Rid of U.S. Barriers to U.S. Exports," *Heritage Foundation Backgrounder,* April 22, 1982, pp. 1–10; Gary K. Bertsch, "U.S. Export Controls: The 1970s and Beyond," *Journal of World Trade Law,* January–February 1981, pp. 67–82.

6. *Balancing the National Interest: U.S. National Security Export Controls and Global Economic Competition* (Washington, D.C.: National Academy of Sciences, 1987). Also see Wayne Abernathy, "How Export Controls Defend the National Interest," *Heritage Foundation Backgrounder,* June 30, 1987, pp. 1–10.

7. Lionel H. Olmer, "USSR Pipeline Sanctions," *National Journal,* September 25, 1982, p. 1655; Paul Freedenberg, "U.S. Export Controls: Issues for High Technology Industries," *National Journal,* December 18, 1982, pp. 2190–93.

8. *Statement by the Honorable G. Fred Bergsten, Assistant Secretary of the Treasury for International Affairs, before the Committee on Banking, Housing and Urban Affairs,* March 6, 1979, p. 3.

9. Joon N. Suh, *"Voluntary" Export Restraints and Their Effects on Exporters and Consumers: The Case of the Footwear Quotas* (St. Louis: Washington University, Center for the Study of American Business, 1981).

10. Murray L. Weidenbaum and Michael C. Munger, "Protection at Any Price?" *Regulation,* July–August 1983, pp. 14–18. See also David G. Tarr and Morris E. Morkre, *Aggregate Costs to the United States of Tariffs and Quotas on Imports* (Washington, D.C.: Federal Trade Commission, 1985).

11. Arthur T. Denzau, *How Import Restraints Reduce Employment* (St. Louis: Washington University, Center for the Study of American Business, 1987).

12. A Chinese boycott of American agricultural products in 1983 reduced U.S. exports to China by more than one-third. Christopher S. Wren, "U.S. Exports to China Drop," *New York Times,* January 25, 1984, p. 24.

13. Jane S. Little, "Intra-Firm Trade," *New England Economic Review,* May–June 1987, pp. 46–51.

14. Office of Technology Assessment, *The U.S. Textile and Apparel Industry* (Washington, D.C.: Government Printing Office, 1987).

15. Robert Crandall, "Import Quotas and the Automobile Industry: The Costs of Protectionism," *Brookings Review,* Summer 1984, pp. 8–16.

16. Charles F. Sabel and Gary B. Herrigel, "Losing a Market to a High-Wage Nation," *New York Times,* June 14, 1987, p. 2F.

17. This agreement between the Caterpillar Tractor Company and the United Auto Workers Union replaced, after a lengthy strike, an earlier provision that provided for a bonus of two hours' pay for each week worked. "A Strike-Weary Caterpillar Knuckles Under," *Business Week,* May 2, 1983, p. 30.

18. A study in the early 1980s reported that the typical auto factory absenteeism in Japan averaged 1.6 percent, whereas in the United States it ranged from 7 to 11 percent. See William J. Abernathy, James E. Harbour, and Jay M. Henn, "Productivity and Comparative Cost Advantages: Some Estimates for Major Automotive Producers" (Draft report to the Department of Transportation, Transportation Systems Center, February 13, 1981).

19. For a convenient compendium of the relevant data, see Comptroller General, *The U.S. Trade Deficit: Causes and Policy Options for Solutions* (Washington, D.C.: General Accounting Office, 1987).

20. By including a variety of foreign countries in their studies and by using varying base periods for comparisons, each researcher in this field has come up with different precise estimates. But they are all variations on the same theme. See W. Michael Cox, "A New Alternative Trade-Weighted Dollar Exchange Rate Index," *Federal Reserve Bank of Dallas Economic Review,* September 1986, pp. 20–28.

21. See Jeffrey H. Bergstrand, "The U.S. Trade Deficit: A Perspective from Selected Bilateral Trade Models," *New England Economic Review,* May–June 1987, pp. 19–31.

22. Barry Bosworth, "Notes on the Competitiveness Debate" (Unpublished manuscript, 1987).

23. Martin Feldstein, "Correcting the World Trade Imbalance" (Unpublished manuscript, December 1986). See also Stephen Morris, *Deficits and the Dollar* (Washington, D.C.: Institute for International Economics, 1985); Otmar Emminger, *The Dollar's Borrowed Strength* (New York: Group of Thirty, 1985).

24. Quoted in Fred Anklam, Jr., "Free Trade Issue Heads for a Congressional Free-for-All," *USA Today,* May 5, 1986, p. 6A.

25. Gerry Weiner et al., "Eye on Canada," *Atlantic Community Quarterly,* Spring 1987, p. 93.

26. Norman S. Fieleke, "The Buy-American Policy of the United States Government," *New England Economic Review,* July–August 1969. The Missouri law also requires cities to adopt procurement guidelines that reflect the "Buy American" philosophy. Phyllis Hyman, "Cities Must 'Buy American,'" *Clayton Citizen-Journal,* September 4, 1987, p. 3A.

27. See Roy Boyd, "Lumber Transport and the Jones Act," *Bell Journal of Economics,* Spring 1983, pp. 202–12.

28. For detail, see Murray L. Weidenbaum, *Business, Government, and the Public,* 3d ed. (Englewood Cliffs, N.J.: Prentice-Hall, 1986), chap. 12.

29. Stephen L. Lande and Craig Van Grasstek, *The Trade and Tariff Act of 1984* (New York: Lexington Books, 1986), p. 4; William R. Cline, "Protectionism: An Ill Trade Wind Rises," *Wall Street Journal,* November 6, 1984, p. 30.

30. Joseph P. Kalt, *The Impact of Domestic Environmental Regulatory Policies on U.S. International Competitiveness,* Discussion Paper Series (Cambridge: Harvard University, Kennedy School of Government, 1985).

31. William R. Cline, "Long-Term Change in Foreign Trade Policy of the United States," in Joint Economic Committee, *The International Economy: U.S. Role in a World Economy* (Washington, D.C.: Government Printing Office, 1980), p. 214.

# Notes

32. Comptroller General, *Controlling Foreign Investment in National Interest Sectors of the U.S. Economy* (Washington, D.C.: General Accounting Office, 1977).

33. Dorothy Christelow, "Japan's Intangible Barriers to Trade in Manufacturing," *Federal Reserve Bank of New York Quarterly Review*, Winter 1985–86, pp. 11–18. See also Arthur J. Alexander and Hong W. Tan, *Barriers to United States Trade in Services* (Santa Monica: Rand Corporation, 1985).

34. Russell Baker, "Lawyers for Cars," *New York Times*, June 8, 1983, p. 27. My lawyer friends tell me that Baker's aim could be accomplished more swiftly by sending ten economists instead of all those lawyers.

35. Ingo Walter and Kent A. Jones, "The Battle over Protectionism: How Industry Adjusts to Competitive Shocks," *Journal of Business Strategy*, 1982, pp. 37–46.

36. Murray L. Weidenbaum, "The Assault on International Trade," *National Review*, December 28, 1984, pp. 29–33.

37. Sven Arndt, "Trade Problems and Trade Policies," *AEI Economist*, November 1985, pp. 1–7; John N. Yochelson, "Internationalization of the U.S. Economy," in John N. Yochelson, Alan Stoga, and Penelope Hartland-Thunberg, *U.S. Leadership in the Changing World Economy* (Washington, D.C.: Center for Strategic and International Studies, 1986), pp. 1–24.

## Chapter 7

1. Murray L. Weidenbaum and Michael J. Athey, "What Is the Rust Belt's Problem?" in Chalmers Johnson, ed., *The Industrial Policy Debate* (San Francisco: ICS Press, 1984), pp. 117–32. For a different view, see Stephen S. Cohen and John Zysman, *Manufacturing Matters* (New York: Basic Books, 1987).

2. Ira Magaziner and Robert Reich, *Minding America's Business* (New York: Vintage, 1982), p. 375.

3. Lester Thurow, "The Great Stagnation," *New York Times*, October 17, 1982, sec. 6, pp. 32, 36.

4. Warren M. Anderson, "Remarks at the KMG Main Hurdman International Partners Meeting" (San Francisco, Calif., September 11, 1985), p. 2.

5. Paul W. McCracken, "The Rust Belt's Coming Revival," *Wall Street Journal*, March 30, 1987, p. 16.

6. David G. Tarr and Morris E. Morkre, *Aggregate Costs to the United States of Tariffs and Quotas on Imports* (Washington, D.C.: Federal Trade Commission, 1985). Another domestic factor is the tendency for American industry to use less steel. Congressional Budget Office, *The Effects of Import Quotas on the Steel Industry* (Washington, D.C.: Government Printing Office, 1984), p. 32.

7. Richard McKenzie with Stephen D. Smith, *The Loss of Textile and Apparel Jobs: The Relative Importance of Imports and Productivity* (St. Louis: Washington University, Center for the Study of American Business, 1986).

8. "Fastest-Growing Occupations, 1986–2000," *New York Times*, October 11, 1987, sec. 12, p. 6. See also George T. Silvestri and John M. Lukasiewicz, "Occupational Employment Projections: The 1984–95 Outlook," *Monthly Labor Review*, November 1985, pp. 42–57.

9. *Economic Report of the President, January 1987* (Washington, D.C.: Government Printing Office, 1987), table B-40, and Bureau of Labor Statistics monthly releases on the employment situation.

10. Richard B. McKenzie with Stephen D. Smith, *The Good News about U.S. Production Jobs* (St. Louis: Washington University, Center for the Study of American Business, 1986).

11. *Economic Report, 1987,* table B-11.

12. By 1900, service employment exceeded manufacturing employment, by a ratio of eight to five. Bureau of the Census, *Historical Statistics of the United States,* pt. 1 (Washington, D.C.: Government Printing Office, 1975), p. 137.

13. This section draws heavily on Donald F. Barnett and Robert W. Crandall, *Up from the Ashes: The Rise of the Steel Minimill in the United States* (Washington, D.C.: Brookings Institution, 1986).

14. William H. Miller, "The Phony War between High Tech and Low Tech," *Industry Week,* October 3, 1983, p. 39. See also National Science Foundation, "Manufacturing Employment Becomes Increasingly Technological," *Science Resources Studies Highlights,* March 10, 1983, pp. 1–4.

15. John Holusha, "Deere & Co. Leads the Way in Flexible Manufacturing," *Des Moines Register,* January 29, 1984, p. 10F.

16. John Naisbitt, *Megatrends* (New York: Warner Books, 1982), p. 71.

17. Ibid.

18. D. Bruce Merrifield, "The Forces of Change Restructuring the U.S. and World Economies (Presentation to Human Resources Services, Inc., New York City, October 22, 1986), pp. 8–9; Leonard L. Lederman, "Science and Technology Policies and Priorities: A Comparative Analysis," *Science,* September 4, 1987, p. 1127.

19. Harold Lever, "America Is Too Tough on Itself," *International Economy,* October–November 1987, p. 79.

20. The following section draws on Murray Weidenbaum with Richard Burr and Richard Cook, *Learning to Compete* (St. Louis: Washington University, Center for the Study of American Business, 1986).

21. Cindy Skrzcki, "The Upside of Downsizing," *Washington Post Weekly,* October 10, 1987, p. 20.

22. "Major Work Stoppages: 1986," *U.S. Department of Labor News,* March 6, 1987, pp. 1–2.

23. "Employment Cost Index—March 1987," *U.S. Department of Labor News,* April 28, 1987, table 1, and earlier issues.

24. Henry Eason, "Keeping Afloat in the Import Flood," *Nation's Business,* September 1985, pp. 42–46.

25. James A. Leaky, "Toyota Production System—Just in Time, Not Just in Japan," *CIM Review,* Fall 1984, pp. 59–66.

26. *1985 General Motors Public Interest Report* (Detroit: General Motors Corporation, 1985).

27. Seymour Lusterman, *Foreign Competition and U.S. Trade Policies* (New York: Conference Board, 1985).

28. John F. Welsh, "World Competitiveness: An Emerging Domestic Reality" (Address to the Economic Club of Chicago, February 20, 1986); "The Changing Character of General Electric," *Wall Street Journal,* July 23, 1987, p. 3.

29. Quoted in Eason, "Keeping Afloat," p. 46.

30. Donald B. Thompson, "Back to Basics, Confronting the Competitiveness Challenge," *Industry Week,* December 10, 1984, pp. 74–80.

31. "Working with Suppliers Improved the Quality of Steel Bought by Ford," *Purchasing,* April 24, 1986, p. 26.

32. Quoted in Jeffrey Leib, "Auto Makers Seek Quality," *New York Times,* August 8, 1985, Business section, p. 1.

33. David A. Garvin, "Quality on the Line," *Harvard Business Review,* October 1983, pp. 65–73.

34. The French historian Fernand Braudel furnishes a colorful description of the business attitude of successful English entrepreneurs several centuries ago: ". . . the rich

# Notes

Manchester merchants, or the manufacturers from Yorkshire and Coventry who went on horseback all over the English countryside delivering their goods in person to the shopkeepers. . . ." Braudel, *The Wheels of Commerce* (New York: Harper & Row, 1982), p. 76.

35. Robert Reich, *Tales of a New America* (New York: Times Books, 1987).

36. National Science Foundation, "Employment of Ph.D. Scientists and Engineers in Industry Continues to Increase," *Science Resources Studies Highlights*, March 13, 1987, p. 1; Conference Board, *Research and Development* (New York: Conference Board, 1986), p. 2; National Science Foundation, "Despite Continuing High Level of Defense-Related R & D Spending, Growth in Nation's R & D Effort Slows," *Science Resources Studies Highlights*, March 27, 1987, p. 3.

37. Anne Watzman, "Pittsburgh Battles Back with High-Tech Attack," *Mid America Outlook*, Fall 1985, pp. 5–7.

38. Doug Podolsky, "Automation Is the Best Hope for Solving Erosion of Trade Balances in Manufactures," *Manufacturing Competitiveness Frontiers*, September 1987, pp. 2–3.

39. Watzman, "Pittsburgh Battles," pp. 5–6.

40. *Economic Report, January 1987*, table B-43.

41. "Japanese Firms Operating in U.S. Are Outperforming American Competitors," *Manufacturing Productivity Frontiers*, April 1985, pp. 34–35.

42. Martin Starr and Nancy E. Bloom, *The Performance of Japanese-Owned Firms in America: A Survey Report* (New York: Columbia University, Graduate School of Business, 1985).

43. "Korean Contractors Trekking Home," *Engineering News Record*, August 22, 1985, pp. 113–14.

## Chapter 8

1. Pension Benefit Guaranty Corporation, *Analysis of Single Employer Defined Benefit Plan Terminations, 1977* (Washington, D.C.: Government Printing Office, 1978), p. 1.

2. This section draws heavily on my earlier article "Strategies for Responding to Corporate Takeovers," in Murray Weidenbaum and Kenneth Chilton, eds., *Public Policy toward Corporate Takeovers* (New Brunswick: Transaction Press, 1988).

3. Quoted in John Greenwald, "The Great Takeover Debate," *Time*, April 22, 1985, p. 44.

4. Quoted in Congressional Research Service, *The Role of High Yield Bonds (Junk Bonds) in Capital Markets and Corporate Takeovers: A Report to the Subcommittee on Telecommunications, Consumer Protection and Finance of the Committee on Energy and Commerce of the U.S. House of Representatives* (Washington, D.C.: Government Printing Office, 1985), p. 26.

5. Alfred D. Chandler, Jr., "How the Heirs of Sloan and DuPont Are Faring," *Across the Board*, May 1986, p. 28.

6. Quoted in Benjamin J. Stern, "Not Worthy of the Name? Investment Banking Isn't What It Used to Be," *Barron's*, July 13, 1987.

7. Peter F. Drucker, "Corporate Takeovers—What Is to Be Done," *Public Interest*, Winter 1986, p. 3; see also Felix Rohatyn, "Junk Bonds and Other Securities Swill," *Wall Street Journal*, April 18, 1985, p. 30.

8. See the studies cited in Richard E. Cook, *What the Economics Literature Has to Say about Takeovers* (St. Louis: Washington University, Center for the Study of American Business, 1987).

9. Quoted in Congressional Research Service, *High Yield Bonds*, p. 27.

10. Michael C. Jensen, "Takeovers: Folklore and Science," *Harvard Business Review*, November–December 1984, p. 1114.

11. Murray Weidenbaum and Stephen Vogt, "Takeovers and Stockholders: Winners and Losers," *California Management Review*, Summer 1987, pp. 157–68.

12. David J. Ravenscraft and F. M. Scherer, *Mergers and Managerial Performance*, Working Paper no. 137 (Washington, D.C.: Federal Trade Commission, Bureau of Economics, 1986), p. 2.

13. F. M. Scherer, "Takeovers: Present and Future Dangers," *Brookings Review*, Winter–Spring 1986, p. 20.

14. Stephen A. Rhoades, "The Operating Performance of Acquired Firms in Banking before and after Acquisition," Staff Paper (Washington, D.C.: Board of Governors, Federal Reserve System, 1985).

15. Ravenscraft and Scherer, *Mergers and Managerial Performance*, pp. 1–37.

16. Senate Committee on Finance, *Federal Income Tax Aspects of Hostile Takeovers and Other Corporate Mergers and Acquisitions* (Washington, D.C.: Government Printing Office, 1985).

17. Charles A. Peck, *Top Executive Compensation* (New York: Conference Board, 1986), pp. 6–7.

18. Gordon Donaldson and Jay W. Lorsch, *Decision Making at the Top: The Shaping of Strategic Direction* (New York: Basic Books, 1983), p. 28.

19. Harold Stieglitz, *Chief Executives View Their Jobs* (New York: Conference Board, 1985), p. 8.

20. Donaldson and Lorsch, *Decision Making*, p. 7.

21. This section draws on Murray Weidenbaum and Richard Cook, "Impacts of Takeovers on Financial Markets," in Weidenbaum and Chilton, eds., *Corporate Takeovers*.

22. Paul A. Volcker, letter to Senator William Proxmire, dated November 8, 1985, pp. 1–2. plus attachments.

23. Quoted in "The Great Takeover Debate," *Time*, April 22, 1985, p. 46.

24. Preston Martin, *Statement before House Committee on Banking, Finance and Urban Affairs* (Washington, D.C.: Board of Governors of the Federal Reserve System, May 3, 1985), p. 2.

25. "Junk Bond Funding for M&A," *Mergers & Acquisitions*, July–August 1986, p. 50.

26. James Balog, "Financing and Restructuring for a Competitive World" (Address to the Valley National Bank Investment Management Forum, October 1985), p. 4.

27. Louis Perlmutter, "Takeovers: The Current Outlook" (Presentation to the Economic Club of Chicago, March 3, 1986), p. 13.

28. Martin Lipton and Andrew R. Brownstein, "Takeover Responses and Directors' Responsibilities—An Update," *Business Lawyer*, August 1985, pp. 1403–30, and Lynn E. Browne and Eric S. Rosengren, "Should States Restrict Takeovers?" *New England Economic Review*, July–August 1987, p. 13.

29. Quoted in David A. Vise, "The Boesky Scandal Has Finally Galvanized Congress," *Washington Post Weekly*, January 26, 1987, p. 21.

30. Martin Lipton, "Takeover Abuses Mortgage the Future," *Wall Street Journal*, April 5, 1985, p. 12.

31. Arthur J. Goldberg, "How Wall Street Takeovers Should Be Curbed," *Christian Science Monitor*, January 7, 1987, p. 11.

32. Browne and Rosengren, "Restrict Takeovers?" pp. 18–19.

33. Randall Smith, "Fed Rule Restricting the Use of Junk Bonds in Takeovers Is by Most Accounts Ineffective," *New York Times*, August 18, 1986, p. 43.

34. Computed from data in *Mergerstat Review 1986* (Chicago: W. T. Grimm & Co., 1987).

35. Quoted in Murray L. Weidenbaum, "Probing the Government's Role in Hostile Takeover Attempts," *Christian Science Monitor*, April 26, 1985, p. 18.

# Notes

36. See Murray L. Weidenbaum, *The Future of Business Regulation* (New York: Amacom, 1980).

37. *Economic Report of the President, January 1985* (Washington, D.C.: Government Printing Office, 1985), p. 211.

38. *Social Responsibilities of Business Corporations* (New York: Committee for Economic Development, 1971), p. 22.

39. See Murray L. Weidenbaum, "Updating the Corporate Board," *Journal of Business Strategy,* Summer 1986, pp. 77–83.

40. See Ralph Nader and Mark J. Green, eds., *Corporate Power in America* (New York: Grossman Publishing, 1973).

41. Lester B. Korn and Richard M. Ferry, *Twelfth Annual Board of Directors Study* (New York: Korn/Ferry International, 1985), p. 2.

## Chapter 9

1. Felix Rohatyn et al. *Promoting Economic Growth and Competitiveness* (Washington, D.C.: Industry Policy Study Group, 1986).

2. *Strategy for a Vital U.S. Economy* (New York: Business Roundtable, 1984), pp. 14–15.

3. Arthur T. Denzau and Clifford M. Hardin, *A National Development Bank: Ghost of the RFC Past* (St. Louis: Washington University, Center for the Study of American Business, 1984).

4. Cited in Murray L. Weidenbaum, *Business, Government, and the Public,* 3d ed. (Englewood Cliffs, N.J.: Prentice-Hall, 1986), p. 249.

5. Leonard Silk, *Economics in the Real World* (New York: Simon and Schuster, 1984), p. 276.

6. Congressional Budget Office, *Federal Support of U.S. Business* (Washington, D.C.: Government Printing Office, 1984).

7. Office of Management and Budget, *Special Analyses, Budget of the United States Government, Fiscal Year 1988* (Washington, D.C.: Government Printing Office, 1987), Special Analysis F.

8. Congressional Budget Office, *Charging for Federal Services* (Washington, D.C.: Government Printing Office, 1983), p. 4.

9. Congressional Budget Office, *U.S. Shipping and Shipbuilding* (Washington, D.C.: Government Printing Office, 1984), p. 102.

10. James K. Hickel, *The Chrysler Bail-Out Bust* (Washington, D.C.: Heritage Foundation, 1983), p. 2. See also James M. Bickley, *Overviews of the Lockheed, New York City, and Chrysler Loan Guarantee Programs* (Washington, D.C.: Congressional Research Service, 1980); Brian M. Freeman and Allan I. Mendelowitz, "Program in Search of a Policy: The Chrysler Loan Guarantee," *Journal of Policy Analysis and Management* 1 (1982): 443–53.

11. Senate Committee on Banking, Housing, and Urban Affairs, *Chrysler Corporation Loan Guarantee Act: Hearing on Oversight of the Chrysler Corporation Loan Guarantee Act of 1979* (Washington, D.C.: Government Printing Office, 1980); House Committee on Banking, Finance, and Urban Affairs, *Oversight Hearing on the Chrysler Corporation Loan Guarantee Act and the Status of the U.S. Automobile Industry.* (Washington, D.C.: Government Printing Office, 1980).

12. Arthur T. Denzau, *Will an "Industrial Policy" Work for the United States?* (St. Louis: Washington University, Center for the Study of American Business, 1983).

13. Michael Porter, "Where the Excellence Is," *Across the Board,* September 1987, p. 31.

14. John S. Heckman and John S. Strong, "Is There a Case for Plant Closing Laws?" *New England Economic Review,* July–August 1980, pp. 3–4.

15. Richard B. McKenzie, *Fugitive Industries: The Economics and Politics of Deindustrialization* (San Francisco: Ballinger, 1984).

16. Lester Thurow, *The Zero Sum Society* (New York: Basic Books, 1980), p. 77.

17. David L. Birch, *Job Creation in America* (New York: Free Press, 1987).

18. *1982 Government Giveaway Guide* (Lynbrook, N.Y.: Classified Reports, 1982).

19. Paul A. Samuelson, "Toting Up the Victories—and Problems," *New York Times,* August 30, 1987, p. F3.

20. Adam Smith, *An Inquiry into the Nature and Causes of the Wealth of Nations* (New York: Modern Library, 1937), p. 14.

21. Porter, "Where the Excellence Is," p. 29.

22. "Excerpts from Soviet Study on the Need for an Overhaul of the Economy," *New York Times,* August 5, 1983, p. 4.

## Chapter 10

1. Presidential statement on signing the Social Security Act of 1935. Quoted in Roger A. Freeman, *Does America Neglect Its Poor?* (Stanford: Hoover Institution, 1987), p. 6.

2. Ibid.

3. Bureau of the Census, *Money Income and Poverty Status of Families and Persons in the United States* (Washington, D.C.: Government Printing Office, 1985).

4. Bureau of the Census, *Estimates of Poverty Including the Value of Noncash Benefits* (Washington, D.C.: Government Printing Office, 1984).

5. Michael Novak et al., *The New Consensus on Family and Welfare* (Washington, D.C.: American Enterprise Institute, 1987).

6. William Julius Wilson, *The Truly Disadvantaged* (Chicago: University of Chicago Press, 1987).

7. Freeman, *Neglect Poor?* p. 11.

8. Cited ibid, pp. 11–12.

9. Ibid., p. 15.

10. Rajni Bonnie Ohri, "Moving towards Welfare Reform," *U.S. Chamber of Commerce Policy Working Papers,* September 1987, p. 7.

11. Charles Murray, *Losing Ground* (New York: Basic Books, 1984), p. 9.

12. Quoted in John N. Wilford, "A Tough-Minded Ecologist Comes to Defense of Malthus," *New York Times,* June 30, 1987, p. 25.

13. William A. Darity, Jr., and Samuel L. Myers, Jr., "Do Transfer Payments Keep the Poor in Poverty?" *American Economic Review,* May 1987, p. 218.

14. David M. Blau and Philip K. Robins, "Labor Supply Response to Welfare Programs," *Journal of Labor Economics,* January 1986, p. 94.

15. Freeman, *Neglect Poor?* p. 16.

16. Robert Rector, "Welfare Reform That Is Anti-Work, Anti-Family, Anti-Poor," *Heritage Foundation Backgrounder,* September 23, 1987, p. 4.

17. Alicia H. Munnell, "The Current Status of Our Social Welfare System," *New England Economic Review,* July–August 1987, pp. 4–5.

18. Richard B. Freeman, "Cutting Black Youth Unemployment: Create Jobs That Pay as Well as Crime," *New York Times,* July 20, 1986.

19. Robert Lerman, "Do Welfare Programs Affect the Schooling and Work Patterns of Young Black Men?" in Richard B. Freeman and Harry J. Holzer, eds., *The Black Youth Employment Crisis* (Chicago: University of Chicago Press, 1986), pp. 403–47.

# Notes

20. Novak et al., *Family and Welfare,* p. 30.

21. I. A. Lewis and William Schneider, "Hard Times: The Public on Poverty," *Public Opinion,* June–July 1985, table 1.

22. Douglas J. Besharov, "Go Slow on Welfare Reform," *Wall Street Journal,* March 18, 1987, p. 24.

23. Kevin R. Hopkins, *Welfare Dependency* (Washington, D.C.: Hudson Institute, 1987), p. 8.

24. Douglas J. Besharov, Alison Quin, and Karl Zinsmeister, "A Portrait in Black and White: Out-of-Wedlock Births," *Public Opinion,* May–June 1987, p. 45; Novak et al., *Family and Welfare,* chap. 3; Freeman, *Neglect Poor?* pp. 28, 31; Comptroller General, *Child Support: Need to Improve Efforts to Identify Fathers and Obtain Support Orders* (Washington, D.C.: General Accounting Office, 1987).

25. Freeman, *Neglect Poor?* p. 37.

26. Daniel P. Moynihan, "The Crisis in Welfare," *Public Interest,* Winter 1967. Cited in Freeman, *Neglect Poor?* p. 34.

27. Peter A. Morrison, *Changing Family Structure: Who Cares for America's Dependents?* (Santa Monica: Rand Corporation, 1986).

28. Senate Republican Policy Committee, *Welfare Reform* (Washington, D.C.: (processed), June 1987), pp. 8–9.

29. Novak et al., *Family and Welfare,* p. 13.

30. Ibid., p. 5. This statement was signed by professional researchers at a wide range of institutions: American Enterprise Institute, Brookings Institution, Foundation for Child Development, Harvard University, Heritage Foundation, Hoover Institution, Institute for Educational Affairs, Manhattan Institute, New York University, Princeton University, and Rockford Institute.

31. Martin Anderson, *Welfare* (Stanford: Hoover Institution, 1978), p. 153.

32. Ibid., p. 163. Anderson's tough position represents only a partial return to the biblical injunction "In the sweat of thy face shalt thou eat bread . . ." (Genesis 3:19).

33. Novak et al., *Family and Welfare,* chap. 7.

34. Hopkins, *Welfare,* pp. 4, 27.

35. The San Diego work program became nearly twice as effective when an unsuccessful job search was followed by some type of mandatory work experience. Comptroller General, *Work and Welfare* (Washington, D.C.: General Accounting Office, 1987), p. 27.

36. Novak et al., *Family and Welfare,* chap. 7. See also Domestic Policy Council, *Up from Dependency: A New National Public Assistance Strategy: A Report by the Low Income Opportunity Working Group* (Washington, D.C.: The White House, 1986).

37. Robert D. Reischauer, "Welfare Reform: Will Consensus Be Enough?" *Brookings Review,* Summer 1987, p. 5.

38. Alan L. Otten, "Poor Will find That Many Jobs Are Out of Reach," *Wall Street Journal,* May 27, 1987, p. 56; Congressional Budget Office, *Work-Related Programs for Welfare Recipients* (Washington, D.C.: Government Printing Office, 1987).

39. Edward T. Duffy, "Investments in People Pay Dividends," *St. Louis Post-Dispatch,* May 21, 1987, p. 3B.

40. Robert Rector and Peter T. Butterfield, "Reforming Welfare: The Promises and Limits of Workfare," *Heritage Foundation Backgrounder,* June 11, 1985, pp. 1–12.

41. Frances Fox Piven and Barbara Ehrenreich, "Workfare Means New Mass Peonage," *New York Times,* May 30, 1987, p. 15.

42. Reischauer, "Welfare Reform," p. 5; Barbara Bergmann, "Family Issues in the Next Presidential Election," *National Economists Club Summary,* September 17, 1987, p. 1.

43. See Hopkins, *Welfare,* pp. 1–35.

44. Michael Harrington, *The New American Poverty* (New York: Holt, Rinehart, and Winston, 1984), p. 179.

# Notes

## Chapter 11

1. William Echikson, "Environmental Problems Are Explosive Issue for East Bloc," *Christian Science Monitor*, November 14, 1987, p. 9.
2. "Attitudes on the Environment," *New York Times*, April 17, 1983, p. 17.
3. Comptroller General, *How to Dispose of Hazardous Waste* (Washington, D.C.: General Accounting Office, 1978), pp. 5–14.
4. Robert C. Mitchell and Richard T. Carson, "Protest, Property Rights, and Hazardous Waste," *Resources*, Fall 1986, p. 6.
5. Quoted in Geraldine Cox, "The Dangerous Myth of a Risk-Free Society" (Address at Drexel University, Philadelphia, February 19, 1987), p. 3.
6. *A Study of the Attitudes of the American Public toward Improvement of the Natural Environment* (Washington, D.C.: National Wildlife Federation, 1969).
7. "Opinion Roundup," *Public Opinion*, February–March 1982, p. 37.
8. Council on Environmental Quality, *Environmental Quality, 1980* (Washington, D.C.: Government Printing Office, 1980), table 10-1.
9. Quoted in Peter Osterlund, "EPA at 15," *Christian Science Monitor*, December 5, 1985, p. 8.
10. Ibid.
11. "Growing Garbage Cans," *Christian Science Monitor*, July 9, 1987, p. 17.
12. Council on Environmental Quality, *Environmental Quality, 1986* (Washington, D.C.: Government Printing Office, 1986).
13. William D. Ruckelshaus, "Plateau of Hope: Some Perspectives on Environmental Achievement" (Remarks to the National Press Club, May 22, 1984), p. 11.
14. "Chemicals," *St. Louis Post-Dispatch*, June 4, 1987, p. 12A
15. *Dioxin in the Environment* (Summit, N.J.: American Council on Science and Health, 1984), p. 5.
16. "The Changing Economics of Waste Management," *Chemecology*, February 1987, p. 2.
17. Comptroller General, *Illegal Disposal of Hazardous Waste* (Washington, D.C.: General Accounting Office, 1985), p. i.
18. "Waste Not, Want Not," *Journal of American Insurance*, Third Quarter 1987, p. 3.
19. My colleague James Davis suggests a more focused subsidy—the payment of cash to each resident of the area, with the payment rising, or falling, with the distance from the dump site.
20. Mitchell and Carson, "Hazardous Waste," pp. 6–8.
21. "Desert Fight for Nuclear Dump," *San Francisco Chronicle*, March 14, 1987, p. 5. See also Philip J. Bourque and R. Haney Scott, "Let States Bid for Nuclear Waste Repository," *Pacific Northwest Executive*, October 1986, p. 1.
22. Luther J. Carter, "U.S. Nuclear Waste Program at an Impasse," *Resources*, Summer 1987, pp. 2–4.
23. Comptroller General, *Hazardous Waste*, p. 9.
24. Philip Shabecoff, "EPA Report Says Agency Is Focusing on Wrong Problems," *New York Times*, February 19, 1987, pp. 1, 14.
25. National Research Council, Committee on Scientific and Regulatory Issues Underlying Pesticide Use Patterns and Agricultural Innovation, *Regulating Pesticides in Food* (Washington, D.C.: National Academy Press, 1987).
26. Office of Technology Assessment, *Annual Report to the Congress, Fiscal Year 1986* (Washington, D.C.: Government Printing Office, 1986), p. 41.
27. Joel S. Hirschhorn and Kirsten U. Oldenburg, "Preventing Pollution Is No End-of-Pipe Dream," *Across the Board*, June 1987, p. 11.

28. "Superfund—It's Time for a Waste-End Fee," *CMA News,* January 1984, p. 16.

29. "Case Histories Detailed—Corporate Imagination, Cooperation, Practicality Lead to Environmental Progress," *Roundtable Report,* March 1984, pp. 1–3.

30. Allen Kneese et al., eds., *Managing the Environment* (New York: Praeger, 1971); Frederick R. Anderson et al., *Environmental Improvement through Economic Incentives* (Baltimore: Johns Hopkins University Press, 1978).

31. Craig E. Reese, *Deregulation and Environmental Quality* (Westport, Conn.: Quorum Books, 1983), pp. 95–105, 147–53.

32. Comptroller General, *Hazardous Waste: Federal Civil Agencies Slow to Comply with Regulatory Requirements* (Washington, D.C.: General Accounting Office, 1986).

33. Comptroller General, *Superfund: Civilian Federal Agencies Slow to Clean Up Hazardous Waste* (Washington, D.C.: General Accounting Office, 1987), p. 3.

34. Vic Fazio, "Needed: A Military Superfund," *Christian Science Monitor,* October 3, 1985, p. 18.

35. Comptroller General, *Hazardous Waste Management at Tinker Air Force Base* (Washington, D.C.: General Accounting Office, 1985), p. 4.

36. See, for example, Andy Bigford, "City Will Stop River Dumping," *Aspen Daily News,* July 21, 1987, p. 1.

37. John A. Jaksch and Henry M. Peskin, "Nonpoint-Source Water Pollution," *Resources,* Winter 1984, p. 25.

38. "Cancer and Environment: Higginson Speaks Out," *Science,* September 28, 1979, p. 1363.

39. Harry Demopoulos, "Environmentally Induced Cancer . . . Separating Truth from Myth" (Talk to the Synthetic Organic Chemical Manufacturers Association, Hasbrouck Heights, N.J., October 4, 1979), pp. 1–6. For another study with similar conclusions, see R. Doll and R. Peto, "The Causes of Cancer: Quantitative Estimates of Avoidable Risks of Cancer in the United States Today," *Journal of the National Cancer Institute* 66 (1981): 1191–308.

40. Bureau of the Census, *Statistical Abstract of the United States, 1987* (Washington, D.C.: Government Printing Office, 1986), p. 69.

41. Bruce N. Ames, *Six Common Errors Relating to Environmental Pollution* (Louisville, Ky.: National Council for Environmental Balance, 1987).

## Chapter 12

1. For detail, see Murray L. Weidenbaum, *The Future of Business Regulation* (New York: Amacom, 1980); Murray L. Weidenbaum, "The Hidden Tax of Government Regulation," *Economic Affairs,* December 1986–January 1987, pp. 14–18.

2. Paul N. Tramontozzi with Kenneth W. Chilton, *U.S. Regulatory Agencies under Reagan* (St. Louis: Washington University, Center for the Study of American Business, 1987), table 1.

3. Quoted in an interview in *Fortune,* September 10, 1979, p. 94.

4. William M. Wardell, "Therapeutic Implications of the Drug Lag," *Clinical Pharmacology and Therapeutics,* January 1974, pp. 73–96.

5. William M. Wardell, *Testimony before the Senate Committee on Labor and Public Welfare, Subcommittee on Health,* Washington, D.C., September 27, 1974.

6. This section draws on material in Murray L. Weidenbaum, "Liberation Economics: The Benefits of Deregulation," *Policy Review,* Summer 1987, pp. 12–16.

7. See George W. Douglas and James C. Miller III, *Economic Regulation of Domestic Air Transport* (Washington, D.C.: Brookings Institution, 1974).

8. John R. Meyer et al., *The Economics of Competition in the Transportation Industries* (Cambridge: Harvard University Press, 1959); Thomas Gale Moore, *Freight Transportation Regulation* (Washington, D.C.: American Enterprise Institute, 1972).

9. Marver Bernstein, *Regulating Business by Independent Commission* (Princeton: Princeton University Press, 1955).

10. George J. Stigler, "The Theory of Economic Regulation," *Bell Journal of Economics and Management Science,* Spring 1971, pp. 3–21; Sam Peltzman, "Towards a More General Theory of Regulation," *Journal of Law and Economics,* August 1976, pp. 211–40.

11. Theodore Keeler, "Airline Regulation and Market Performance," *Bell Journal of Economics and Management Science,* Autumn 1972, pp. 399–424; W. A. Jordan, *Airline Regulation in America* (Baltimore: Johns Hopkins University Press, 1970).

12. Murray L. Weidenbaum, *Government-Mandated Price Increases* (Washington, D.C.: American Enterprise Institute, 1975).

13. Martin Derthick and Paul J. Quirk, *The Politics of Deregulation* (Washington, D.C.: Brookings Institution, 1985), pp. 257–58.

14. Murray L. Weidenbaum and Robert DeFina, *The Cost of Federal Government Regulation of Economic Activity* (Washington, D.C.: American Enterprise Institute, 1978).

15. "Dick and Jane Visit the Farm: Editorial," *Omaha World-Herald,* June 15, 1976.

16. Executive Order 12291, November 27, 1974 (President Ford); Executive Order 12044, March 24, 1978 (President Carter); Executive Order 122191, February 17, 1981 (President Reagan).

17. George C. Eads and Michael Fix, eds., *The Reagan Regulatory Strategy* (Washington, D.C.: Urban Institute Press, 1984), pp. 15–41.

18. Tramontozzi and Chilton, *Regulatory Agencies,* tables 1 and 2.

19. David R. Graham and Daniel P. Kaplan, "Airline Deregulation Is Working," *Regulation,* May–June 1982, pp. 26–32; Comptroller General, *Increased Competition Is Making Airlines More Efficient and Responsive to Consumers* (Washington, D.C.: General Accounting Office, 1985); Robert E. Mabley and Walter D. Strack, "Deregulation—A Green Light for Trucking Efficiency," *Regulation,* July–August 1982, pp. 36–42; Theodore E. Keeler, *Railroads, Freight, and Public Policy* (Washington, D.C.: Brookings Institution, 1983); Thomas G. Moore, "Rail and Truck Reform—The Record So Far," *Regulation,* November–December 1983; Andrew S. Carron, "The Reorganization of Financial Regulation," *Brookings Review,* Spring 1984.

20. James L. Gattuso, "What Deregulation Has Meant for Airline Safety," *Heritage Foundation Backgrounder,* November 12, 1986, pp. 1–11.

21. Richard B. McKenzie and William Shughart II, *Has Deregulation of Air Travel Affected Air Safety?* (St. Louis: Washington University, Center for the Study of American Business, 1986).

22. Steven Morrison and Clifford Winston, *The Economic Effects of Airline Deregulation* (Washington, D.C.: Brookings Institution, 1986).

23. "Airlines Before and After," *National Journal,* June 20, 1987, p. 1586.

24. Agis Salpukas, "The Crunch at Airlines' Hubs," *New York Times,* October 12, 1987, p. 23.

25. Kenneth Labich, "Blessings by the Truckload," *Fortune,* November 11, 1985, pp. 138–44; James L. Gattuso, "Time to Complete Trucking Deregulation," *Heritage Foundation Backgrounder,* January 16, 1986, pp. 1–12.

26. Sylvia Nasar, "Productivity Perks Up," *Fortune,* September 28, 1987, p. 62.

27. Robert D. Hershey, Jr., "Airline Deregulation Debated," *New York Times,* August 28, 1986, p. 21; James L. Gattuso, "The Consumer Rail Equity Act: Returning to the Dark Days of Regulation," *Heritage Foundation Backgrounder,* June 5, 1987, pp. 1–10.

28. Lester Lave, "A New Wave of Environmental Laws Looms," *Wall Street Journal,* December 17, 1986, p. 20.

# Notes

29. *American Petroleum Institute v. OSHA*, No. 78-1253 (5th Circuit, 10-5-78).

30. Peter Huber, "Who Will Protect Us from Our Protectors?" *Forbes*, July 13, 1987, p. 57.

31. The discussion between Senators Griffin and Muskie on the Clear Air Act of 1970 furnishes an insight into the contemporaneous congressional attitude. Here is a sample (*Congressional Record*, September 21, 1970, pp. S16095–96):

> *Muskie:* We think . . . this is a necessary and reasonable standard . . . if the industry cannot meet it, they can come back. . . .
> *Griffin:* . . . without the kind of scientific knowledge that is needed—without the hearings that are necessary and expected, this bill would write into legislation concrete requirements that can be impossible. . . .

## Chapter 13

1. The best available indicator of the prevailing private-sector forecast is contained in the monthly *Blue Chip Economic Indicators*, compiled by Robert J. Eggert and issued by Capital Publications, Inc., Alexandria, Virginia.

2. See Murray L. Weidenbaum, "The Case for Making Economic Forecasts," *Challenge*, July–August 1986, pp. 54–56.

3. See Economic Forum, *The Long-Range Outlook: Bliss, Déjà Vu, or Collapse?* (New York: Conference Board, 1986).

4. "Solum certum nihil esse certi." In *Home Book of Quotations* (New York: Dodd Mead, 1967), p. 227.

5. *Long-Term U.S. Economic Outlook* (St. Louis: Laurence H. Meyer and Associates, 1987). See also Betty W. Su, "The Economic Outlook to 1995," *Monthly Labor Review*, November 1985, pp. 3–16; *Long-Term Forecasts, 1984–1994* (New York: A. Gary Shilling, 1984); Lora S. Collins, *The U.S. Economy to 1990* (New York: Conference Board, 1985).

6. "The U.S. Economy to 1995," *Conference Board Perspectives*, 1987, no. 6.

7. *The Federalist* (New York: Modern Library, 1937), p. 260.

8. Arthur Okun, *Equality and Efficiency: The Big Tradeoff* (Washington, D.C.: Brookings Institution, 1975).

9. John Shannon, "The Return to Fend-for-Yourself Federalism: The Reagan Mark," *Intergovernmental Perspective*, Summer–Fall 1987, p. 37.

## Chapter 14

1. M. Kathryn Eickhoff, "The Outlook for U.S. Policy" (Presentation to the Conference Board, Chicago, May 29, 1987).

2. Clifford M. Hardin, Kenneth A. Shepsle, and Barry R. Weingast, *Public Policy Excesses: Government by Congressional Subcommittee* (St. Louis: Washington University, Center for the Study of American Business, 1981).

3. See Congressional Budget Office, *Reducing the Deficit: Spending and Revenue Options* (Washington, D.C.: Government Printing Office, 1987).

4. Lawrence J. Korb, "A Blueprint for Defense Spending," *Wall Street Journal*, May 20, 1987, p. 32. "One of the major contributing factors is a systematic bias in DOD cost estimating practices that encourages the use of optimistic cost assumptions while excluding actual cost experience and the reality of the budgeting process environment." Comp-

troller General, *Underestimation of Funding Requirements in Five Year Procurement Plans* (Washington, D.C.: General Accounting Office, 1984), p. 1.

5. Lawrence J. Korb, "The Reagan Defense Budget and Program: The Buildup That Collapsed," *Cato Journal* (in press); *Statement of Robert F. Hale, Assistant Director, National Security Division, Congressional Budget Office, before the Committee on the Budget, U.S. House of Representatives,* September 14, 1987, p. 9.

6. Korb, "Blueprint," p. 32.

7. Kevin R. Hopkins, *Welfare Dependency* (Washington, D.C.: Hudson Institute, 1987).

8. Ibid.

9. Quoted in Steven Solomon, "American Laboratories, Foreign Brains," *New York Times,* July 19, 1987, p. F8.

10. Such federal statutes are listed in *Federal Attorney Fee Awards Reporter,* June 1981, p. 2. For description of typical cases, see James T. Bennett and Thomas J. DiLorenzo, *Destroying Democracy: How Government Funds Partisan Politics* (Washington, D.C.: Cato Institute, 1985), pp. 103–9.

11. J. Richard Crout, *The Nature of Regulatory Choices* (Rochester: University of Rochester Medical Center, 1978), p. 10.

12. Albert M. Wojnilower, *A Trade Deficit for All Seasons* (New York: First Boston, Inc., 1987), p. 11.

13. Jack N. Behrman, *The Rise of the Phoenix: The United States in a Restructured World Economy* (Washington, D.C.: International Economic Policy Association, 1987).

14. See Robert D. Hormats, "Economic Everest Awaits the Next President," *New York Times,* July 19, 1987, p. 25E.

15. Lawrence Malkin, *The National Debt* (New York: Henry Holt, 1987), p. 272.

16. See Peter Hooper and Catherine L. Mann, "The U.S. External Deficit: Its Causes and Persistence" (Paper presented for a conference at the Federal Reserve Bank of St. Louis, October 23, 1987), pp. 83–85.

17. Don R. Conlan, *A Tourist's Eye View of the Soviet Economy* (Los Angeles: Capital Strategy Research, Inc., 1987), p. 4.

# INDEX

# Index

Holmes, Sherlock, 9
Honda, 181
Hoover, Herbert, 172
Hopkins, Kevin, 197, 272
Household International, 161
Huber, Peter, 242
Hudson Institute, 197, 202
Hugo, Victor, 19

IBM, 98, 153
Income redistribution, 18
Industrial policy, 170–88; aid to business, 175–83; bailouts, 183–87, 278–79; Chrysler Corporation Loan Guarantee Act, 180; foreign experience, 181–82; planning agency, 172–74; plant closing laws, 182–83
Industrial production, 130, 132
Institute for Defense Analysis, 81
Inter-American Development Bank, 124
International trade, 277–78; barriers, 121–25; export barriers, 111–12; policies, 117–19; protectionism, 113–17; U.S. deficit, 119–21, 125–128
International trade legislation: Buy American Act of 1933, 122; Export Administration Act, 111; Jones Act (Merchant Marine Act of 1936), 122–23; Surface Transportation Assistance Act of 1978, 122; Trade Act of 1974, 123

Jacobs, Irwin, 151
Japan: Ministry of International Trade and Industry, 181
Johnson, Lyndon B., 8, 17, 192, 193; Great Society, 25, 33, 193
Johnson, Thomas S., 158
Johnston, Jr., J. Bennett, 46, 215
Jones & Laughlin, 140

Kahn, Alfred, 236
Kennedy, John F., 6, 171, 191; New Frontier, 33
Kidder, Peabody & Co., 142
King Canute, 127, 182
King George II, 95

Kirkland, Lane, 33, 151, 171, 172, 174
Korb, Lawrence, 271
Korean War, 86
Kurtz, Jerome, 93

Labor legislation: Davis-Bacon Act, 65; Employee Retirement Income Security Act (ERISA), 150, 229; Occupational Safety and Health Act, 209
Labor programs: unemployment compensation, 177; workers compensation, 177
Lave, Lester, 241
Lazard Frères, 158, 170
Lehman, John, 66
Lever, Lord Harold, 138
Levi Strauss & Company, Inc., 98
Lockheed Corp., 74, 178, 278
*Los Angeles Times*, 196
Love Canal, 211, 212
Lustron Corporation, 173

Magaziner, Ira, 131
*Mainichi Daily News*, 114
Makin, John, 37
Malkin, Lawrence, 285
Manufacturing: CAD/CAM, 137, 141; cost of production, 139–42; growth industries, 135–36; industries' "rust belt", 129; just-in-time inventory system, 141; product quality, 143–44; research and development, 145–46
Maskus, Keith E., 115
Mayo Clinic, 145
Mazda, 181
McClure, James, 215
McCracken, Paul, 110, 132
McDonnell Douglas Corporation, 72, 81
MCI Corp., 235
McKenzie, Richard, 11
Metcalf, Joseph, 79
Moynihan, Daniel Patrick, 198
Munger, Michael C., 115
Murray, Charles, 194

National Bureau of Economic Research, 195

# Index

# Index